Women and the Americ...

WOMEN and the AMERICAN CITY

Edited by
Catharine R. Stimpson,
Elsa Dixler,
Martha J. Nelson,
and Kathryn B. Yatrakis

The University of Chicago Press
Chicago and London

The articles in this volume originally appeared in *Signs: Journal of Women in Culture and Society,* supplement to volume 5, number 3 (Spring 1980). The original publication was supported by funding under a Grant/Cooperative Agreement with the U.S. Department of Housing and Urban Development. The author and publisher are solely responsible for the accuracy of the statements and interpretations contained in this publication, and such interpretations do not necessarily reflect the views of the government.

The University of Chicago Press, Chicago 60637
The University of Chicago Press, Ltd., London

Library of Congress Cataloging in Publication Data
Main entry under title:

Women and the American city.

   "Articles . . . originally appeared in Signs: journal of women in culture and society, supplement to volume 5, number 3 (spring 1980)."
   Includes bibliographical references and index.
   1.   Cities and towns—United States—Addresses, essays, lectures.   2.   Women—United States— Addresses, essays, lectures.   3.   City and town life—United States—Addresses, essays, lectures.
4.   Urban policy—United States—Addresses, essays, lectures.   5.   Women in community development— United States—Addresses, essays, lectures.
6.   Women's rights—United States—Addresses, essays, lectures.   I.   Stimpson, Catharine R.
II.   Signs.
HT123.W55   305.4'2'0973   80-53136
ISBN 0-226-77478-3
ISBN 0-226-77479-1 (pbk.)

Cover photograph by Kee Chang, Chicago Association of Commerce and Industry, 130 S. Michigan Ave., Chicago, Illinois 60603.

Contents

Foreword

This book is the result of a grant from the U.S. Department of Housing and Urban Development's Office of Policy Development and Research, which I headed from 1977 to 1980. I am particularly proud that *Signs* received one of those grants. My admiration for its editor and the quality of its scholarship is long standing, and its pages provide a uniquely suitable forum for exploration of one of our foremost concerns—women and cities.

The issues that face women and our communities are inextricably linked. In fact, the very word "city" is a she. In French, in German, in Italian, "city" carries the feminine gender: *la ville, die Stadt, la citta.* In Egyptian hieroglyphics, "town" as well as "house" may stand as symbols for "mother." The word "metropolis" derives from the Greek for "mother" and "city." Athens, the most distinguished city-state in history, was named after the goddess of wisdom, Athena. And to push it a bit further, I like to think the Big Apple, cognomen of my favorite city, is called that in association with Eve, the mother of us all.

These references are not accidental. While the women's movement has quite rightly tried to bring a woman's ties to home into perspective with the other forces that work toward her happiness, the fact still exists that women *do* have a special relationship with home—and therefore, with towns and cities.

Yet the contributions of both our cities and our women are too often undervalued. More critically, their needs are frequently ignored.

This book makes a major contribution to addressing those needs. Through an examination of the many ways in which the fates of women and cities are intertwined, it can foster dialogue, encourage further research, and stimulate action. And act we must. In addition to problems inherited from the past, we are faced with staggering changes that have swept our society in the last few years.

The profile of the typical American family has been radically altered. In the past decade, families headed by women have grown at a rate ten times faster than the two-parent family. Today, one-quarter of all American households are headed by women. The percentage of women in the labor market has increased from 29 percent in 1950 to 40 percent today.

Many of those working women are mothers with children. In 1978, more than half of all mothers with children under eighteen were in the labor force. It is predicted that by 1990 only one out of every four women with children will remain at home.

Moreover, those women who work outside the home always have more than one job because it is they who remain primarily responsible for child care and housework. Their needs in cities, therefore, are commonly different from those of men.

If our families are to thrive—indeed if they are to survive—in our cities, we need a new vision that helps both women and their communities to adjust to the overwhelming changes in life-style that have overtaken us.

We need to strive for a nonsexist city—one in which the urban design takes into account the problems of women who head their own households, who work at jobs (usually lower paying than those of men), who often have less education than men and fewer opportunities to improve themselves.

The women whose work appears in the following chapters—and the increasing number of women involved in all aspects of city development and scholarship—provide reason to hope that we will indeed create and act on a new urban vision.

I do not mean to suggest that men are insensitive to cities or that there is a "woman's view" that radically differs from a man's. Urban blight will not disappear because women are in top policy making jobs, nor will unemployment or all the problems connected with day care. But when women as well as men are operating at every level of decision making, then we *can* expect a more balanced, synergistic approach to our urban problems.

We might also expect that, among their many contributions, women will emphasize the importance of nurturing—a traditionally feminine role. For if we have been able to teach men that women have more than a nurturing role to play in the world, perhaps it is time for us to teach cities how to nurture their people and provide for their needs. The cities should learn quickly. After all, the city *is* a she.

DONNA E. SHALALA, *President*
Hunter College of the
City University of New York

Preface

Catharine R. Stimpson

Three hypotheses underlie this book: The American city has both enhanced and constricted women's lives; the experience of men and women in American cities is quite significantly different; and, finally, studies of such divergences and their effects are original, suggestive, and necessary. Of course, this single text cannot provide a complete analysis of women and the city, a final synthesis of women's studies and urban studies. Instead, we hope to reveal a vital field of inquiry and some of the maps now being drawn of it. Indeed, three of our sections—a massive review essay by Gerda R. Wekerle, a series of research notes, and two book reviews—prove how many of these maps already exist. Together, these contributions provide a fresh, comprehensive account of the thinking about women and cities.

In our first articles, Jo Freeman and Ann R. Markusen offer two analyses of contemporary urban policy and suggestions for change that would benefit women. The next articles use history to illuminate current concerns. Elizabeth Ewen explores the response of immigrant women to the modern city and to the mass culture it supported. Marilyn Gittell and Teresa Shtob succinctly describe the role of women in urban politics and community organizations, a recurring theme in this book. Galen Cranz outlines the surprising influence of our thinking about femininity and masculinity on the design of urban parks and on ideologies of urban leisure. Susan Saegert also analyzes some connections between notions of gender and urban/suburban life. Four pieces then discuss some of the difficulties cities can impose on women. Marsha Hurst and Ruth Zambrana present case studies of minority women, primarily Hispanic, who use the health facilities of a poor New York neighborhood. Elizabeth W. Markson and Beth B. Hess reveal the problems of growing old in the city. Margaret T. Gordon, Stephanie Riger, Robert K. LeBailly, and Linda Heath investigate women's fear and experience of crime. Helena Z. Lopata writes about the restrictions that existing transportation systems impose on women's mobility.

Such articles speak of the harshness, the penalties, of urban life. However, they also emphasize women's strengths and promote, implicitly and explicitly, a belief in both the possibilities of cities and the resilience of human character. They suggest that "people are capable of acting together, and capable of acting not just for themselves, but for their brothers and sisters."[1] In Dolores Hayden's essay, the vision of a city free from discrimination articulates this capacious conviction most clearly. If our contributors are realistic about American women in the modern city, they also refuse to believe in blind submission to difficulty.

We are grateful to the Department of Housing and Urban Development for a generous grant that underwrote the costs of a special issue of *Signs: Journal of Women in Culture and Society* that was the basis of this book.[2] I am happy to acknowledge the guidance of an editorial advisory committee—Astrid E. Merget, Francine F. Rabinovitz, Richard Sennett, Margaret C. Simms, and Roberta Steinbacher, and the able, energetic help of three coeditors—Elsa Dixler, Martha J. Nelson, and Kathryn B. Yatrakis. I am sure that we all hope that this book will be of use to scholars and students, to policymakers and citizens alike.

Douglass College
Rutgers University

[1]Interview with Frances Fox Piven, "Slicing the Big Apple," *Liberation* 19, nos. 8–9 (Spring 1976); quote from p. 18.

[2]"Women and the American City," *Signs: Journal of Women in Culture and Society* 5, no. 3, suppl. (Spring 1980): S1–S274.

Women and Urban Policy

Jo Freeman

Any analysis of the impact of urban policy on women is complicated by the absence of an urban policy. While the Department of Housing and Urban Development (HUD) has been in place since 1965 and hundreds of policies and laws affecting urban areas have been promulgated in the last forty years, there is no coordinated, directed policy with specific programs to achieve important goals. From this perspective, President Carter's announcement early in his term that he would present a national urban policy was a major step. The fact that his "policy" was largely a smorgasbord of already existing programs capped by some new ideas that Congress did not pass into law reflects the difficulty of creating coherence out of chaos when there is no consensus on goals and many vested interests with stakes in specific means.

Within the arena of urban policy are several recognized but unresolved conflicts for which Carter's proposals did not display a clear preference. One of the most overwhelming is the sheer diversity of urban conditions. The phrase "urban crisis" suggests pervasive decay, but an ordering of cities by an "urban hardship index"[1] shows that the crisis is concentrated in the older cities of the Midwest and Northeast, and "within these cities, to certain areas that have been characterized in recent years by a rapid process of decentralization."[2] In part, the highly

I would like to thank Georgia Strasburg, David Baer, Ilana Bain, and many anonymous federal bureaucrats for their invaluable assistance in preparing this article.

1. Paul R. Dommel, James W. Fossett, and Richard P. Nathan, "Cities in Crisis: The Impact of Federal Aid" (Washington, D.C.: League of Women Voters Education Fund, December 1977), pp. 1–2.

2. Paul R. Dommel and Richard P. Nathan, "The Cities," in *Setting National Priorities: The 1978 Budget,* ed. Joseph A. Pechman (Washington, D.C.: Brookings Institution, 1977), p. 283.

1

differentiated and localized nature of urban problems makes them difficult to solve. Our federal system gives representation on the national level to states, not cities, and disproportionate representation to states with lower populations. In the bargaining over the allocation formulas necessary to secure congressional passage of the legislation, less needy areas frequently get a significant share of the resources.[3] Similarly, once funds are divided up, the governing unit often uses them to maintain basic services, primarily in those areas from which the most votes come, or to lower taxes.[4] Consequently, any attempt to provide more aid for the most needy localities would require a budgetary increase or a reduction in funds available to many areas currently receiving them.

Another problem is what would be an appropriate "solution" to the urban crisis. The two most frequently discussed strategies are revitalization and adjustment. The revival strategy "seeks to restore large cities to the roles they had in the past, though with perhaps not precisely the same activities. This includes attracting back both economic activities and households that have moved elsewhere. This strategy emphasizes permanent capital investments to make cities more competitive with suburban locations and forms of aid that geographically tie their recipients to the community."[5] The "adjustment" strategy accepts the decline of cities as irreversible and seeks only to ameliorate the subsequent problems. This is done by making it easier for the population to move to places of greater economic opportunity and by providing transitional aid as services are reduced. Needless to say, city governments are not likely to find the adjustment strategy desirable, and even the most depressed cities contain a significant number of voters.

I

Although students of urban problems acknowledge the importance of race in the creation of "crisis conditions," it is rare for anyone to look at the sex composition of cities or of depressed neighborhoods. Perhaps after the next census when figures for metropolitan areas will be available on a block-by-block basis, such an analysis can be undertaken. Yet even on an aggregate basis, it is clear that central cities have a disproportionate share of women, especially women who are elderly or solely responsible for families.

3. Howard E. Shuman, "Congress, the President, and Urban Policy" (paper delivered at the annual meeting of the American Political Science Association, New York, 1978).

4. David A. Caputo, *Urban America: The Policy Alternatives* (San Francisco: W. H. Freeman, 1976), pp. 146–47.

5. Anthony Downs, "Urban Policy," in *Setting National Priorities: The 1979 Budget,* ed. Joseph A. Pechman (Washington, D.C.: Brookings Institution, 1979), p. 174.

In 1977, the central city area contained 115 women over the age of fourteen for every 100 men, compared with a sex ratio of 108 for non-metropolitan areas and 107 for suburban ones. In the central city population over age sixty-five, the ratio rises to 157 women for every 100 men. Almost 7 percent of the central city population consists of women over age sixty-five, compared with 4.4 percent who are elderly men[6] (see table 1). The distribution of female-headed families is similarly skewed. The percentage of families maintained solely by women is twice as great in the central cities as in the suburbs (20.7 percent compared with 10.9 percent). Approximately 40 percent of all families, with and without children under eighteen, live in the suburbs, but only a little over 30 percent of all female-headed families live there. This is heavily weighted by the number of black female-headed families, over 60 percent of which are concentrated in the cities (see table 2). Despite the popular idea that suburbs are the place where children are raised, there are no significant differences in family distribution by the presence or absence of children under age eighteen or in the number of children per family.[7] Race and sex of family head are much better predictors of whether a family will live in the central city than are presence or number of children under eighteen.

Table 1

Number of Women per 100 Men for Total Population over Age Fourteen and over Age Sixty-five, 1977

	Central Cities		Suburban		Nonmetropolitan	
	Over 14	Over 65	Over 14	Over 65	Over 14	Over 65
White	114	164	106	140	106	131
Black	122	128	110	127	122	163
Total...............	115	157	107	140	108	133

SOURCE.—Computed from U.S. Department of Commerce, Bureau of the Census, *Social and Economic Characteristics of the Metropolitan Population: 1977 and 1970,* Current Population Reports, ser. P-23, no. 75 (Washington, D.C.: Government Printing Office, November 1978), tables 1, 4.

6. U.S. Department of Commerce, Bureau of the Census, *Social and Economic Characteristics of the Metropolitan Population: 1977 and 1970,* Current Population Reports, Ser. P-23, no. 75 (Washington, D.C.: Government Printing Office, November 1978), tables 1 and 4. The Bureau of the Census defines "central city" as the one to three largest incorporated areas within a Standard Metropolitan Statistical Area (SMSA). "Suburban," used here instead of the census's term, "outside central city," refers to the remainder of the SMSA. Thus many central cities have major "suburban-like" areas in them, and many suburbs or nonmetropolitan areas may contain small but highly urbanized sections in them. "Nonmetropolitan" means the rest of the country after the SMSAs are subtracted. Thus an analysis by census tract, or by block, is really necessary to establish the degree of concentration of women in specific locales.

7. Ibid., table 7.

Table 2

Percentage of Families, and Female-headed Families, with and without Children under Eighteen, by Place of Residence, 1977

	Central Cities				Suburban				Nonmetropolitan			
	With Children		Without Children		With Children		Without Children		With Children		Without Children	
	Female	All	Female	All	Female	All	Female	All	Female	All	Female	All
White	32	22	36	26	40	44	35	40	28	34	29	34
Black	62	55	65	58	16	21	11	18	22	24	24	24
Total	42	26	41	28	32	41	31	38	26	33	28	34

Source.—Computed from U.S. Department of Commerce, Bureau of the Census, *Social and Economic Characteristics of the Metropolitan Population: 1977 and 1970,* Current Population Reports, ser. P-23, no. 75 (Washington, D.C.: Government Printing Office, November 1978), table 7.

Note.—"Female" denotes female-headed families.

As one might predict from the above, city women are less likely to be married and living with their husbands than their suburban or rural counterparts. In 1977, one out of three central city households was maintained by a person living alone or only with nonrelatives, compared with one in five suburban households. Fifty-nine percent of such persons, urban and suburban, were women[8] (see table 3).

Why are single women, with or without children, so concentrated in cities? At one time the answer would have been because of jobs. The labor force participation rates of women for the decennial censuses show that the more urban the environment, the higher the female participation rate. In earlier censuses, where the metropolitan/ nonmetropolitan distinction is not made but that between urban, rural nonfarm, and rural farm is, the differences are even greater.[9] Yet by 1977 this trend appears to have stopped and almost reversed itself. While the 1977 figures, taken from the Current Population Survey, are not perfectly comparable to the more comprehensive census, the margin of error is not great enough to obscure the fact that now more women work who live in the suburbs than who live in the central cities. No longer do jobs appear to be the reason women are concentrated in the cities, although those who do work are more likely to work full time (see tables 4, 5).

If jobs are no longer the reason, perhaps a better one is the availability of affordable housing. Women earn considerably less than men, even when they work full time. Fewer women than men are employed, and even when income from all sources is taken into account, women's median income is only 39 percent that of men's (see table 6). As Downs has explained,

> Most new housing is built on vacant land around the edges of built-up areas and according to very high standards of quality legally required by local zoning and building codes. Therefore, it is too expensive for most households. This legal exclusion of the poor and near-poor from new growth areas results in spatial separation of most middle- and upper-income households from most poorer ones. The former are concentrated in newer neighborhoods in the periphery of the metropolitan area (and a few close-in neighborhoods). The poor are concentrated in neighborhoods with the oldest and most deteriorated housing, generally in the center of the metropolitan area.[10]

Women heading families, and single-woman households, are considerably less likely than men to have a middle- or upper-middle-level

8. Ibid., table 5.
9. For the 1950 census, see vol. 2, pt. 1, table 50; for 1940 see vol. 2, pt. 1, table 17; for 1930 see vol. 3, pt. 1, table 30.
10. Downs, p. 165.

income. Consequently, an analysis by the Department of Housing and
Urban Development concluded that "nearly half of all female heads of
household must spend one-fourth or more of their cash incomes on
[adequate housing]. Less than 20 percent of *all* households need do the
same."[11] The same analysis argued that "by spending up to one-fourth

Table 3

Percentage of All Persons over Age Fourteen Married and
Living with Their Spouses in 1977

	Central Cities		Suburban		Nonmetropolitan	
	Female	Male	Female	Male	Female	Male
White	58	51	64	60	62	66
Black	32	40	43	52	36	45
Total	47	54	59	63	59	63

Source.—Computed from U.S. Department of Commerce, Bureau of the Census, *Social and Economic Characteristics of the Metropolitan Population: 1977 and 1970*, Current Population Reports, ser. P-23, no. 75 (Washington, D.C.: Government Printing Office, November 1978), table 4.

Table 4

Labor Force Participation Rates by Sex and by Place of Residence, 1960–77 (%)

	Total		Central City		Suburban		Nonmetropolitan	
	W	M	W	M	W	M	W	M
1977	48.0	75.7	48.2	73.5	50.0	79.9	45.4	73.6
1970	41.8	75.8	44.7	75.1	41.8	79.4	38.6	72.3
1960	35.5	78.6	40.6	79.7	34.4	81.7	31.6	75.1

Source.—U.S. Department of Commerce, Bureau of the Census, *Social and Economic Characteristics of the Metropolitan Population: 1977 and 1970*, Current Population Reports, ser. P-23, no. 75 (Washington, D.C.: Government Printing Office, November 1978), table 11; ser. P-23, no. 37, table 13.
Note.—W = women, M = men.

Table 5

Percentage of Civilian Income Recipients Who Are Year-round Full-Time
Workers, by Place of Residence and Sex, 1977

	Central City	Suburban	Nonmetropolitan
Women	32.0	30.2	26.3
Men	51.8	57.6	50.7

Source.—U.S. Department of Commerce, Bureau of the Census, *Money Income in 1977 of Families and Persons in the United States*, Current Population Reports, ser. P-60, no. 118 (Washington, D.C.: Government Printing Office, 1979), table 41.

11. U.S. Department of Housing and Urban Development, Office of Policy Development and Research, *How Well Are We Housed? 2. Female Headed Households* (Washington, D.C.: Government Printing Office, November 1978), p. 18.

Table 6

Median Income by Place of Residence, Women's as Percentage of Men's, 1977

	Central City	Suburban	Nonmetropolitan	Total
All income recipients	45.7	35.2	38.8	38.9
Year-round full-time workers ...	61.6	57.9	60.0	58.4

SOURCE.—Computed from U.S. Department of Commerce, Bureau of the Census, *Money Income in 1977 of Families and Persons in the United States,* Current Population Reports, ser. P-60, no. 118 (Washington, D.C.: Government Printing Office, March 1979), table 41.

of their income on housing, 80 percent of all American households should be able to obtain unflawed, uncrowded housing, but only 53 percent of all female-headed households can be expected to find adequate housing for the same proportion of income."[12]

Even when women can afford decent housing, they cannot always find it—or rent it. Although there are no scientifically verifiable data documenting sex discrimination in housing, a 1975 "Report on Sex Discrimination in Five American Cities" found sex discrimination pervasive. "Three facially neutral criteria surfaced during the Hearings and Workshops as prevalent practices in the rental industry for refusing to rent to women: (1) Children are not allowed. (2) Prefer married couples. (3) Sorry—no single roommates."[13] Other practices were described that also have discriminatory effects: refusing to rent a two-bedroom apartment to a single woman with a female, but not a male, child, or refusing to count as income alimony payments or public assistance. It may not be due to lack of income alone that 73 percent of households in public housing are headed solely by women.[14]

Although women are major beneficiaries of direct housing subsidies, both for privately owned and public housing, they are much less likely to benefit from another major government housing subsidy program—tax breaks for homeowners. Estimates of savings to homeowners through income tax deductions of property tax and mortgage interest payments range from $7 to $12 billion, considerably more than $3 billion of budget outlays in 1977 for direct housing subsidies.[15] Simply by knowing the lower incomes of women, one is not surprised to learn that of the 48.8 million owner-occupied homes in the United States in 1977, only 18 percent are owned by women heading households. Of this small percentage, 45 percent are owned by women over age sixty-five—suggesting that widowhood rather than personal resources or conscious intention is the main stimulus.[16] While discrimination may have been a major cause of low homeownership rates prior to passage in 1974 of the Equal Credit Opportunity Act[17] and of an

12. Ibid., p. 15.
13. U.S. Department of Housing and Urban Development, Office of the Assistant Secretary for Fair Housing and Equal Opportunity, *Women and Housing: A Report on Sex Discrimination in Five American Cities*, prepared by the National Council of Negro Women (Washington, D.C.: Government Printing Office, June 1975), p. 36.
14. Unpublished data from the Department of Housing and Urban Development, Management Information System, Subsidized Housing Admissions and Continued Occupancy, 1978.
15. Henry Aaron, *Shelter and Subsidies* (Washington, D.C.: Brookings Institution, 1972), chap. 4; *Special Analyses: Budget of the United States Government, Fiscal Year 1976* (Washington, D.C.: Government Printing Office, 1975), pp. 108–9.
16. Unpublished data, Department of Housing and Urban Development, Annual Housing Survey (1977), table A-1.
17. Equal Credit Opportunity Act, P.L. 93-495.

act prohibiting sex discrimination in housing and housing finance,[18] as it was then deemed good business practice,[19] there are no hard data on sex discrimination in the sale and financing of houses since then. However, HUD's feeling is that, next to low income, women's greatest barrier to owning their own homes is ignorance of how to do it and what it involves.[20] The department has created a Woman and Mortgage Credit Project to inform lenders of the credit worthiness of women and to educate women on their rights and opportunities in obtaining credit and housing finance. The project is still too new to evaluate.

A second reason women live in cities is the availability of public transportation. A survey done in 1969 by the Federal Highway Administration showed that of those over age sixteen, men were 40 percent more likely than women to have driver's licenses. When disaggregated by place of residence, the percentage of men with licenses varied little, while that of women varied enormously. Only 32.5 percent of women over age sixteen in cities of 1 million or more had driver's licenses (see table 7). Not surprisingly, when cars are used, men are 50 percent more likely to be drivers than are women. Women are 50 percent more likely than men to use intracity mass transit—though the figures are very small compared with the total number of trips involved.[21] Although the per-

Table 7

Percentage of Persons Sixteen Years of Age and Older with Driver's Licenses, by Place of Residence, 1969

Place of Residence	Percentage with Driver's Licenses		
	Males	Females	Total
Unincorporated areas	90.0	68.8	79.2
Incorporated places:			
Under 5,000	90.9	67.4	78.8
5,000–24,999	90.5	66.9	78.2
25,000–49,999	87.8	66.4	76.6
50,000–99,999	84.5	54.5	68.3
1,000,000 and over	68.2	32.5	48.8
Total incorporated	85.4	58.1	70.9
Total	87.0	61.5	73.6

Source.—U.S. Department of Transportation, Federal Highway Administration, *Nationwide Personal Transportation Study, Characteristics of Licensed Drivers*, Report no. 6 (Washington, D.C.: Government Printing Office, April 1973), p. 8.

18. Section 808(b) of the Housing and Community Development Act (amending Title VIII of the 1968 Civil Rights Act), P.L. 93-384.

19. Senate Committee on Banking, Housing, and Urban Affairs, *Home Mortgage Disclosure and Equal Credit Opportunity* (Washington, D.C.: Government Printing Office, 1976).

20. Interview with Jo Ann McGeorge, project director for the Women and Mortgage Credit Project of the Economic Affairs Department of the Office of Policy Development and Research, Department of Housing and Urban Development.

21. U.S. Department of Transportation, Federal Highway Administration, *National Personal Transportation Study: Mode of Transportation and Personal Characteristics of Tripmakers*, Report no. 9 (Washington, D.C.: Government Printing Office, November 1973), appendix C, tables 3, 5.

centages for the national survey are small, studies that concentrate on particular cities show the same pervasive sex differences. Controlling for income, age, and other variables only partially eliminates the differences in use of cars versus public transportation or even walking. Studies of preferences even show that men are much more "antitransport" than women are. As Lalita Sen summarized, "The results clearly endorse the viewpoint that women are more likely to use some form of public transportation than men, both for work and discretionary trips and have a more favorable attitude toward transit and the use of public funds to subsidize transit."[22]

II

The concentration of women and female-headed families in the city is both cause and consequence of the city's fiscal woes. Women live in cities because it is easier and cheaper for them to do so, but because fewer women are employed, and those that are receive lower pay than men, they do not make the same contribution to the tax base that an equivalent population of men would. Concomitantly, they are more dependent on public resources, such as transportation and housing. For these reasons alone urban finances would be improved by increasing women's employment opportunities and pay. Yet nothing in our current urban policy is specifically geared to improving women's financial resources. There are some proposed incentives to business to create more jobs, but not necessarily ones that would utilize the skills women currently have. The most innovative proposal was a tax credit for new hires from certain groups with particularly high unemployment rates. None of the seven targeted groups were women.[23]

The Carter administration also proposed (but Congress did not pass) that $3 billion be authorized for labor-intensive public works. This is a standard ploy for quickly increasing employment in industries subject to cyclic unemployment. Because the unemployment rate dropped, the administration does not intend to reintroduce the proposal. However, since it is a standard countercyclical move, which will likely be used

---

22. Lalita Sen, "Travel Patterns and Behavior of Women in Urban Areas" (paper prepared for the Department of Transportation Conference on Women's Travel Issues: Research Needs and Priorities, September 17–20, 1978), p. 9; see also Alice E. Kidder, "Transportation Problems of Low Income Women as Members of the Transportation Disadvantaged," ibid.; Joyce Fanning Madden and Michelle J. White, "Women's Work Trips: An Empirical and Theoretical Overview," ibid.; A. H. Studenmund, Larry C. Kerpelman, and Marian T. Otts, "Women's Travel Behavior and Attitudes: An Empirical Analysis," ibid.

23. U.S. Department of the Treasury, Internal Revenue Service, *Targeted Jobs, Tax Credit and WIN Credit,* Publication 906 (Washington, D.C.: Internal Revenue Service, February 1979).

again, it is worth understanding its implications for women.[24] Public works proposals quickly create a lot of jobs, but they primarily require muscle power or construction skills few women have gained. Without parallel programs to recruit and train women for public works jobs, they will principally employ men. The government has created extensive training programs to recruit and prepare blacks for the construction trades, and these programs have been quite successful. The equivalent programs for women are small, very new, and largely funded through local Comprehensive Employment and Training Act (CETA) grants.

The Comprehensive Employment and Training Act is the major source of training funds, though it is administered primarily on a local level. The reauthorization in 1978 did contain some provisions directed at women—for example, a displaced homemakers program—but these are miniscule compared with the entire CETA budget authorization. Although many women have been trained by CETA programs, they are a lower percentage than the national unemployed population.[25] While the wide variety of programs under CETA will not be analyzed here, it is worth noting that some are heavily female (e.g., the Work Incentive Program for welfare recipients) and some are heavily male (e.g., the Job Corps for underprivileged youth). In all programs, but especially in the heavily female ones, women receive fewer jobs than men after training. The jobs are heavily concentrated in traditionally female areas and pay less.[26] Unfortunately, beyond these aggregate statistics, we do not know what the impact of CETA on women has been: whether it reinforces traditional employment patterns or whether it helps women learn skills and find jobs they would otherwise not hold, even though they are in female-dominated occupations. The Employment and Training Administration has funded a large CETA evaluation project, but the consequences of CETA for women are not one of the principal concerns.

Unless the impact of CETA and other government programs on women is specifically examined, it is likely that in the future they will primarily help men, as they have in the past. The consequences can be seen in the poverty statistics. If one compares the percentage of families in poverty by race and sex of family head, poverty has been declining over time—but not at the same rate for everyone. The decline for female-headed families has only been slight, but that for families with an adult man in them has been significant. Indeed, the absolute number of female-headed families in poverty has increased,[27] despite the fact that

24. Library of Congress, Congressional Research Service, "Urban Policy: Status of the President's Proposals," by Keith H. Bea. Issue brief no. IB77103 (May 21, 1979).

25. U.S. Department of Labor, Employment and Training Administration, *Employment and Training Report of the President* (Washington, D.C.: Government Printing Office, 1978), p. 42.

26. Ibid., chap. 2.

27. U.S. Department of Commerce, Bureau of the Census, *Characteristics of the Population below the Poverty Level: 1977,* Current Population Reports, ser. P-60, no. 119 (Washington, D.C.: Government Printing Office, March 1979), p. 4.

women have been entering the labor force at a very rapid rate. As a result, poverty, which was once identified as a minority problem, is more and more becoming a *female* problem (see table 8). This is so because women can no longer depend on men as the major source of their continuing economic support. At the same time, women are more and more likely to be a—often the—major source of economic support for children. One-third of recent marriages end in divorce,[28] and 18.6 percent of all children under eighteen live in one-parent households. An estimated 45 percent of the children born in 1977 will reside in a one-parent family sometime before they reach the age of eighteen.[29]

Thus, although most people marry, few women spend their entire lives out of the labor force. Although "only 15.5 percent of all American families consist of a working husband, a wife who is not in the labor force, and one or more children under 18 years of age," our economic and employment policies are still made on the assumption that this is the *average* family.[30] This bias is pervasive. Until recently, the United States Census always assumed that every family had *one* head and that head was always a husband, if he were present. Families were either "female headed" (i.e., with no man) or "male headed." Although political pressures are forcing a change in this definition,[31] the determination to cling to the ideal of male precedence is found in the current tripartite division of families into "female headed," "husband/wife," and "*other* male head" (italics added).

Economic policy is similarly made on the assumption that each fam-

Table 8

Percentage of Families in Poverty, 1959 and 1977

	Female Headed		Husband-Wife and Male Headed	
	White	Black	White	Black
1959	34.8	65.4	13.3	43.3
1977	24.0	51.0	4.8	13.3
Decline	31.0	22.0	63.9	68.8

SOURCE.—U.S. Department of Commerce, Bureau of the Census, *Money Income and Poverty Status of Families and Persons in the United States: 1977 (Advance Report),* Current Population Reports, ser. P-60, no. 116 (Washington, D.C.: Government Printing Office, July 1978), table 16.

28. U.S. Department of Commerce, Bureau of the Census, *Numbers, Timing, and Duration of Marriages and Divorces in the U.S.: June 1975,* Current Population Reports, ser. P-20, no. 297 (Washington, D.C.: Government Printing Office, October 1976), p. 4.

29. Paul C. Glick, "Who Are the Children in One-Parent Households?" (paper delivered at the Council on Early Childhood Conference on Children of One-Parent Households, Detroit, Wayne State University, May 1979), p. 7.

30. Janet L. Norwood, "New Approaches to Statistics on the Family," *Monthly Labor Review* (July 1977), p. 31. Some computations even assume exactly two children, a boy age thirteen and a girl age eight.

31. Ibid., p. 33.

ily has one primary wage earner, all others being secondary. The primary wage earner is the one who earns the most. This view is often used to discount the current high unemployment rate as not representing real hardship because a significant proportion of the unemployed are married women.[32] In fact, President Carter's original welfare reform plan (not passed by Congress) provided that welfare recipients would be given one public service job per family and specified that the person to get that job would be the one who worked the most hours or earned the most in the preceding six months.[33] Because of this preference for men, the Department of Labor estimated that men would have received 50 percent of the public service jobs, even though they are only 19 percent of the adults on welfare.[34]

The long-range economic problems of women and their children will not be solved until we recognize that employment is still the primary means by which income is distributed. Although somewhat erratic, the job market is nonetheless more reliable and more accessible than marriage as a means of economic support. Furthermore, in the long run it is more feasible for the government to equalize access to the labor force than to make up for failures of marriage through welfare and other transfer payments. However, for women to be on an economic par with men, it is necessary to guarantee their right to equal labor force participation and equal benefits from that participation. The idea that every able-bodied person who desires a job has a right to it is a new one. It took a major economic catastrophe, the Depression, to convince the public and the policymakers that the provision of adequate jobs was a social responsibility. This was embodied in the Employment Act of 1946.[35] Yet, in 1978, it was thought necessary to make still another attempt "to translate into practical reality the right of all Americans who are able, willing, and seeking to work to full opportunity for useful paid employment at fair rates of compensation." Even this Full Employment and Balanced Growth Act is more an expression of hope than a series of practical programs.[36] Nothing in it, or in other government employment policies, recognizes that women face a different economic reality than men do.

What is needed to bring women's employment situation up to par with men's is not merely more government programs but an entire re-

32. For documentation and analysis of this view, see Kay L. Schlozman, "Women and Unemployment; Assessing the Biggest Myths," in *Women: A Feminist Perspective,* ed. Jo Freeman (Palo Alto, Calif.: Mayfield Publishing Co., 1979), pp. 290–312.

33. Nancy Gordon, "Women's Roles in Welfare Reform," discussion with Arnold Parker and Jodie Allen, *Challenge* (January–February 1978), pp. 45–50.

34. U.S. Department of Commerce, Bureau of the Census, *Money Income in 1977 of Families and Persons in the United States,* Current Population Reports, ser. P. 60, no. 118 (Washington, D.C.: Government Printing Office, 1979), table 49.

35. P.L. 79-304.

36. P.L. 95-523.

conceptualization of women's role in the labor force. We must recognize that all adults have responsibility for the support of themselves and their children regardless of their individual living situation, and that all are entitled to policies which will facilitate the carrying out of this responsibility, regardless of sex, marital, or parental status. Guaranteeing equal labor force participation goes beyond equal employment opportunity. This merely asserts that women who are like men should be treated like men and accepts as standard the traditional male life-style. That standard, in turn, assumes that one's primary responsibility should and can be one's job, because one has a spouse (or spouse surrogate) whose primary responsibility is the maintenance of home and family obligations. Most women cannot fit these assumptions because of our traditional conception of the family and women's role in it. Despite the fact that only 15.7 percent of all persons over age eighteen are spouses in husband/wife families with children under eighteen in which only the husband works, our entire social and economic organization assumes this as the norm. Couples who share family responsibilities, or singles who take them all on, pay a price for deviance.

The right of equal labor force participation would recognize that society should provide the support services necessary to fulfill one's family obligations rather than assume that such services will be provided by another member of the family (usually a wife). It also recognizes that job opportunities should be available to fit a variety of life-styles, rather than the traditional one of primary wage earner with dependent spouse. Key to providing equal labor force participation is increasing the availability to women of all jobs and the benefits from them. Although occupational segregation by sex has remained well entrenched for most of this century, it has never faced a concerted effort to eliminate it. While there is no comprehensive strategy for accomplishing this as yet, enough has been written about the tactics for doing so to make further analysis unnecessary here.

There has also been much analysis of the need for, or lack of need for, child care. However, this has never been done within the framework proposed here: guaranteeing equal labor force participation. Thus child care has been looked at as a problem of working women who have to work. It has been viewed not as a right but as a form of subsidy for the disadvantaged. Government publications state that impoverished female family heads would work if child care facilities were available but that "the cost of child care would have to be weighed against their earning capacity."[37] If a woman earns less than the cost of caring for her children, it is deemed a bad social investment. This view fails to consider the opportunity cost to the woman from not working, even though lack of

---

37. U.S. Department of Commerce, Bureau of the Census, *Characteristics of the Population below the Poverty Level* (n. 27 above), p. 7.

continuity in the labor force is acknowledged as a significant cause of lower lifetime earnings. It does not acknowledge how the lack of child care impedes her ability to get training for more than the most menial jobs or employer expectations of her ability and willingness to take on more demanding ones. Nor does it take into account the effect on children of being raised on welfare, without having any primary role models who are gainfully employed. In short, our current national policy is that women should pay the financial and opportunity costs of raising the next generation, unless they are able to find a mate willing to share these with them.

As employed women struggle with family burdens that men are not yet willing to share, they must also cope with a structure of time that assumes a traditional role allocation. The forty-hour, five-day week requires that one be ready and available to work at exactly the same hours that businesses and agencies with which one conducts aspects of one's private life are open. When women assume full-time jobs, they are often able to limit or adjust the private side of family work to fit their employment responsibilities. It is much more difficult to adjust the family work requiring public contact. Women are more likely to be part-time workers than men because having hours free during the work day is the only way they can deal with the conflicts between their worker and family roles. The rigid and inflexible hours of the standard work week, coupled with the long-standing employer assumption that the serious (and promotable) employee is one whose first obligation is to the job, is another way in which women experience discrimination.[38] Measures for dealing with these conflicts have generally been proposed under the rubric of "alternate work schedules." While these arose out of a concern for the quality of work life and management's concern for increasing worker satisfaction in order to increase productivity, their benefits to women have not been overlooked.

Three major forms of nontraditional schedules have been broached: the four-day work week, flexible working hours, and part-time employment. In addition, organized labor has also favored cutting the standard work week to less than forty hours (usually thirty) without loss of pay, although if business hours were similarly cut, this would not relieve schedule conflicts for women.

In theory, the four-day work week would permit both women and men free time to tend to family responsibilities or to engage in leisure without requiring loss of wages. It would also decrease commuting time. This assessment assumes that agencies and businesses remain open the standard five days, so that family and personal obligations requiring public contact can be performed. If this were not to be the case, a four-

38. Juanita M. Kreps and R. J. Leaper, "Home Work, Market Work, and the Allocation of Time," in *Women and the American Economy,* ed. Juanita Kreps (Englewood Cliffs, N.J.: Prentice-Hall, Inc., 1976).

day work week would just make it harder to resolve conflicts between work and private life. Furthermore, such a division of the week would separate the home from the job even more, a consequence of the industrial revolution that has frequently been criticized. Part-time employment has been very much a women's issue. Yet as long as there is still a standard full-time schedule, part-time employment runs a real risk of becoming a female ghetto. Already 66.7 percent of all part-time employees are women; 29.3 percent of employed women, compared with 10.1 percent of employed men, work part-time.[39] Part-time jobs are rarely responsible ones, and those in them often find their promotion opportunities limited. Currently, the fringe benefits available to part-time employees are fewer than those available to full timers, though prorating is not unfeasible. Flexi-time, in which workers choose their own daily hours as long as certain core hours are maintained, appears to be the only innovative schedule for which there is some evidence that it helps women.[40] Even here the data are too limited to predict the consequences for women of widespread adoption. Fortunately, because many government agencies and several industries are experimenting with it, results may be evident in a few years.

Another possibility that has not been widely discussed is to lengthen the work day or week. Although shift work and twenty-four-hour operation is common in some industries, it has never been proposed for the white-collar sectors. Yet, as long as an individual's standard work week were not to exceed the current forty hours, lengthening the work period has many attractive features. Time conflicts would be reduced. One could work one's normal hours and still find public agencies and private businesses open for the conduct of private life. One could go to the post office to pick up undelivered mail, be at home for repair people, go to the doctor or dentist or a child's teacher without having to take leave from one's job. If shifts were staggered, the rush-hour pressure on transportation systems could be relieved, and the peak load problems of the utilities partially ameliorated. Even a slight extension of the work day would have a beneficial effect on the unemployment rate by creating more jobs and would provide for better utilization of buildings and other facilities. Finally, this would be a much easier policy for the government to pursue than any of the others implied or specified in this paper. Not only could the federal government extend the hours of its own agencies through administrative order, but public service employment could be targeted to extension of services by state and local agencies. This would also help curb the much lamented "substitution effects," in which state and local governments substitute federal money for their own tax dollars

39. Department of Labor, Bureau of Labor Statistics, "Special Labor Force Report," 216, table A.

40. J. Walker, C. Fletcher, and D. Macleod, "Flexible Working Hours in Two British Government Offices," *Public Personnel Management*, vol. 4 (1975).

rather than use it all to create more jobs. One could encourage private employers similarly to extend their hours and increase their employment through tax breaks and credits for associated expenses, although this might not be desirable or necessary. For those employers who cater to the public, the mere existence of a buying public at other than the standard hours might be sufficient to stimulate extended hours.

III

These proposals for improving the employment opportunities of women are most quickly and beneficially pursued in a city, where people, needs, and resources are most concentrated. Public transportation systems, on which women depend more than men, are already in place in the older cities, the very ones that need to be revitalized. Housing is there, too, although it also needs an infusion of funds and skilled labor to make much of it livable. While 95 percent of that skilled labor is male, model programs now exist to train women in construction and other crafts necessary to rehabilitate the housing. A significant expansion of these could provide many underemployed and poor women with high-paying jobs that would not require the years of professional education necessary for white-collar jobs which pay equivalent salaries. It is also easiest in the city to be employed in one of the better-paying professions, and, if one is married, for both members of a professional couple to be adequately employed. If enough such couples were attracted back into the city, it would provide the tax base to support the social programs that eroded with the middle-class flight to the suburbs. As Eli Ginzberg, chair of the National Commission for Employment Policy, has argued, "The new trends to later marriages, low births, and the increased career interests of educated women provide the city with an opportunity to attract and retain professional couples, both of whom hold good jobs and are career oriented."[41]

The city is also the place where alternative work schedules can be most efficiently developed and hours extension prove most profitable. More use of public buildings and spreading out the use of transportation facilities would be, in the long run, much more economical than our present system of concentrated use. Extended hours would also enhance the safety of the streets. Numbers increase safety, safety increases numbers. Adding to the hours public agencies and buildings are open would raise the number of people needing the streets and public transportation systems, to the benefit of all.

41. Eli Ginzberg, "The Corporate Headquarters Complex in New York City" (New York: Conservation of Human Resources Project, Columbia University, 1977), p. xxix.

In brief, our cities can be great arenas for experimentation in life-styles not based on the traditional sex-role allocations, places where women and men can live more equally without paying a price for deviancy and where all persons can fulfill more efficiently and productively the obligations of their work and private lives without having constantly to juggle serious conflicts. To have the programs and the policies to make this possible requires that our decision makers shed both traditional conceptions of the family and restricted ideas of appropriate sex roles. It requires acknowledging the person as the basic unit of society, with both a private and a productive life, and creating the support structure and the employment possibilities necessary to make this a reality.

Brooklyn, New York

Photograph by Mel Rosenthal

City Spatial Structure, Women's Household Work, and National Urban Policy

Ann R. Markusen

This paper investigates the interrelationship between city spatial structure, women's household work, and urban policy. It first differentiates between two types of work in urban space: wage-labor production and household reproduction of labor power, generally and incorrectly ignored in analyses of urban spatial structure and dynamics by neoclassical location theorists and Marxist urbanologists alike. I contend that social reproduction, organized within the patriarchal household where an unequal internal division of labor favors men, profoundly affects and explains the use of urban space. The paper then presents a theoretical argument regarding the evolution of contemporary urban spatial structure. It argues that the dominance of the single-family detached dwelling, its separation from the workplace, and its decentralized urban location are as much the products of the patriarchal organization of household production as of the capitalist organization of wage work. While this arrangement is apparently inefficient and onerous from the point of view of women, it offers advantages to men and poses contradictions for capitalism.

Challenging such patriarchal structuring of urban space are residential choices that certain demographic groups are currently making. New spatial developments—such as retirement communities, gentrification (urban renewal for upper- and middle-income households), and the growth of small towns—suggest that the dominant urban decentralized form of housing and land use may pose major obstacles to efficient household production. A second, and less anarchic, challenge is from the women's movement. Since the 1960s women have organized to

I would like to thank Heidi Hartmann, Marc Weiss, Constance Blake, Patricia Morgan, Margaret Hilton, Gerda Wekerle, and Joyce Chelouche for extensive comments and enthusiasm for the topic.

change land-use laws, to restructure the patterns of housing ownership and housing-unit structure, to form urban cooperatives for child care and other sharing of household work, and to restructure the urban transportation system. Nevertheless, current patterns of homeownership, real estate construction practices, and the permanency of urban physical structure are formidable barriers to the nonpatriarchal restructuring of urban space.

The analysis of urban spatial structure from a feminist perspective leads ultimately to a questioning of national urban policy. How has it influenced such structure in the past? Does the current policy debate encompass women's concerns? A review of the Carter policy proposed in 1978 shows that its focus on investment stimulation and city fiscal crisis would not have appreciably helped women, especially with issues of the household division of labor in urban space. The final section presents a vision of a feminist national urban policy.

Production and Social Reproduction in Urban Space

Human energy is largely spent in one of two activities: the production of commodities for market exchange and the reproduction of labor power. The former is organized, at least in capitalist society, within the institution of plants, shops, or offices, where employers hire workers (i.e., buy their labor power) for wages in order to produce commodities such as food, clothing, and shelter, machines, insurance, and so on. These are then sold to consumers or other employers for prices that more than cover wages and costs of production. Both neoclassical and Marxist economic analysts, studying the relationships among employer, worker, and output, seek to explain the conditions under which workers enter the labor market (labor force participation), under which their labor power may not be purchased by employers (unemployment), and by which certain levels of output are forthcoming from the use of certain production processes (productivity).

Similar studies look at the composition of output as a function of both demand (consumer's purchases) and supply (production conditions), and at the savings and spending behavior of workers, who receive wages, and of corporations and capitalists, who receive profits. Such studies contribute to the construction of aggregate Keynesian indicators, such as Gross National Product, and to interpretations of their causation that will guide a government intervention meant to perfect the operation of the production sphere. Marxist accounts emphasize different features of the same production process, particularly the exploitation of labor power and the inherent tendency toward crisis. Marxists consequently derive opposing views of the causes of capitalist economic problems, predicting that a socialist transformation is required to solve production-sphere problems.

In the urban setting, these production concerns take on a spatial dimension. As urban economic problems, production problems become those of the transportation of employees to work (the journey to work), of the availability of desirable production space (including rights to pollute), of the fit of skills of a local population to regional industrial structure, and the multiplier process whereby locally generated income and locally stimulated production result in further increases in output and income in secondary and tertiary sectors. Neoclassical urban economic studies, at both the micro and macro level, aim at so characterizing the production process in urban space that government policy can substitute in cases of market failure (pollution control), strengthen or subsidize the market where it is weak (transportation), and stimulate the aggregate level of activity in a local economy when it is recessed (countercyclical revenue sharing). In Marxist versions, urban problems stem from the very structure of capitalism, because both economic crisis and class conflict produce contradictions in urban structure and governance.[1]

While these are generally considered to be the "economic" realities of urban life, the sphere of social reproduction, or reproduction of the production sector workforce, is equally economic in the sense that it, too, requires labor time. Social reproduction involves the activities of both government and households that reproduce both current and future generations of labor power. These include the direct provision of the conditions of physical and mental health, cooked meals, personal services, education, maintenance of living conditions, and child care. However, the organization of social reproduction, meaning the context surrounding the use and compensation for labor time of the household workers involved, is quite different from the terms under which labor is hired and organized in the capitalist wage-labor sector.

Of the two basic institutions involved in social reproduction, government hires workers in much the same way that private businesses do. However, government does not compensate laborers strictly on the basis of productivity, does not aim to make a profit on their labor, and does not derive revenues from the sale of labor-produced output. It instead raises funds via a complex taxation system. Demands for public sector outputs are registered, not by a market process, but by a political system where voter-elected representatives determine levels of output and tax payments. Much more needs to be understood about the way in which the public sector operates, and the ways in which the structuring of urban space conditions the efficiency and equity of the local public sector. In minor ways, the recently proposed national urban policy addresses certain of these conditions by proposing incentives to metropolitan areas to adopt tax-sharing schemes and by requiring neighborhood citi-

1. Neoclassical work can be sampled in such periodicals as the *Journal of Urban Economics;* Marxist work in the *International Journal of Urban and Regional Research.*

zen participation in certain public sector urban programs. Another subject worthy of research is the interrelationship between household production and local public sector structures.

Of greater interest to us now, however, is the structuring of social reproduction in the household realm of urban society. Most economists and other social scientists treat the household as a social and economic unit without disaggregating it to its individual members. Conventional economic analysis treats the household as a consuming and resource-owning unit, whose sole relationships to wage-labor and commodity markets consist of supplying labor to and consuming the output of the commodity production process. Similarly, Marxist analyses of the household under capitalism have emphasized its function as a private sphere absorbing the alienation of the capitalist workplace[2] and even as a triumph of the working-class family preventing complete proletarianization.[3] Both types of analysis obscure the role that household members, chiefly women, perform in the reproduction of labor power and the social relationships of the household in which it takes place.

In urban space, the location and organization of households are generally considered of economic interest only as the locational source of labor power and buying power. Neoclassical studies hypothesize that household-location decisions are primarily a function of the journey to work and secondarily reflect preferences for accessibility to open space, good public services, retail markets, and housing quality.[4] Even the term "journey to work" suggests, incorrectly, that no work is done in the household. The locational outcomes are always presented as utility-maximizing decisions undertaken by the household as a whole. They have not been analyzed as decisions per se about production input required in the reproduction of labor power (e.g., minimizing travel time to schools, to health care, to markets, and to recreation). Nor has household-location analysis considered conflict among the members of the household, particularly between those who are primarily engaged in the capitalist labor market and those primarily responsible for social reproduction activities (especially when working as wage labor also), that is, conflict between men and women or husbands and wives.

The Marxist feminist literature[5] is beginning to correct these omis-

2. Eli Zaretsky, "Capitalism, the Family, and Personal Life," pts. 1 and 2, *Socialist Revolution* 3, nos. 1–2 (January–April 1973): 69–125, and 3, no. 3 (May–June 1973): 19–70.

3. Jane Humphries, "The Working-Class Family, Women's Liberation and Class Struggle: The Case of Nineteenth Century British History," *Review of Radical Political Economics* 9, no. 3 (Summer 1977): 25–41.

4. William Alonso, "Metropolis without Growth," *Public Interest* 53 (Fall 1978): 68–86.

5. Sheila Rowbotham, *Women's Consciousness; Man's World* (London: Penguin Books, 1973); Dorothy Smith, "Women, the Family, and Corporate Capitalism," *Berkeley Journal of Sociology* 20 (1975–76): 55–90; Heidi Hartmann, "The Unhappy Marriage of Marxism and Feminism: Towards a New Union," *Capital and Class* 3 (Summer 1979): 45–72; Ann R. Markusen, "Feminist Notes on Introductory Economics," *Review of Radical Political Economics* 9, no. 3 (Summer 1977): 1–18.

sions. It argues that the household is not a passive consumption unit, but one in which people reproduce their labor power, of both current and future generations, through a process that involves considerable male/female division of labor, extensive expenditure of labor time, and particular composition of output that has its own quality and distributional patterns. Even though more than half of all adult women under age sixty-five work for wages, they still bear the primary responsibility for household work. The products of their labor are meals, clean and mended clothes, home health care, preschool education of children, financial and transportation services, and so on. Yet, the economic nature of this activity is largely hidden by the informal economic contract involved. Marriage, this view argues, is an implicit rather than an explicit contract for the exchange and organizational control of labor power in the household.

Household Production, Women's Roles, and the Structuring of U.S. Urban Space

The most striking aspects of modern U.S. city spatial structure are the significant spatial segregation of residence from the capitalist workplace, the increasing low-density settlement, and the predominant single-family form of residential housing. Most contemporary analysts variously ascribe these developments to the rise of mass production techniques, to the automobile, to FHA mortgages, and to class and racial segregation. None of the analyses mentions woman's household work, household social relations, or patriarchy as primary determinants of this structure. Feminists critical of urban structure claim that current forms are inefficient for social reproduction and reinforce women's roles as household workers and as members of the secondary labor force. Yet no one has systemically critiqued the myopia of both neoclassical location theory and Marxist urban spatial theory by documenting the centrality of the patriarchal form of household organization as a necessary and causal condition responsible for contemporary urban structure and its problems.

Hayford has explored the relationship of patriarchy to community structure throughout human history.[6] Our more specific concern here is with the spatial form produced by the conjuncture of patriarchy and capitalism in advanced industrial countries. By patriarchal structuring of social reproduction, I follow the definition of Hartmann, in which the labor power of women within a capitalism system is employed partially or wholly in the service of men in the household and where the returns to both women's and men's labor are contained in the family wage, which the man controls. Women's work involves the same basic activities that

6. Alison Hayford, "The Geography of Women: An Historical Introduction," *Antipode* 6, no. 2 (1974): 1–6.

occur in capitalist production, but organized differently. A woman produces a meal for the household by purchasing raw material inputs at the grocery store or by growing a garden, combining them with her labor time, energy, and machine power provided by kitchen equipment, and serving them to household members. In contrast, her hired counterpart in the restaurant may do the same things, but her service is sold for a price that covers both her own wages and her employer's required return on investment. The productivity and efficiency of household production in the former case are just as important as in the latter, except that in the latter the market test is the willingness of the consumer to buy the restaurant meal at the price covering costs, while the quality and costliness of the household meal are directly "tested" by household members' satisfaction, and the implicit price is represented by the expenditure of household income and time.

The organization of household production has not been without its students and efficiency-promoting studies. Beginning in the middle of the nineteenth century, home economics specialists investigated ways of increasing the efficiency and quality of household production. They introduced mechanized techniques (sewing, washing, and dishwashing machines; vacuum cleaners; etc.), and they rationalized organization of women's time, using methods reminiscent of scientific management in the factory. Such efficiency concerns, however, have accepted the nuclear household as the unit of analysis. Most home economists have confined their prescriptions to changes within the household, rather than to changes in the size, composition, or spatial organization of households in urban places, including their juxtaposition to other institutions that supply inputs into the household production process. A few considered collective kitchens and apartment hotels, but for the most part dramatic changes in household organization were championed by utopians: Charlotte Perkins Gilman, for instance, in *Herland*,[7] her feminist utopia originally published in 1915, and Melusina Fay Peirce in her 1868–71 campaign for cooperative housekeeping in Cambridge, Massachusetts.[8]

Similarly, few treatments of optimal household location in urban space try to account for the maximization of efficiency in household production. Most location models assume that the household chooses between "*the* journey to work" (implying only one wage worker) and various consumption goods such as housing, open space, and public sector services. Gravity models (models that weight the multiple spatial orientations of the firm, e.g., toward sources of inputs and markets for outputs, by the transportation costs between each in order to predict the profit-maximizing location) have not been developed for intraurban household location. The exclusion of household production from the

7. Charlotte Perkins Gilman, *Herland* (New York: Pantheon Books, 1979).

8. Dolores Hayden, "Melusina Fay Peirce and Cooperative Housekeeping," *International Journal of Urban and Regional Research* 2, no. 3 (October 1978): 404–20.

calculus for urban spatial location is damaging, because it may lead to erroneous conclusions about the ability of certain urban policies to affect spatial form or to a blindness regarding the vulnerability of urban form to changes in household structure.

The fundamental separation between "work" spheres and home corresponds roughly to the division of primary responsibility between adult men and women for household production and wage labor, at least historically. Since patriarchy is the organizing principle of the former sphere, urban spatial structure must be as much a product of patriarchy as it is of capitalism. Patriarchy may thus contribute to and condition urban problems. The recent literature by feminists critiquing urban structure, both the single-family household and its spatial decentralization, argues that current patterns are inefficient for women because they result in wasted labor time and curtailed access to jobs and other facets of urban life.[9] Popular accounts, such as Betty Friedan's critique of women's household experience in *The Feminine Mystique* and Marilyn French's detailing of suburban housework in the bestselling novel *The Women's Room*,[10] also document the waste and alienation inherent in the current structure of urban housing, suburban neighborhoods, and intraurban transportation networks. Further proof can be discerned in the efforts by various women's groups and community organizations to protect existing forms of suprahousehold nonmarket production and collective consumption and to extend them further in the spheres of housing, child care, and other shared neighborhood services.

If these contentions regarding the inefficient structuring of urban space are true, why do women continue to choose household production roles in the existing urban structure? Primarily because their choices are so limited. In household decisions men and women are conditioned by the limited range of their options, a fact which conventional location analysis obscures. The major force encouraging women to remain in the household sector is the inaccessibility of jobs in the capitalist labor market, and the occupational segregation that keeps women's wages at strikingly low levels and women confined in low-skill, no-advancement jobs.

9. Dolores Hayden and Gwendolyn Wright, "Architecture and Urban Planning: Review Essay," *Signs: Journal of Women in Culture and Society* 1, no. 4 (Summer 1976): 923–33; R. Palm and A. Pred, "A Time-geographic Perspective on the Problem of Inequality for Women," in *Women in Society*, ed. P. Burnett (Chicago: Maroufa Press, 1977); David Popenoe, *The Suburban Environment: Sweden and the United States* (Chicago: University of Chicago Press, 1977); Wendy Sarkissian, "Planning as If Women Mattered: The Story of Brown Hills," mimeographed (Berkeley: Department of Landscape Architecture, University of California, 1978); Gerda Wekerle and Novia Carter, "Urban Sprawl: The Price Women Pay," *Branching Out* 5, no. 2 (1978): 12–14; Eva Gamarnikow, "Introduction to the Special Issue on Women and the City," *International Journal of Urban and Regional Research* 2, no. 3 (October 1978): 390–403.

10. Betty Friedan, *The Feminine Mystique* (New York: Dell Publishing Co., 1963); Marilyn French, *The Women's Room* (New York: Summit Books, 1977).

These conditions, in turn, have been traced to patriarchal compromises struck between male workers and capitalist employers, where the primary incentive for male workers to oppose women's incorporation into wage labor was the level of service and power men commanded in the household.[11] Even when women work for wages, and a majority do, their lower pay reinforces their role as supplemental breadwinners for the household, and they continue to bear the primary responsibility for housework.

A second, and tempering, observation must be made. Given the quality and paucity of the alternatives, women's control over their own working conditions may be greater in the household workplace than in a factory or service establishment. Of course, this may not be universally true; some husbands require extraordinary cleanliness and service on command, and some use physical violence to enforce their demands. Household production organized in single-family units permits some variation of tasks and development of a higher level of skills, compared to the specialization and deskilling generally enforced in the lower ranks of the labor market, a station to which most women would be assigned if working as wage labor. This consideration of quality of working conditions cautions us against concluding that household production per se is inefficient. A feminist society, in which oppressive household divisions of labor were eliminated, might still choose to perform many tasks in the reproduction of labor power within a modified form of household.

But, if contemporary urban spatial structure is dysfunctional for most women, then it must be functional or efficient from the point of view of capitalism or patriarchy or both. To distinguish between the two, we must look at the ways in which the conditions governing women's household production in urban settings have evolved with developments in the capitalist workplace and in the patriarchal household. Capitalist structuring of twentieth-century society has profoundly influenced the household, both directly through its requirements for the type of labor power to be reproduced and indirectly through its organization of commodity production. Increasingly, because of its hierarchical elaboration of the labor force, the capitalist production sphere required dramatically different conditions for the rearing of children. This has resulted in class-differentiated neighborhoods with tremendous responsibility for child care devolving upon women in individual households. Women may collaborate in the decision to live in suburbia, because, given the options, suburban locations offer safer, less crime-ridden, and less racially tense environments for both blacks and whites for bringing up children. Furthermore, since the types of household labor involved in caring for children are dissimilar from those involved in reproducing the labor

11. Heidi Hartmann, "Capitalism, Patriarchy, and Job Segregation by Sex," *Signs: Journal of Women in Culture and Society* 1, no. 3, pt. 2 (Spring 1976): 137–69; Ruth Milkman, "Women Workers and American Trade Unions," *Socialist Review* (1980), in press.

power of adults, it may be that differentials in quality, productivity, and required labor time result in the relatively high incidence of households with small children in metropolitan suburban locations.

Second, capitalist organization of land and housing as commodities brokered by the real estate industry, built by the construction industry, and financed by the banking sector, has found current patterns of residential decentralization and single-family dwellings profitable. However, such profitability need not require this particular spatial form. For instance, in the absence of the patriarchal nuclear family, these same industries might have made just as much profit off the construction, sale, and financing of high-density, urban apartment-like living quarters accommodating various forms of household composition. It is true that the single-family form of housing is more amenable to the type of recycling of urban space that occurs with blockbusting, speculation, and continual construction and destruction of housing values. Nevertheless, this argument cannot explain the single-family unit; more accurately, it reflects its popularity. The housing and land use recycling process has, however, indirectly promoted the isolation of the suburban household worker by eroding the extended family and community network that previously helped informally to collectivize household work in urban areas. The dynamics of urban land use increasingly result in the wholesale slummification or renewal of neighborhoods, a process that undermines entire ethnic communities and disperses their residents. This is also a function of the increasing labor mobility required by employers, which produces individual household migration patterns, both intraurban and interregional, that disrupt long-term community ties.

A final factor in the individualization of urban household work has been the restructuring of the income basis for retired people toward social security and pensions and away from inclusion in family support systems. This development has eliminated the need for generations to occupy the same household or to settle near each other. Incomes of the elderly are frequently insufficient to support residence in the same neighborhood as those of their sons and daughters. As a result of age segregation of urban and even regional space (seniors moving to Florida and Arizona), women have lost the propinquity of parents and other older neighbors as child carers. Di Leonardo's work[12] indicates that in Italian urban communities of all classes, integenerationally shared household arrangements have been a primary motivational reason for women's dedication to household work and have frequently eased work duties through sharing. While an individual woman might be glad to escape her mother-in-law, on the whole this nuclear fragmentation of the family appears to increase the relative inefficiency in household pro-

---

12. Micaela Di Leonardo, "La Vita Nuova: Class, Work and Kinship among Italian-American Women in California" (Ph.D. diss., University of California, Berkeley, 1980).

duction for women, though not necessarily for patriarchal relations or for capitalism as a whole.

While individual employers may benefit from mobility of labor within cities and regions, and while certain industries may have actively promoted and profited from the evolution of contemporary urban spatial form (the durable-goods industries, for instance), there are other ways in which the present form of household production in urban space is inefficient for capitalist production requirements. First, the continued absorption of women's labor time in the household prevents them from being available as wage workers to a production sector that is always in search of cheap labor. Second, current urban household spatial structure requires large commuting costs and considerable duplication of the household production apparatus, which become part of the basic living costs of workers that employers must cover in the wage.

It is unnecessary to attempt to unravel completely the relationship between patriarchy and capitalism in promoting contemporary labor spatial structure. While eliminating capitalism does not necessarily end patriarchy, as the socialist countries show, it is not clear that we could eliminate patriarchy without transforming capitalism. Some argue that patriarchy indirectly serves capitalism by dividing the workforce and blunting class consciousness.[13] However, acceptance of this view does not require a corollary that *all* forms and products of patriarchal relationships are functional for capitalism. Even if the current urban structure is efficient for capitalism as a whole, one can make a case that it is functional for patriarchy, and that the widespread indifference to women's concerns about its inefficiency can be attributed mainly to patriarchal, rather than capitalist, ideology.

How do men benefit from contemporary urban spatial structure? I can offer several hypotheses. First, the "ideal" single-family, detached, urban or suburban dwelling embraces the contemporary patriarchal form of household organization. Within it, the man (when present) is generally considered the head of household (until the current census, he was officially so), the primary wage earner, and the major support of the household. This form discourages extended family or community sharing of housework; deploys the machinery of housework in individual units, which makes sharing difficult; and replaces collective play space (parks) with individual yards. The journey to work of the husband tends to dominate location decisions, and the distance to jobs, combined with inadequate public transportation, discourages women from working for wages. The publicly subsidized (FHA) propagation of homeownership entails significant commitments on the part of both women and men to maintenance work on the individual structure, toil that is confined and controlled within the household unit.

13. Rowbotham (n. 5 above).

Second, the apparently wasteful expenditure of women's labor time under such circumstances underscores the nature and maintenance of power and privilege of men in the patriarchal household unit. Veblen argued years ago that men receive satisfaction from the conspicuous consumption of women's labor time in the household: the more waste apparent, the more social status accruing to them.[14] If this motive prevails, productivity of women's time in the household is not important, and a concern with it would directly conflict with accrual of status. Feminist historians have observed that working-class women as well as men aspired to replicate the upper-class family, where women did not have to work for a wage, but would instead perform the role of household manager and servant. The lack of interest in household efficiency in the larger spatial context also reinforces the illusion that only men "really" work and "provide" for their families. At any rate, we can conclude that in general, American men have not registered complaints about the waste of women's labor time, or inefficiency, of dispersed, residential, single-family dwelling patterns.

A third, and nonconflicting, hypothesis concerns the quality of output achievable under the patriarchal form of household organization. The advantages of this form of organization include the flexibility of scheduling of certain services (meals, recreation, etc.) and the potentially higher quality of home-cooked meals, homegrown vegetables, and personally tailored services. (Of course, such personally crafted services could be worse, as well!) In this sense, the current form of household production may not be inefficient, that is, wasteful of women's labor time. This argument would hold if women's preferences coincide with men's preferences; given the alternatives, women may indeed enjoy their own home-cooked meals and may prefer taking care of their own children to cheap restaurants or for-profit custodial child care. But it may also benefit men at women's expense. Flexible and quality meals for husbands may require the squandering of women's labor time.

We are, of course, dealing with shifting definitions of efficiency. In the argument regarding quality of household output, the "efficiency" of a home-cooked meal depends on which side of the dinner table you occupy. While it appears that men as a rule gain from the current organization of household production, these gains are qualified by their position as wage-earning workers. It is possible that such personal service could become very expensive with certain changes in capitalist workplace organization, commodity composition, and women's resistance. For instance, if women's wages were to rise enough to make their wage labor attractive; if women were to demand full partnership in household work; and if the quality and price of market-produced child care, meals, and so on were to improve substantially, men might agree

14. Thorstein Veblen, *The Theory of the Leisure Class* (New York: Macmillan Co., 1899).

more readily to women's wage work, with a diminution of the quality and privilege associated with full-time household work, and to restructuring of the household in urban space. Nevertheless, the single most significant factor in the structure of the patriarchal household is the derogation of primary responsibility for household labor upon women. If men were to assume their share of responsibility for housework and child care, then we might experience significant changes in household structure and spatial location in urban areas. Such an event might show us just how inefficient contemporary household production patterns really are. Similarly, the question of whether current patterns are functional for capitalism depends upon the net effects on profit produced through such arrangements and, further, on the way in which patriarchal concessions to male workers are necessary to the maintenance of a docile workforce.

Of course factors other than the patriarchal form of household production influence location decisions and housing choices, particularly race and class characteristics and the relationship between households and wage-labor work locations. Furthermore, American individualism has undoubtedly coincided with patriarchal household structure to promote the single-family suburban housing that is more common in U.S. cities than in European ones. Yet, the central theoretical point stands: patriarchy profoundly shapes American urban spatial structure and dynamics. It implies that the dismantling of patriarchal household arrangements might call for dramatic restructuring of cities.

The Reshaping of Urban Space

Patriarchy is not a static system. Currently under widespread attack by the women's movement, it also must accommodate itself to changes in capitalism, particularly the increasing availability of commodity substitutes for household labor (child care, restaurant meals, and so on). In unorganized as well as organized ways, changes are taking place in urban living arrangements that foreshadow the future evaluation of urban spatial structure. For instance, three significant demographic changes have occurred in the 1970s in the United States that involve new forms or locations of household production. Their emergence contributes substance to the argument that decentralized urban single-family households are not the most efficient workplaces for the reproduction of labor power and human life. Each instance involves a different segment of women in the population, but all three suggest significant efficiencies deriving from a more integrated use of urban space or a more collective form of household or neighborhood structure.

The first phenomenon is gentrification, that is, the reverse migration of middle- and upper-income residents to urban centers, bringing housing rehabilitation or rebuilding with them. While no urban analysts have pursued this explanation, it seems clear that gentrification is in large part a result of the breakdown of the patriarchal household. Households of gay people, singles, and professional couples with central business district jobs increasingly find central locations attractive. Particularly important has been the success of both gays and women in the professional and managerial classes in gaining access to decent-paying jobs. Gentrification must also be ascribed to the growth of high-income professional and managerial jobs per se in big cities, where the needs of contemporary large-scale corporations have concentrated jobs associated with the control and management of large-scale economic enterprises and with government-related activity.[15]

Gentrification in large part corresponds to the two-income (or more) professional household that requires both a relatively central urban location to minimize journey-to-work costs of several wage earners and a location that enhances efficiency in household production (stores are nearer) and in the substitution of market-produced commodities (laundries, restaurants, child care) for household production. In some areas, such as the SoHo district in New York City, large networks of women-headed households share child care and other household production activities in a well-organized manner. The flexibility in designing living space out of converted lofts enhances this collectivization and permits variation in household composition.

Second is the movement of retired households to relatively nonurban settings, all the way from southern New Jersey and the Upper Peninsula in Michigan to retirement colonies like Leisure World in Florida and in the Southwest. While these households generally remain nuclear, the division of labor between men and women frequently breaks down. One striking feature of these communities is that they provide relatively easy access to the normal range of inputs in the household production process, eliminating the difficulties posed by urban and suburban traffic, parking, and high taxes. Condominiums reduce the household maintenance tasks. Such communities are experiencing the revival of noncommodity production and barter among residents, women and men alike, with a more explicit emphasis on the quality of household production. Retirement housing is also frequently more collective in shared space and facilities. Buildings or complexes may include group dining facilities, group recreational facilities, and small health-care and therapy centers.

Finally, there is striking evidence that the fastest growing American communities are small and medium-sized towns, not urban areas.[16] Although suburbs continue to be developed, the total suburban popula-

---

15. Stephen Hymer, "The Multinational Corporation and the International Division of Labor," in Stephen Hymer, *The Multinational Corporation: A Radical Critique*, ed. R. Cohen et al. (Cambridge: Cambridge University Press, 1979).

16. Alonso (n. 4 above).

tion is not rising rapidly, and many urban areas as a whole are experiencing depopulation. While decentralization of employment and the relatively lower cost of living are most often cited as causes, my own informal observations suggest that women are frequently strong proponents of such moves, because they provide greater possibilities for shared child care and greater community involvement in social reproduction. Such places also involve easier access to jobs, even though they may not offer better pay than those available in urban areas. I have noticed, for example, that wives of construction workers who are regionally mobile often choose to live permanently in small towns rather than cities because they make household life easier while their husbands migrate to seasonal jobs.

These latter two examples are not cases of the breakdown of patriarchy per se but of household and urban spatial patterns that have evolved from a breakdown of the patriarchal structuring of household production. In fact, both of the latter cases may be explained as reactions to the extraordinary success of that form in dominating the housing stock and the spatial array of urban residences. In the former case, older people frequently find it inefficient to continue to live in, maintain, and pay taxes on a large house which previously operated as the workplace for rearing children. The homogeneity of single-family neighborhoods makes it nearly impossible to find alternative housing in the same area. The choice to migrate to another region entirely may be more a hallmark of the destruction of any meaningful or accessible social unit larger than the family than a product of the cessation of wage work or the search for a warmer, healthier climate. Similarly, the migration to small towns of nuclear families not tied to urban labor markets signals the inefficiency of household production imposed by the patriarchal urban form, particularly its destruction of access for women to collective help with household production, to jobs, and to urban amenities.

However, just as patriarchy will not disappear without organized resistance, the trends we have just discussed cannot be counted on anarchically to undermine the patriarchal structuring of households and urban space. The sobering reality of this form of urban spatial structure is its permanence. It is literally constructed in brick and concrete. Therefore, its existence continues to constrain the possibilities open to women and men seeking to form new types of households and to reorder the household division of labor. The fact that housing, the primary workplace for social reproduction, is also the major asset for many people tends to reinforce the single-family, patriarchal shape of housing and neighborhoods. Builders, and people buying from them, worry that innovative housing forms will not have a resale value. People interested in suprafamilial communal living situations have generally had to either migrate to rural areas where they could construct their own housing or to older central city areas where they could convert large old housing units (originally built for extended families or boarders). Efforts by lesbians and other organized groups (e.g., a church group in Detroit) to take over entire neighborhoods are severely hampered by the individualization of land-ownership patterns and the legal sanctity of property. Developers, through urban renewal, may use public domain powers to clear entire sections of urban land for private business development, but community and neighborhood groups have no such access to eminent domain for efforts to collectivize living space for the tasks of social reproduction. The dominance of the single-family, detached dwelling in a decentralized urban spatial structure reinforces people's ideas of what forms of household structure are possible and penalizes them materially if they wish to pursue other visions.

Since the resurgence of the women's movement in the late 1960s, women who wish to change their living arrangements and household responsibilities, or to increase their options for doing so, have found it necessary to attack the structural determinants of patriarchal household urban form directly. The women in SoHo successfully fought city zoning ordinances that prohibited the types of units they wanted to construct out of old lofts. Ettore's study[17] of lesbian ghettos in Britain documents their struggle to secure access to the city, through forms of squatting and collectivized households, in living arrangements not mediated by marriage. In many urban areas, women have set up cooperative child care and other forms of cooperatives that help alleviate the burdens of housework.[18] Women have found regulations of the welfare state that presume the patriarchal family is the normal household unit and that are frequently oppressive to men as well as women (e.g., the refusal of HEW until recently to grant aid to dependent children to fathers).

The widespread activism of women in urban struggles around housing, child care, and neighborhood preservation has generally been neglected in the literature on urban social movements.[19] Feminist critics of this literature point out that because women's struggles have frequently been over issues bearing on conditions of social reproduction, they are invisible to the students of urban social movements, who identify urban problems as capitalist, not patriarchal, phenomena.[20] Furthermore, the literature frequently overemphasizes the role of men in such movements and misrepresents the goals and strategy of the organizations. While

17. E. M. Ettore, "Women, Urban Social Movements, and the Lesbian Ghetto," *International Journal of Urban and Regional Research* 2, no. 3 (October 1978): 499–520.

18. Anna Whyatt, "Cooperatives, Women, and Political Practice," *International Journal of Urban and Regional Research* 2, no. 3 (October 1978): 538–57.

19. Manuel Castells, *The Urban Question: A Marxist Approach*, trans. Alan Sheridan (Cambridge, Mass.: M.I.T. Press, 1977); Janice Perlman,"Grassroots Participation from Neighborhood to Nation," in *Citizen Participation in America*, ed. Stuart Langdon (Lexington, Mass.: Lexington Books, 1976).

20. Hilary Rose, "In Practice Supported, in Theory Denied: An Account of an Invisible Urban Movement," *International Journal of Urban and Regional Research* 2, no. 3 (October 1978): 521–37; Gamarnikow (n. 9 above).

leadership may be male, the main organizing in many urban struggles has been accomplished by women, who tend to know their neighborhoods better, who build collectivization of household labor into many community group organizing efforts, and who seem to opt for a form of organization that permits them to continue their household work.[21] Recently formulated socialist strategies for transforming urban structures, such as Stone and Hartman's program for housing,[22] have as a rule completely ignored the role of social reproduction and household labor in structuring urban space. Such plans also neglect to ask women what types of housing and changes in the organization of urban space would alleviate the unequal patriachal division of household labor. The Stone/Hartman strategy, for instance, would leave untouched the basic single-family housing unit. Nor does it include any explicit expectation that a socialist housing strategy should alleviate women's household working conditions.

The National Urban Policy Debate

All women are affected by the limited choices offered in urban space. In addition to local struggles, a major means for reshaping urban spatial structure is national urban policy. How well has urban policy addressed feminist concerns with household and urban form? Clearly since World War I, U.S. policy has reinforced the nuclear family, detached dwelling, decentralized urban structure. A review of the most recent set of urban proposals at the national level does not promise much relief. Wekerle[23] has attacked them, because they ignore women's urban needs, specifically the limited proposals for low-income housing, and because of the absence of new programs for improved transportation, certain types of urban infrastructure, and welfare programs. But, urban policy debate is significant more for its omission of women's concerns than any deliberate attempt to preserve existing spatial structure. While the most recently proposed policy has floundered in Congress, its scrutiny reveals the conspicuous absence of the feminist perspective. In March 1978, the Carter administration unveiled its National Urban Policy, designed to fulfill campaign promises to an urban constituency, including black groups, that had supported Carter's election bid. They had been patient, particularly since the urban policy had been assigned sec-

---

21. See, e.g., Ronald Lawson and Stephen Barton, "Sex Roles in Social Movements: A Case Study of the Tenant Movement in New York City," *Signs: Journal of Women in Culture and Society* 6, no. 2 (Winter 1980), in press.

22. Michael Stone and Chester Hartman, "Housing, a Marxist Analysis and a Socialist Program" (paper presented at Cornell University Conference on Progressive Planning, Ithaca, New York, April 1979).

23. Gerda Wekerle, "A Woman's Place Is in the City," mimeographed (Toronto: York University, 1978).

ondary priority while the Carter administration undertook its first major policy initiative, energy, and since the energy policy, as a whole, had assumed an antiurban bias.[24]

The urban policy identified two major problems that characterized U.S. cities in the late 1970s: declining economies (some central cities, some suburbs, and even entire metropolitan areas), and attendant urban fiscal crises experienced by their local governments. The first integrated and explicit urban policy, it implicitly embraced a theory that the urban crisis occurring in many different U.S. cities can best be reversed by a major attempt to revive private economic activity, thereby mitigating high levels of unemployment, plumping city tax bases, and diminishing such decline-related expenditures as welfare. More than any previous urban-oriented federal policy, this one aimed at underlying causes rather than such symptoms as poor housing or unemployed people. Supposedly, the new attack on basic economic conditions would generate the income and quality of public sector services that would, in turn, prompt improved housing and human welfare.

Thus the keystones of the package were its business-oriented stimulants, particularly the National Development Bank (NDB), the targeted investment tax credit (ITC), the Employment Tax Credit at the federal level, and the fiscal stimulants of Soft Public Works and renewal of Supplemental (previously antirecessionary) Assistance for the local level. The NDB would offer loans and grants to private businesses to expand production in urban areas. The targeted ITC would soften the antiurban bias of the proposed extension of the 10 percent ITC by adding on an additional 5 percent tax rebate for building in troubled urban, as opposed to suburban or rural, areas. The Employment Tax Credit would permit employers who expanded their urban workforce to deduct a percentage of the new payroll from their federal corporate income tax liability. The Soft Public Works program would expand jobs (part union labor, part hard-core unemployed) in the construction industry through rehabilitation and insulation projects on public buildings. Supplemental Assistance would extend the then-existing countercyclical revenue-sharing program, in which large grants went to cities with unemployment rates sharply above the national average, mostly large northeastern and midwestern cities like New York and Detroit. While the proposed urban policy contained a number of housing and neighborhood programs, such as community health centers, community anticrime programs, and housing rehabilitation loans, the proposed dollar commitments to these types of program were small. By far, the largest financial commitment (over 90 percent) would go into the investment-inducing and fiscal solvency proposals (see table 1).

24. Ann Markusen and Jerry Fastrup, "The Regional War for Federal Aid," *Public Interest* 53 (Fall 1978): 87–99.

Whether the Carter investment-oriented programs would, in fact, stimulate employment is not at all clear, since they are heavily biased in favor of highly capital intensive redevelopment. They include no direct requirement that private-firm beneficiaries be accountable for the net number of jobs created (including those eliminated by new developments) or generate new tax revenue to cover the additional public sector services that their expansion would require.[25] At any rate, this question is now moot, since neither the ITC nor the NDB proposal passed Congress.[26] An extension of the regular investment tax credit did pass, and although it is to include rehabilitation, its bias is toward new

Table 1

New Urban Initiatives, 1979–81
(Fiscal Years, in Millions of Dollars)

Function and Program	Budget Authority		
	1979	1980	1981
National resources and environment	40	15	15
Transportation	200	200	200
Community and regional development:			
Public works	1,000	1,000	1,000
National Development Bank	2,360	3,405	3,620
Community development corporations	20	20	20
Urban parks and recreation facilities	150	150	150
Housing Rehabilitation Loan Program (sec. 312)	150	150	150
Self-help development program	15	15	15
Community Development Credit Unions	12	. . .	. . .
Urban Volunteer Corps (new, ACTION)	40	40	40
Loan guarantees*	(2,200)	(3,800)	(5,000)
Education, training, employment, and social services	172	172	172
Targeted Employment Tax Credit	(1,500)	(1,500)	(1,500)
Investment Tax Credit Extension†	(200)	(200)	. . .
Community anticrime programs	10	10	10
Health–Community Health Center	50	50	50
State incentive grants	200	200	200
Supplementary fiscal assistance	. . .	660	. . .
Totals:			
Budget authority outlays	4,419	6,087	5,642
Revenue reductions	(1,700)	(1,700)	(1,500)
Loan guarantees	(2,200)	(3,800)	(5,000)
Total effect of proposals	8,319	11,587	12,142

Source.—Adapted from President Carter's speech to Congress, "New Partnership to Conserve America's Communities," March 27, 1978, Washington, D.C.
Note.—Figures in parentheses are not outlays, but revenue foregone and value of guarantees.
*Nonbudgetary. Figures represent the value of loans guaranteed. Cost to the taxpayer depends on rate of default.
†Figures are questionable. Much higher figures for the investment tax credit extension are found in Luger (n. 27) on the order of $8,400 per year in lost revenues.

25. The National Urban Policy Collective, "Carter's National Urban Policy," mimeographed (Berkeley: Department of City and Regional Planning, University of California, 1978).

26. Marc Weiss and Erica Shoenberger, "Carter's New Urban Strategy," *In These Times* (February 28, 1979), p. 17.

building and rebuilding rather than maintenance. New building heavily favors rapidly growing regions and suburban areas, not the most problematic areas. The extension can thus be expected to continue to encourage the suburbanization and regional shift of employment.[27] A version of the employment tax credit did pass, but only after it was divorced from the urban policy and rolled into the general tax reform bill.

The major successes to date in the Carter program are those policy innovations that the executive branch could implement without Congressional approval or appropriations, namely, Carter's pledge to perform urban impact analyses of new federal policy initiatives and his pledge to redirect federal procurement and federal facility location to needy regional economies. Yet even these efforts define "impacts" and "needs" in terms of conventional economic criteria such as employment, income, and local government tax and expenditures.

The perspective implicit in the national urban policy debate is that the urban problem consists only of the behavior of economic aggregates. In other words, if we could equalize (and lower) unemployment rates and equalize (and raise) public expenditures across cities and suburbs, we would have solved the urban problem. Lower unemployment could be achieved by investment and employment incentives; higher public expenditures could be achieved through state and federal increases in revenue sharing and grants. Restored health to the basic economic indicators of urban unemployment and city fiscal solvency would reflect increased well-being and security of urban residents. More jobs would increase incomes and reduce unemployment; a solvent city would be able to reduce taxes, expand social services, and stem the out-migration of business. Equalization across cities and regions could be achieved by spatial targeting of both policy types.

It is difficult to discern exactly what the net effects of a Carter-type new urban policy on women might be. Most of the proposals are aimed at improving employment or income, without targeting beneficiaries by class, race, or sex. They do not chart the complex process by which increases in employment and income filter through a local economy, displacing some jobs, restructuring some neighborhoods, increasing some types of public services, and lowering taxes for some groups. A business receiving a grant or subsidy would not have to guarantee job creation or worry about its impact on the restructuring of urban space, such as destruction of existing neighborhoods to build a new subsidized inner-city plant. In this sense, the policy is worse than urban renewal, which at least invested residents with legal rights to relocation assistance. The policy as a whole does little to help women, especially with problems of the urban structuring of household production.

Housing programs have constituted a major exception to this rec-

27. Michael Luger, "The Unintended Regional Employment Consequences of Business Tax Incentives," mimeographed (Berkeley: Department of Economics, University of California, 1978).

ord. However, housing policy has traditionally been a pro-production policy in disguise, aimed more at stimulating the construction sector, thereby boosting real estate and building industry profits and expanding jobs for construction workers, than at providing decent housing (part of social reproduction) for the population.[28] As Wekerle has pointed out,[29] the strongest housing emphasis in the Carter urban policy lies in its new rehabilitation program. Yet rehab loans can only benefit professional and upper-income women, who have only recently gained access to credit. Moreover, Carter's proposed program cuts both public housing and Section 8 funds, though these housing programs and purchase subsidies for low-income households are the most likely to reach low-income households. If anything, the Carter policy might be expected, through these mechanisms, to widen the gap between working-class and professional/managerial-class women. No part of the policy appears to address either the employment problems of lower-income women or the inefficiency of household production imposed by current patterns of urban structure. Thus, while the housing programs may aid the dismantling of patriarchal household relations in one class segment, they may by omission reinforce them for women in other class locations.

More by its omission than by its content, the national urban policy debate has not been concerned with the particular problems that women face in the urban environment as household workers, many of which assume crisis proportions in this era of change in family structure and in women's participation in the labor force. While it is not a policy that purports to deal with urban spatial dynamics directly, its focus on investment location, and its assumption of continued housing and transportation policies that do favor current patterns, betray its belief that women's spatial concerns are not important. The policy does nothing to encourage commercial, residential, and workplace reintegration or greater choice in housing form. In fact, to the extent that it encourages and perpetuates the replication of existing urban structure and function, with its massive-scale segregation of workplace and household and its emphasis on single-family dwellings, we can more grimly conclude that it perpetuates women's problems with the urban environment and does little to eliminate the burdens of patriarchy.

Toward a Feminist National Urban Policy

Since urban spatial structure and housing form is such an important constraint on women's ability to change household work roles, national

28. Stone and Hartman (n. 22 above); Marc Weiss, "The Origins and Legacy of Urban Renewal," in *Urban and Regional Planning in an Age of Austerity*, ed. P. Clavel, W. Goldsmith, and J. Forester (New York: Pergamon Press, 1980); Joel Friedman, Judith Kossy, and Mitt Regan, "Working within the State: Progressive Roles for Planners," ibid.

29. Wekerle (n. 23 above).

urban policy should be a major target for feminists. The Department of Housing and Urban Development should rank high with departments concerned with labor, health, education, and welfare as a major agency charged with policy responsibilities central to women. HUD's programs should be scrutinized for their impacts on women and new initiatives should be proposed and demanded.

What would a national urban policy that addressed women's issues look like? Perhaps if we could map this out, we could better assess current national urban policy. The answer grows out of our criticisms of the current structuring of urban space for household production and from a more general critique of social structures that impede women's progress and that could be addressed at the urban level. First of all, the most pressing issue for both women's involvement in the labor force and for economizing on household production involves child care. Without some form of socialized child care, women with young children will remain tied primarily to household production locations. Three solutions are possible: sharing informally through extended-family arrangements and neighborhood co-ops; publicly producing child care; and privately producing, for profit, child care. Each currently exists on a limited basis. Each has serious consequences for both the quality of child-care services and the labor-force participation of women. No thorough study of the implications of each as a prototype system has been done. Clearly, the problem is urban in nature: Should child care be provided cooperatively in small neighborhood complexes or single-family homes, by the public sector in public buildings (like elementary education) on a larger neighborhood scale, or in private enterprises in neighborhood or regional shopping centers? The alternative location— at the plant, office, or shop—has received little attention, even though it has interesting possibilities for parent/worker involvement in child care and for efficiency in journey-to-work trips.

A second issue, also of significance, is the type of housing available in urban areas. Women living without men but with children (a rapidly growing group), and groups of single adults, have difficult times both in adapting existing housing to their needs and in obtaining access to it. Restricted credit opportunities are only one of several discriminating barriers. We have no way of knowing what types of households people would choose to live in, given a choice, but we can say that these choices have not existed in the past, nor do they exist in the present. Federal policy might (as it does in the energy business) invest in research and development and experimental projects with various forms of collective and nonpatriarchal housing.

A third set of policies would encourage and subsidize the reintegration of uses in urban space to enhance the efficiency of the household production sector. These policies might pioneer and provide incentives to small-scale commercial development; to the decentralization of jobs in small establishments; to efficiencies in the use of urban space, such as more park space in place of endless private front yards; fine-grained transportation systems; etc. While I leave the design of these to my imaginative sisters, I might suggest one criterion that could be used to judge the desirability of such projects (net of other costs): the elimination of unnecessary labor time expended in individual travel (excluding public transportation time which can be used to read newspapers or books or to socialize), in individual yard improvement and grooming, in individual meal preparations, child care, and so on. Other criteria must address both the quality of output and the quality of women's working conditions.

Of course, the efficiency of household production cannot be gauged without considering its market-produced substitutes and its alternative employment opportunities for household (mainly women) workers. No urban policy focused on household production could be satisfactory for women without parallel all-out attack on discrimination in employment. The value of women's labor time in household production can only be accurately assessed if full value is accorded women's work in the wage-labor market.

Finally, a feminist urban policy would establish a new research agenda. This would explore the theoretical understanding of the relationship between patriarchal household form, urban housing, and spatial structure. It would pursue extensive empirical work to document the cost in women's labor time and the working conditions within the household resulting from various aspects of urban structure. It would develop and introduce a new type of cost/benefit calculus for judging the efficiency and social welfare of such public projects as transportation systems, housing, and urban infrastructure (parks, streets, utilities). This calculus would evaluate the effects of such projects on the household division of labor and its productivity. It would design, propose, and experiment with policies and projects that would directly address household production concerns, increase women's choices, and alleviate the onerous division of household labor. It would investigate the proper levels of government or form of collective organization that should be charged with reshaping elements of urban structure. Such a research agenda, which would undoubtedly uncover many creative possibilities, would end the invisibility of women's concerns within both the academy and the agencies that shape urban policy.

Department of City and Regional Planning
University of California, Berkeley

City Lights:
Immigrant Women and the
Rise of the Movies

Elizabeth Ewen

American life, from 1890 to 1920, was marked by dramatic growth and massive uprooting. New industries were built, national markets for consumer goods developed, and the urban metropolis became a distinct social environment. Rapid industrial change created an explosion of energies that redefined the social content of American society and resulted in the formation of a new culture, a modern urban way of life. Within this general environment, two developments are important to examine.

The first is a massive immigration: over 23 million people from eastern Europe and southern Italy came to the United States and settled in primarily urban centers. They were to labor in and populate a maturing industrial society, but they emerged from semi-industrial peasant and artisan backgrounds where the social institutions of family and community organized and maintained a customary culture. For these people, the migration represented a crisis in the fabric of their lives, deeply experienced in the home and the family, the usual realm of women. The new urban world threatened the basis of traditional womanhood, forcing women to look in two directions simultaneously: to the past for strength to sustain life in the present and to the future to find new means of survival. This double vision impinged directly on family life and created strains on the customary expectations of the mother-daughter relationship. One generation, the mothers, had grown to maturity in European society. Urban life challenged the sense of survival and perception they had brought with them when they migrated to the United States. The next generation, the daughters, although touched by the experience of the Old World, were much more the children of the metropolis. Their lives were caught up in social dynamics beyond the frame of old-world understandings.[1]

Simultaneously, within the cities, we can see the rise of new cultural images—billboards, signs, advertising, the electric lights of Broadway—pressing themselves on people's attention, creating a new visual landscape of possibility. An urban and distinctly American culture proclaims itself in image form, demanding response and notice, as strange to small-town Americans as it was to incoming immigrants. Viola Paradise of the Immigrant Protective League analyzed the social complexity of this new cultural formation: "The very things which strike the native born [Americans] as foreign seem to her [the new immigrant] as distinctly American: the pretentiousness of signs and advertisements, the gaudy crowded shop windows, the frequency of fruit stands and meat markets, her own countrymen in American clothes . . . she sums it all up as 'America.' "[2] For immigrants in particular, one of the most powerful components of this new urban culture was the development of moving pictures. In a world of constant language barriers, the silent film was compelling and accessible. Silent pictures spoke primarily to urban immigrant audiences of women and children, themselves caught up in the social drama of transformation.

This article will look at the interaction between the social experiences of immigrant women and the images that confronted them in their daily lives. It is not a history or aesthetic of silent film, but an attempt to understand women's history in relation to "the agencies of mass impression,"[3] a term once used to describe the development of modern urban

1. Some of the material used in this essay comes from Elizabeth Ewen, "Immigrant Women in the Land of Dollars, 1890–1930" (Ph.D. diss., State University of New York at Stony Brook, 1979), to be published by Pantheon Press, New York, in 1980. I will refer primarily to the experiences of Italian and Jewish women migrating to New York City during this period. In order to highlight the mother-daughter relationship, I have de-emphasized the role of fathers in family life. For an exploration of this theme, see Alice Kessler-Harris's introduction to Anzia Yezierska's *Breadgivers* (New York: Doubleday & Co., 1925; reprint ed., New York: George Braziller, Inc., 1975), as well as the novel itself. The source material documenting the lives of immigrant women comes mainly from three sources: contemporary novels and autobiography, social work material, and oral history. I have made extensive use of the archives of the Oral History Project: 1890–1930, City University of New York, New York City, directed by Herbert Gutman and Virginia Yans-McLaughlin from 1974 to 1976. For secondary materials, see Virginia Yans-McLaughlin, *Family and Community: Italian Immigrants in Buffalo, 1890–1930* (Ithaca, N.Y.: Cornell University Press, 1977); Charlotte Baum, Paula Hyman, and Sonya Michel, *The Jewish Woman in America* (New York: Dial Press, 1976); and Judith Smith, "Our Own Kind: Family and Community Networks in Providence," *Radical History Review* 17 (April 1977): 99–120. I would like to thank Stuart Ewen for his support and helpful criticisms.

2. Viola Paradise, "The Jewish Girl in Chicago," *Survey* 30 (1913): 700–703, see esp. p. 701.

3. Malcolm Wiley and Stuart Rice, "The Agencies of Communication," in *Recent Social Trends in the United States: Report of the President's Research Committee on Social Trends* (New York: McGraw-Hill Book Co., 1933), p. 209.

culture in image form. The movies will be viewed as an exemplary piece of a cultural environment that interacted, over time, with the social history of its audience. Film is but one example of the association between the large-scale displacement of people and the rise of the agencies of mass impression in American history. Radio also developed within the framework of domestic migration, and television within the contours of large-scale migrations from the country to the city, from the city to the suburbs.[4] In each case, the changing demographic and industrial patterns created the context for an audiovisual culture designed to fill the gaps and fissures of experience. The agencies of mass impression became a new electronic voice in the social landscape of everyday life, explaining away the past, preparing people for participation in a new present.

One arena of transformation was the home. As modern industry socialized production, a historical crisis developed in the interior structure of the household that made imperative the reconstruction of the home, the family, the social roles of women, and the subjective experience of daily life.[5] On the one hand, women increasingly entered the industrial work force. The expanding consumer industries assembled a female work force to be employed in the new ready-made clothing, food, appliances, perfumes, and cosmetics industries and to work in various capacities associated with modern forms of corporate and retail distribution: typing, secretarial work, and sales.[6] On the other hand, these new industries changed the status of the home itself. Their goods and services altered decisively the fabric of daily life and work *inside* the home. The working woman and the modern housewife stand at two poles of the same historical moment.

Adaptation to city life required a constant struggle. Old-world societies, whether in eastern Europe or southern Italy, were rooted still in resources drawn from nature: gardens, home production, and systems of family and community support.[7] In the New World, wages and

4. See Robert Sklar, *Movie-made America* (New York: Random House, 1975), pp. 3–33; and Raymond Williams, *Television* (New York: Schocken Books, 1975) pp. 9–31.

5. See Robert S. Lynd and Alice Hanson, "The People as Consumers," in *Recent Social Trends;* William Ogburn, "The Family and Its Functions," in *Recent Social Trends;* Batya Weinbaum and Amy Bridges, " The Other Side of the Paycheck: Monopoly Capital and the Structure of Consumption," *Monthly Review* 28 (July 1976): 88–103.

6. Of course, this trend develops with the Industrial Revolution of the nineteenth century, but rapid industrialization brings this historical tendency to fruition. See Alice Kessler-Harris, "Stratifying by Sex: Understanding the History of Working Women," in *Liberating Women's History*, ed. Berenice Carroll (Champaign: University of Illinois Press, 1975); Rosalyn Baxandall, Elizabeth Ewen, and Linda Gordon, "The Working Class Has Two Sexes," *Monthly Review* 28 (July 1976): 1–9.

7. For Italian women, see Phyllis Williams, *South Italian Folkways in Europe and America* (New Haven, Conn.: Yale University Press, 1938), pp. 19–24; Leonard Covello, *The Social Background of the Italo-American School Child* (Totowa, N.J.: Rowman & Littlefield, 1967), pp. 210–20; Yans-McLaughlin, pp. 25–35. For Jewish women, see Baum et al.,

money were the key to survival. In the old cultures, the social labor of women had converted raw materials into household goods; the new-world immigrant mothers had to confront the industrial marketplace to secure the goods necessary for their families' survival and well-being.

In order to make ends meet, most immigrant families adopted a new division of labor. The facts of urban economic life made family cooperation essential. Louise More's study of wage earners' budgets in New York in 1909 provides the crucial observation that "the number of families entirely dependent on the earnings of one person is small when compared with the numbers whose incomes include the earnings of husband, wife, several children, some boarders, gifts from relatives. . . . Several or all of these resources may enter into the total resources of that family in a year. Perhaps this income should more accurately be called the household income, for it represents the amount which comes into the family purse, of which the mother usually has the disbursement."[8] While the father and older children worked for wages outside the home, the mother was central to the family's well-being. As one social worker noted at the time: "It is the mother around whom the whole machinery of family life revolves. The family economy depends on her interests, skills and sense of order. Her economic importance is far greater than that of her wealthier sisters for as income increases . . . the amount of it controlled by the wife diminishes. . . . But in her humble status, her position is thoroughly dignified."[9]

Robert Chapin concluded in his 1909 study of New York working-class life that "while the personal factor does operate in the case of every family . . . the limits with which it may affect the actual sum total of material comforts that make up the living of the family are set by *social forces*. These social forces find expression on the one side in the income which the family receives—that is, in the rate of wages received by the father and others who are at work; on the other side, they are expressed in the prices that have to be paid to get housing, food and other means of subsistence."[10] The common experience for immigrant women on arrival was to "figure the dollar in their home money. They thought they were rich until they had to pay rent, buy groceries, clothing and shoes. Then, they knew they were poor."[11] To maintain home and family in the urban economy demanded a range of skills from the daily negotiations

pp. 66–74; Mark Zborowski and Elizabeth Herzog, *Life Is with People* (New York: International Press, 1952; reprint ed., New York: Schocken Books, 1972), pp. 131–35.

8. Louise More, *Wage Earners' Budgets: A Study of Standards and Cost of Living* (New York: Henry Holt & Co., 1907; reprint ed., New York: Arno Press, 1971), p. 28.

9. Mary Simkhovitch, *The City Workers' World* (New York: Henry Holt & Co., 1917), pp. 79–80.

10. Robert Chapin, *The Standard of Living among Workingman's Families in New York City* (New York: Russell Sage Foundation, 1909; reprint ed., New York: Arno Press, 1971), pp. 249–50.

11. Elizabeth Gurley Flynn, *Rebel Girl* (New York: International Press, 1973), p. 133.

in the marketplace for basic needs, to the careful accumulation of money for rent, to taking in boarders to help make ends meet, to occasional finishing work brought back from the garment shops. In addition, the social demands were equally pressing: from the care of young children, to the daily grind of housework, to the care of the sick, to providing help to neighbors and relatives.

In all of these activities, immigrant mothers faced impossibly high rents, the fear of eviction, high prices for food and clothing, sickness, noise, inferior housing, and times of unemployment and poverty. Barred from access by reasons of sex, class, nationality, language, and custom to most of the institutions of American society, most mothers relied on institutions that were the most familiar and immediate: family and community. Many sought out relatives, neighbors, and other women of the same ethnicity to establish networks of support and common concern. Within the congested tenement districts of New York, new forms of community developed in which women learned from each other and shared the problems of urban life. Elsie Clew Parsons, the well-known contemporary anthropologist, observed:

> One of the most noticeable traits in the life of the average tenement dweller . . . to the eyes . . . of the private visitor . . . is the more or less intimate and friendly intercourse of the families of the house. Washtubs and cooking dishes are borrowed from one another at any hour of the day; a mother leaves her child with a friend across the hall when she goes shopping . . . ; a kindly soul sits up all night with a sick child; yet, in spite of all the little individual acts of service, the whole round of economic activity is entirely independent of every other family.[12]

The borrowing of tools, the lending of service, the exchange of activity became a buffer against the isolation imposed on women as housewives and a mediation between an older, more familiar culture left behind and the chaotic individualizing forces of urban life.

While immigrant mothers were consumed by new realities, fathers and older children were engaged in the world of wage labor and urban institutions outside the home. On the surface, there appears to be a generational split between first-generation immigrant mothers and their daughters. The urban environment created a historic division in the customary expectations of the mother-daughter relationship. The industrial city separated the home-centered experience of mothers from the more social experience of daughters in ways that were painful and difficult to understand. New urban institutions like the public school, the settlement house, the dance halls, and the diversions of the street made claims on the lives of some immigrant daughters, redirecting their activ-

---

12. Elsie Clew Parsons, "The Division of Labor in the Tenements," *Charities and the Commons* 15 (1905): 443.

ity. Unlike their mothers, the immigrant daughters' sense of self, although halting and incomplete, was directed outward. American society was based on a different conception of family life which demanded that adolescents identify with a social world outside the domain of family. Access to that world was dependent on having time and money for the use of the self. The price of admission to new culture was the negation of old-world notions of womanhood; needs appeared for clothing, hairstyles, and makeup necessary to assume the external appearance of an "American," for forms of economic and sexual independence away from maternal authority. While some of these divisions had been experienced back home, the city universalized these new relations.

This, of course, put pressure on the immigrant mothers, who needed their daughters' economic support to maintain the fragile household economy, but who felt threatened by the separate social life demanded by some daughters. Patriarchal culture had deemed the outside world the proper place for men and boys, while young women were expected to stay close to home by the side of their mothers. The struggle to free the self from family bonds was harder to win for daughters than for sons.[13] In general terms, the outside world of American culture was viewed with hostility by most immigrant mothers, who saw these institutions as a direct threat to their ability to carry on cultural traditions and achieve economic viability.

However, one American institution became a realm of shared cultural experience for mothers and daughters: the movies. While immigrant parents battled their daughters' assertion of the right to participate in most of the recreational institutions of the city, *everyone* went to the movies. They became the one American institution that had the possibility of uniting generations and was cross-generational in its appeal. Most film historians agree that the first audiences for motion pictures came primarily from the immigrant working-class neighborhoods of America's largest cities. The movies were a welcome diversion from the hardships of daily life in these communities. By 1909, New York City alone had over 340 movie houses and nickelodeons with a quarter of a million people in daily attendance and a half million on Sundays. *Survey* magazine, the journal of social work, observed that "in the tenement districts the motion picture has well nigh driven other forms of entertainment from the field" and that "it was the first cheap amusement to occupy the economic plane that the saloon [had] so exclusively controlled."[14] Like

13. Since men were more irregular in turning over their wages in full, the mother-daughter bond was vital to the economic viability of family life (see Ewen, pp. 123–31; and Louise Odencrantz, *Italian Women in Industry* [New York: Russell Sage Foundation, 1919], pp. 175–77). For cultural conflicts, see Ewen, pp. 276–323; Marie Concistre, "A Study of a Decade in the Life and Education of the Adult Immigrant Community in East Harlem" (Ph.D. diss., New York University, 1943), reprinted in part in Francesco Cordasco and Eugene Bucchioni, *The Italians* (Fairfield, N.J.: Augustus M. Kelley, Publishers, 1974); Belle Isreals, "The Way of the Girl," *Survey* 22 (1909): 494–97; Baum et al., pp. 115–17.

14. Lewis Palmer, "The World in Motion," *Survey* 22 (1909): 357.

the saloon, it was cheap: a nickel per person, twenty-five cents for the whole family. Unlike the saloon, it was not sex defined; anyone who had a nickel could enter. There, for a low price, families could be enveloped in a new world of perception, a magical universe of madness and motion.

The movies became for immigrants a powerful experience of the American culture which was often denied to them, surrounding them with images, fantasies, and revelations about the New World: "More vividly than any other social agency, they revealed the social typography of America to the immigrant, to the poor. . . . From the outset, the movies were, besides a commodity and a developing craft, a social agency."[15] In *Sons of Italy*, Antonio Mangano described the effects of motion pictures on recently arrived Italians: "Moving pictures were a great attraction, and he went every day to see what new pictures there were on the billboards. . . . Cold chills crept up and down his back as he witnessed thrilling scenes of what he thought was *really* American life."[16] The movies also became a translator of the social codes of American society which could now be unraveled, looked at, interpreted, made fun of, understood. They formed a bridge between an older form of culture inadequate to explain the present and a social world of new kinds of behavior, values, and possibilities; their images and fantasies were a text of explanation, a way of seeing. Like their audience, early movies had not yet found a voice. Silent movies spoke in a more comprehensible language of silence, image, sign, and gesture.

The movies also presented themselves as a release from daily troubles, a world where the realities of daily life were rendered empathetically in comedic or melodramatic form. Movie advertisements pitched themselves to working-class audiences in a tone of compassion:

> If you're tired of life, go to the movies
> If you're sick of trouble rife, go to the picture show
> You'll forget your unpaid bills, rheumatism and other ills
> If you'll stop your pills and go to the picture show.[17]

15. Lewis Jacobs, *The Rise of American Film* (New York: Harcourt Brace & Co., 1939; reprint ed., New York: Teachers College Press, 1969), p. 12. Secondary material fairly contemporary to the period under investigation is often more useful in analyzing historical trends than contemporary film scholarship that asks different questions. For an historian of immigration to discard the material presented in Robert Foerster, *The Italian Emigration of Our Times* (Cambridge, Mass.: Harvard University Press, 1924), or in Isaac Hourwich, *Immigration and Labor* (New York: G. P. Putnam's Sons, 1912), to name but a few, would be an error. The same is true for film scholarship; Jacobs's *The Rise of American Film* or Vachel Lindsay's *The Art of the Moving Picture* (New York: Macmillan Publishing Co., 1915; reprint ed., New York: Liveright Publishing Corp., 1970) are so valuable because of their proximity to the developments under study. Failure to appreciate the viewpoint of the past produces a one-dimensional present-mindedness.

16. Antonio Mangano, *Sons of Italy* (New York: Missionary Education Movement, 1917), pp. 6–7.

17. Cited in Russell Nye, *The Unembarrassed Muse* (New York: Dial Press, 1970), p. 365.

In a sense, the form was an emanation of community. Families went together; local merchants advertised on the screen; people sang along and read or translated captions out loud; the organ played; socializing was common. One observer commented: "Visit a motion picture show on a Saturday night below 14th Street when the house is full and you will soon be convinced of the real hold this new amusement has on its audience. Certain houses have become genuine social centers where neighborhood groups may be found . . . where regulars stroll up and down the aisles between acts and visit friends."[18] The *Jewish Daily Forward* in 1908 commented on the growing popularity of this medium for women and children during the day. "Hundreds of people wait on line. . . . A movie show lasts a half an hour. If it's not too busy you can see it several times. They open at one in the afternoon and customers, mainly women and children, gossip, eat fruit and nuts and have a good time."[19]

If the form was collective, the content of some early movies bore a direct relationship to the historical experience of its audience. Some films depicted a landscape outside of immigration; these brought American history and culture, in the form of westerns, news clips, and costume dramas, to ethnic eyes. Some movies were nativist, racist, and sexist. But many early movies showed the difficult and ambiguous realities of urban tenement life in an idiom that spoke directly to immigrant women. In the early days of the movie industry, there was more of an identity of experience and background between filmmaker and audience. The new medium attracted many immigrant and working-class entrepreneurs into its ranks. Before Hollywood took center stage, the movies were created in primarily urban settings. As Lewis Jacobs, the film historian, observed, "The central figure of adventure comedies was always a common man or woman—the farmer, fireman, policeman, housewife, stenographer, clerk, servant, cook. . . . Such characters were selected because the audience and filmmakers alike were of this class and because of the growing popular interest in the everyday person."[20] From 1903 to 1915, he argues, poverty and the struggle for existence were "favorite dramatic themes." In films with titles like *The Eviction, The Need for Gold, She Won't Pay Her Rent, Neighbors Who Borrow, The Miser's Hoard, Bertha, the Sewing Machine Girl,* and *The Kleptomaniac,* everyday situations were depicted, the causes of poverty were held to be environmental, and economic injustice was deplored.[21]

18. Palmer (n. 13 above), p. 355.

19. Cited in Irving Howe, *World of Our Fathers* (New York: Harcourt Brace Jovanovich, 1976), p. 213; see also Odencrantz, p. 235; and P. Williams, pp. 117–18.

20. Jacobs, p. 17; see also Sklar, pp. 18–30.

21. Jacobs, pp. 69–71. Robert Bremer (*From the Depths: The Discovery of Poverty in the United States* [New York: New York University Press, 1956]) argues that the early movies made a real contribution to the social understanding of poverty as environmental (see pp. 110–12).

More important, these films spoke directly to tensions and contradictions in the world of immigrant mothers. For example, Edwin S. Porter, the director of *The Great Train Robbery,* made a film in 1905, *The Kleptomaniac.* Its theme is justice in a class-defined society. The first sequence shows the arrest of a wealthy woman caught shoplifting trinkets from a department store, the second that of a poor woman, on the brink of starvation, stealing a loaf of bread. The third sequence brings both women to court, wherein the poor woman is jailed and the judge discharges the rich woman. An epilogue sums up the three sequences; we see a figure of Justice blindfolded, holding up a scale. On one side of the scale is a bag of gold; on the other, the loaf of bread. The scale moves in favor of the gold. The blindfold is removed, and the figure of Justice has only one eye, which is fixated on the gold.[22] In *Eleventh Hour,* the slum dwellers are Italian. The father, a street peddler, goes to jail for fighting with a bully who constantly harasses him. When the bully dies, the husband is sentenced to life. The wife pleads with the governor to no avail, as do the children. At the "eleventh hour," the father is released, the family reunited.[23] This film spoke clearly of the defense of the family against legal injustice and harassment.

Sometimes, the immigrant experience itself was the subject of silent movies, for instance, Chaplin's *The Immigrant.* The content of Thomas Ince and Gardner Sullivan's *The Italian* (1911) is revealing in this regard. The film uses a series of dramatic contrasts to depict the social transformation and economic dislocation of immigrant families on New York's Lower East Side. It begins with a romanticized image of Italian life in Venice, where the audience is introduced to Beppo, a gondolier, and Gallia, a young peasant woman. The film develops images of a bounteous and festive Italy. The scene then shifts to the Lower East Side; the new landscape is framed by stark, bleak, realistic images. Beppo has become a poor bootblack, Gallia a housewife in a stifling tenement apartment. Aided by neighbor women, Gallia gives birth to a son, who rapidly becomes quite sick. The doctor explains that the baby is sick from the heat and the impure milk he has been drinking. In 1911, the higher grades of milk were pasteurized and sold in bottles at an expensive price, but the lower grades of unpasteurized milk were sold as "loose" in tenement neighborhoods and carried home in glasses or pails. John Spargo, a well-known social reformer, argued in 1908 that in immigrant neighborhoods "one third of all babies die before five years old of diseases chiefly connected to the digestive tract and a considerable percent of these diseases are definitely known to be caused by milk."[24] In contrast to

22. For another account, see Jacobs, pp. 47–48.

23. Ibid., pp. 70–71.

24. John Spargo, "Common Sense of the Milk Question," *Charities and the Commons* 20 (1908): 544–96, see esp. p. 595; for another account of this powerful movie, see Lindsay, pp. 70–71.

the bountiful imagery utilized to frame peasant life, the image of poisoned milk spoke to the inversion of nature and mothering in industrial America.

At this point a new level of contrast develops. While Beppo and Gallia try to raise money for a supply of bottled, pasteurized milk, the baby languishes and dies. In his travels, Beppo tries to raise money from "The Boss, The Wealthiest Man of the Slums." The Boss denies him, throws him off his car, and has him arrested. Beppo is imprisoned. The Boss also has a sick child, so he uses his money and influence to rope off his elegant house from the public noise that would be fatal to his child. Beppo, out of prison and consumed with hate, sneaks into the Boss's house to harm the child, but he cannot bring himself to do it. While the Boss's child lives, Beppo and Gallia grieve. The contrasts between peasant and urban life, rich and poor, class and family, spoke directly to immigrant mothers: the maintenance of family and the care of children was a class question, since only through access to money could these conditions be transformed. This film provided a prism through which the audience could look at and recognize itself.

In *The Eviction,* a poor man, drunk with his friends, dreams that his wife has sold her wedding ring to save their home and furniture. On awakening, he hurries home to see the landlord removing the furniture from their tenement apartment. Passersby chip in to pay the rent, the husband repents, the wife forgives, and a new life begins for the family.[25] This movie would have made perfect sense to urban immigrant women. Maria Ganz, in her autobiography of New York tenement life, tells of an evicted woman and the community support of her neighbors:

> The evicted woman kept staring at the litter of cheap things in which she must have taken no end of pride and pleasure while she had been gathering them one by one in the making of her home, now left in pieces on the street, a symbol of eviction and destitution. She brought out a china plate from the folds of her dress and placed it on one of the chairs. . . . People would drop pennies, perhaps even nickels and dimes into that plate—enough to save her from being wholly destitute.[26]

Mike Gold, in his autobiography, *Jews without Money,* explained this system of community support: "This is an old custom on the East Side; whenever a family is to be evicted, the neighborhood women put on their shawls and beg from door to door."[27]

Early movies existed outside of the moral universe of correct and

25. See Jacobs, pp. 71–72.

26. Maria Ganz with Nat Ferber, *Rebels: Into Anarchy and out Again* (New York: Dodd, Mead & Co., 1919), pp. 77–78.

27. Mike Gold, *Jews without Money* (New York: Liveright Publishing Corp., 1930), p. 94.

respectable middle-class society. Comedies also mocked respectable ruling elites and looked at authority, social conventions, and wealth with a jaundiced eye. In the Sennett and Chaplin comedies, the artifacts of the new consumer culture became objects of ridicule. Mack Sennett explained the attraction of his films: "Their approach to life was earthy and understandable. They whaled the daylights out of pretension. . . . They reduced convention, dogma, stuffed shirts and Authority to nonsense and then blossomed into pandemonium. . . . I especially liked the reduction of authority to absurdity, the notion that Sex could be funny, and the bold insults hurled at Pretension."[28]

Yet, despite the affinities between audience and early film, it is undeniable that the movies also were an institution of the larger society, subject to its shifts and pulls. If some of the silent movies registered, to some degree, the social and economic problems of urban life, others spoke increasingly to the social and sexual dynamics, the ideological superstructure of an evolving consumer culture. We can begin to perceive the dim outlines of this development if we look more closely at the contradictory experiences of immigrant daughters and their interaction with the silent screen. As we have said, the concerns and experiences of immigrant daughters were somewhat different than the more home-bound problems of their mothers. Their work experience led some of these daughters into active participation in the trade-union movement, political life, and involvement in the suffrage movement.[29] For others, contact with American culture was mainly associated with educational aspirations and cultural transformation.

For many, beguiling ready-made clothes, freer ways of relating to the opposite sex, and new forms of independence from family created compelling and fresh definitions of femininity. As one social worker noted at the time:

> Inevitably, the influences of her new work life, in which she spends nine hours a day, begin to tell on her. Each morning and evening as she covers her head with a crocheted shawl and walks to and from the factory, she passes the daughters of her Irish and American neighbors in their cheap waists in the latest smart styles, their tinsel ornaments and gay hair bows; a part of their pay envelopes go into the personal expenses of these girls. Nor do they hurry through the streets to their homes after working hours, but linger with a boy companion "making dates" for a movie or affair.[30]

28. Cited in Edward Wagenknecht, *The Movies in the Age of Innocence* (Norman: University of Oklahoma, 1962), p. 41. See Sklar's discussion of the relationship between comedy and audience, pp. 104–21. For a feminist counterpoint, see Molly Haskell, *From Reverence to Rape* (Middlesex: Penguin Books, 1973), pp. 61–74.

29. See Alice Kessler-Harris, "Organizing the Unorganizable: Three Jewish Women and Their Union," *Labor History* 17 (Winter 1976): 5–23.

30. Ruth S. True, "The Neglected Girl," in *West Side Studies*, ed. Pauline Goldmark (New York: Russell Sage Foundation, 1914), p. 116.

While most immigrant mothers became reconciled to the fact that their daughters would leave home to go to work or school, it was still expected that the daughters would obey and internalize their mothers' standards of sexual deportment. For the second generation, the gap between home life and work life was acute: "It wasn't that we [the younger generation] wanted to be Americans as much as we wanted to be like other people. . . . We gradually accepted the notion that we were Italians at home and Americans elsewhere. Instinctively, we all sensed the necessity of adapting ourselves to two different worlds."[31] A social worker noted: "The old standards can scarcely be maintained in a modern community where girls work in factories side by side with men. . . ." She continued: "It was impossible for the parents to supervise young women in school or at work . . . the girl naturally thinks that if she can take care of herself at work, she is equally well able to do so at play."[32] To accommodate this necessary cultural transition, some immigrant daughters developed strategies for claiming a part of their income for themselves. Ruth S. True, in her study of working-class life, recorded this example: "Filomena Moresco, whose calm investment of $25 in a pretty party dress, a beaver hat, and a willowed plume was reported as little less than the act of a brigand. If she had withheld twenty cents out of her pay envelope, she probably would have been beaten by her mother. As it was, she appropriated $25 and her high handedness was her protection."[33]

A social contradiction developed. On the one hand, adolescent daughters were reared in the morality of family obligation; "good girls" returned their unopened pay envelopes to their mothers and were obedient to the needs of their families. "Bad girls" snuck or took money out of their envelopes to spend on themselves and defied the wishes of their mothers. Having money to spend on the self was intimately connected to breaking out of the family circle; personal ideas of independence were against the ideology of feminine sacrifice. For example, Agnes Mazza, an Italian garment worker, was a good girl: "I gave my pay envelope to my mother. I wouldn't dare open it up. I'd give it to my mother because I knew she worked for us and I thought this was her compensation. I always stayed close to my mother." Her sister, however, was different.

> She used to open the envelope and take a few dollars for herself if she needed it. They [sister and friends] would come home at 12 o'clock—this was terrible, especially for the Italian people. The neighbors would gossip, would say look at that girl coming home by herself. My mother would talk to her but it did no good. And then one day, my sister wanted to pay board. She was 18. My mother

31. Jerry Mangione, *Mount Allegro* (Boston: Houghton Mifflin Co., 1943), p. 228.
32. Sophonisba Breckinridge, *New Homes for Old* (New York: Harper & Bros., 1921), p. 175.
33. True, p. 112; see also Breckinridge, p. 170; and P. Williams, p. 36.

said, "What do you mean board?" She said, "I give you so much and keep the rest." So my mother said, "Alright, do what you please."[34]

Independence from family obligation implied not only the right to wages, a new physical appearance, and a social life, but, most important, the right to a mate of one's own choice. At issue were not ultimate goals, for both the bad and the good girls had severely limited options, but the means to the future, the means to marriage. In a sense, the initial stages of the sexual revolution of the twentieth century can be identified with this desire for independence on the part of those daughters who broke with family tradition and control to marry men of their own choosing.

Despite the enormous energies and activities of some immigrant daughters in the trade-union and women's suffrage movement, the options open to most women at this time were limited to the appropriation of urban adolescent culture as a wedge against patriarchal forms of sexual control. New, often bewildering dating, courtship, and sexual patterns caused pain and anguish for mothers and daughters alike. While family-dominated culture was repressive, it also presented a known form of courtship and sexual relations. The more anonymous nature of sexual relations in the city created traps for women, and immigrant women were often taken advantage of by strange and unscrupulous men.[35] It was not clear how to delineate a new morality from the connection between economic and sexual independence. It was ironic that those immigrant daughters who worked in the ready-made clothing industry were not paid enough to purchase what they produced and, consequently, had to engage in a family battle for the right to the fruits of their labor. Their inability to purchase an American "appearance" led to anguish and frustration. This problem was not associated only with immigrant life; the conflict between family obligation and more individualized definitions of social life was also felt in the homes of the prosperous middle class.[36]

While the old ways seemed inadequate as a guide to industrial culture, the movies seemed more shaped to the tempo of urban life. Increasingly, the social authority of the media of mass culture replaced older forms of family authority and behavior. The authority of this new culture organized itself around the premise of freedom from customary bonds as a way of turning people's attention to the consumer marketplace as a source of self-definition. This new cultural thrust took on American Victorian culture as much as that of first-generation immigrant parents.

34. Oral interview with Agnes Mazza, CUNY Oral History Project, May 1975; see Yezierska (n. 1 above), pp. 35–36, for a fictional rendition of this theme.

35. See Robert Park and Herbert Miller, *Old World Traits Transplanted* (New York: Harper & Bros., 1921; reprint ed., New York: Arno Press, 1971), pp. 79–80; Baum et al., pp. 116–17.

36. Sklar, pp. 88–91.

The movies became less identified with family entertainment and were utilized increasingly by the young as a space away from family life, a place to escape, to use a hard-won allowance, to sneak a date. As True observed: "There is a signal of restlessness beneath the surface. . . . Into her nature are surging for the first time the insistent needs and desires of her womanhood. She is the daughter of the people, the child of the masses. Athletics, sports, discussions, higher education will not be hers to divert this deep craving. . . . The city bristles with the chances she longs for—'to have fun and see the fellows.' " Because of these needs and the limited options for their expression, "the control of a little money is far more essential to these girls in their search for enjoyment than to girls in another class. There are many doors which a very small coin will open for her."[37]

One of these doors was the movies, where there were "flashing gaudy posters [which] lined the entrances. . . . These supply the girls with a 'craze.' These same needs send them . . . to the matinees. There pictures spread out showing adventure and melodrama which are soul-satisfying."[38] Filomena Ognibene, an Italian garment worker brought up by strict parents, claimed that "the one place I was allowed to go by myself was the movies. I went to the movies for fun. My parents wouldn't let me go out anywhere else, even when I was twenty-four. I didn't care. I wasn't used to going out, going anywhere outside of going to the movies. I used to enjoy going to the movies two or three times a week. But I would always be home by 9 o'clock."[39] Sometimes the movies were used to subvert the watchful eye of parental supervision. Grace Gello recounted that she met her future husband in 1918 through her father. "We kept company for a year and a half. We weren't allowed to go out alone, even with groups of people. My father or mother always accompanied us. But we did meet on the sly. Occasionally, we would take the afternoon off to go to the movies. We didn't do this too much because we were afraid of my father. He would say, 'If I catch you, I'll break your neck.' "[40]

By 1915, the year of D. W. Griffith's *Birth of a Nation,* the movie industry had expanded its initial audience to include middle-class patrons, had moved to the remote environs of Hollywood, and had established the studio form and the star system. The thematic content showed the transition; if some of the earlier images had depicted the urban housewife embattled by the economic forces of the New World, the new film iconography began increasingly to include images of women in flight from or redefining the meaning of home, family, sexual behavior, and social codes. The first female "stars" of the industry were

37. True, pp. 58–59.
38. Ibid., p. 67.
39. Interview with Filomena Ognibene, March 1975.
40. Interview with Grace Gello, April 1975.

cast in roles new to the silent screens: the vamp, the gamine, and, of lesser significance, the virgin.[41] Through the creation of these feminine archetypes, the silent screen began to raise sexual issues and develop imagistic fantasies that bore a relationship to the confusing sexual experiences of immigrant daughters.

The vamp was the symbol of the war between passion and respectability. Theda Bara, born Theodosia Goodman, daughter of a Jewish garment worker from Cincinnati, was created by Fox Studios as one of America's first movie stars. In over forty films from 1915 to 1919, she played the vamp, the woman who flaunts men and social convention to get what she wants. In the American lexicon, the archetype of the sexual woman was European, a woman who used her beauty and passion "to lure some helpless and completely dumb man to his ruin."[42] Underneath this image was a new consciousness about sexual relations. In Theda Bara's own words, ". . . believe me, for every woman vamp there are ten men of the same . . . men who take everything from women, love, devotion, youth, beauty and give nothing in return. *V* stands for vampire and it stands for Vengeance too. The vampire that I play is the vengeance of my sex on its exploiters. You see . . . I have the face of a vampire, perhaps, but the heart of a 'feministe.' "[43] For example, in *A Fool There Was* (1914), Bara portrayed a woman who reduced respectable middle-class men to bumbling idiots, leaving a train of madness and suicide along the way. While this film has little to recommend it as art, its imagery depicts a woman who has broken with social convention, who drinks and smokes with abandon, and who reverses the traditional assumptions of the male-female relationship. In doing so, her image points to a clear critique of the double standard.[44]

The gamine, epitomized by Mary Pickford, was an archetype of female adolescence whose pluck, self-determination, and will allowed her to create a more independent future. Born Gladys Smith into a poor family and forced at an early age to become "father" to her family,[45] Mary Pickford often played a battling tomboy "provoked by a sense of injustice and motivated by the attempt to bring happiness to others."[46] In her many films, she took on repressive fathers, ministers, and moralistic community values and defined for herself her own space. While she was part sweetness, she was also part "hellion . . . morally and physically committed to all out attacks against the forces of bigotry and malicious

41. For a particularly useful analysis, see Sumiko Higashi, *Virgins, Vamps and Flappers* (Montreal: Eden Press, 1978); Haskell, pp. 42–89.

42. Wagenknecht, p. 181.

43. Cited in Higashi, p. 61.

44. For accounts of Theda Bara, see Wagenknecht, pp. 179–81; Higashi, pp. 55–62; and Jacobs, pp. 266–67.

45. Mary Pickford, *Sunshine and Shadow* (New York: Doubleday & Co., 1955), p. 31.

46. Higashi, p. 43.

snobbery that sought to frustrate the proper denouement of a trium-
phant lovely girl."[47] In projecting the image of a spirited adolescent girl
in movies like *Rags* and *Little Annie Rooney,* she was an appealing example
for women who were themselves attempting their own fights against
barriers. Although Mary Pickford occasionally played adult roles, her
screen projection of independence was usually circumscribed by childhood. She herself stated the irony of her position. For Mary Pickford,
"the longing for motherhood was to some extent filled by the little children I played on the screen. Through my professional creations, I became, in a sense, my own baby."[48]

While the vamp and the gamine projected images of sexual freedom
and social independence, the virgin, the Griffith heroine, was, in many
ways, the last holdout of the patriarchal tradition. The virgin, played by
Lillian Gish, was the good woman firmly devoted to the protection of her
virtue against the menace of male passion. While the virgin, as the male
symbol of American womanhood, registered the existence of the new
sexual wilderness, she recoiled against it, seeking protection from its
claims through patriarchal solutions.[49]

The history of these transitional female archetypes displays some
parallels to the social and sexual struggles of the immigrant daughters. If
they were torn between fresh notions of sexuality and constricting family
structures, the vamp and the gamine, who seemed to point the way to
new definitions of femininity, were locked into a constricting star system,
which severely limited their expression and development. Their images
were used by the new studios as building blocks of an expanding industry. By 1919–20, the movie industry had become a major corporate
enterprise, committed to a national rather than a class audience. To
create this audience, some movies opted for images from the consumer
marketplace. Some of the content and form of postwar movies revealed
a new definition of "Americanization," the consumer society as an ideal
way of life. Perhaps early movies had shown an ambivalence toward
urban industrial society, but by 1920 American capitalism's consumer
culture was in full force.[50]

47. James Card, "The Films of Mary Pickford," in *"Image" on the Art and Evolution of the Film,* ed. Marshall Deutelbaum (New York: Dover Publications, 1979). For accounts of Mary Pickford which stress this theme, see Card; Higashi, pp. 41–52; Haskell, pp. 58–61; Wagenknecht, pp. 159–63; and Jacobs, pp. 264–66. Card, Higashi, and Jacobs all stress Pickford's popularity with working-class audiences.

48. Pickford, pp. 350–51.

49. Higashi, pp. 1–15; Haskell, pp. 49–57. For a discussion of the ambiguities of the virgin theme, see Russell Merritt, "Mr. Griffith, *The Painted Lady* and the Distractive Frame," in Deutelbaum, pp. 147–51. In *The Painted Lady,* Blanche Sweet, as the good girl, is driven mad by sexual contradictions, caught as she is between a repressive father, an unscrupulous lover, and the new sexual world represented by makeup and clothing. For analysis of the good-bad girl, see Martha Wolfenstein and Nathan Leitesm, *Movies* (New York: Free Press, 1950), pp. 25–46.

50. See Stuart Ewen, *Captains of Consciousness* (New York: McGraw-Hill Book Co.,

By 1920, a new "formula" for movie making was developed, most notably in the films of Cecil B. DeMille. Realizing that "a new generation of movie goers, not in sympathy with its elders,"[51] was growing up, DeMille redefined the subject matter of film. While the DeMille films continued to explore the sexual dynamics of urban culture, they also began to demonstrate the maturation of a new sexual logic. Instead of the traditional settings of the prewar movies, DeMille "withdrew the curtains that had veiled the rich and fashionable and exhibited them in all the lavish and intimate details of their private lives."[52] The new De-Mille movies created a fantasy world where sex, romance, marriage, and money were intertwined to create a new frame of reference. In movies like *Old Wives for New* (1918), *Male and Female* (1919), *Why Change Your Wife?* (1920), and *Forbidden Fruit* (1920), DeMille gave voice to a crucial myth of modern culture: metamorphosis through consumption.

In the DeMille formula, the key to modern marriage lay in the ability of women to maintain a sexually attractive appearance. In *Old Wives for New*, the plot hinges around a slovenly, lazy wife in danger of losing her dapper husband. In *Why Change Your Wife?* a dowdy, modest woman interested in high culture is embarrassed by her husband's gift of a risqué negligee. The marriage breaks down. The wife then experiences a metamorphosis: she realizes that sexual appeal is crucial and thereafter transforms her appearance by purchasing new clothes. In brief, the vamp had become respectable.[53]

In *Male and Female* and *Forbidden Fruit*, DeMille explores class re-lations through the lens of sexuality and consumption. *Male and Female*, a satire of aristocratic manners, contrasts the exquisitely coiffured and well-mannered mistress (Gloria Swanson) with the sloppy and ill-mannered servant girl, Tweeney. For example, in the first part of the film, each of them eats breakfast. Edward Wagenknecht, a DeMille de-fender, argued that there was a social purpose to the scene: "From Tweeney's eating habits in *Male and Female*, it is just possible that some of the comfortable gum chewers in our 'movie palaces' may have learned that it is not good form to leave your spoon standing in your cup or to cover a whole slice of bread with jelly and then bite into it."[54]

In *Forbidden Fruit*, DeMille recreated the Cinderella myth and gave

1976); Stuart Ewen and Elizabeth Ewen, "Americanization and Consumption," *Telos* 37 (Fall 1978): 42–51; and Helen Lynd and Robert Lynd, *Middletown* (New York: Harcourt Brace & Co., 1929).

51. Benjamin Hampton, *History of the American Film Industry* (Covici, N.Y.: Friede, Inc., 1931; reprint ed., New York: Dover Publications, 1970), p. 221. For an analysis of this change, see Hampton, pp. 197–215; Sklar, pp. 88–92, 122–34; Jacobs, pp. 287–301; and David Robinson, *Hollywood in the Twenties* (New York: A. S. Barnes & Co., 1968), pp. 26–41.

52. Hampton, p. 222.

53. Higashi, pp. 136–42; Hampton, pp. 220–26; Sklar, pp. 91–96; Haskell, pp. 76–77; Jacobs, pp. 335–41, 401–3.

54. Wagenknecht, p. 207.

it a modern twist. The heroine, Mary Maddock, is the wife of a lazy, working-class husband who lives off her earnings. In contrast to a film like *The Italian,* the depiction of working-class marriage here assumes that husbands live off the labor of their wives. Mary is asked by the oil magnate for whom she works to help him and his wife "vamp" another oil magnate in order to close a business deal. They offer her twenty dollars, and she agrees. Replete with Cinderella fantasies, the film details her transformation. The wealthy wife phones for "jewels from Tiffany, gowns from Poiret, and perfumes from Coty." The servants dress her, and a hairdresser does her hair; she has become an object subject to the manipulation of experts. Her new appearance is quite convincing: she has transcended her class. The only obstacle to her success now is her manners. In a key scene, Mary, through cues and imitation, triumphs by choosing the correct fork. The rest of the film revolves around her duty to her husband versus her newly found life and "love" in the upper classes. Ultimately, "Cinderella" wins her love choice and escapes her husband and her class.

In contrast to the earlier movies, the DeMille films demonstrate the new logic of consumption as a way of presenting the self in the urban world, as the essence of the promise of modern life for women. In doing so, these films openly attack the customary assumptions, behavior, and style of the audience and point the way to the appropriation of a new form of self-definition. In this sense, they became an agency of Americanization. After the success of *Why Change Your Wife?* and *Forbidden Fruit,* many producers "turned their studios into fashion shops and the screen was flooded with imitations. . . . Wise wives, foolish wives, clever and stupid wives were portrayed in every variety of domestic situation that gave an opportunity for displays of wealth, money getting, money making, smart clothes and romance."[55] In imitation, movies with titles like *The Amateur Wife, The Misfit Wife, Poor Men's Wives,* and *Behold My Wife* "all lectured to the frump who learns that it is important to remain stylish and good looking after marriage."[56] They emphasized that the metamorphosis of the female self was the new condition for securing the means to survival in modern society—to getting and keeping a husband.[57]

55. Hampton, p. 224.
56. Cited in Jacobs, p. 401. The sexual relationships depicted in these films bear a striking resemblance to the critique of male-female relationships developed by Charlotte Perkins Gilman in *Woman and Economics* (Boston: Small Maynard & Co., 1898). Gilman argues that male capitalist greed and gain in the market and female "sex attraction" in the home constitute the grid of dependency relationships in modern society and create a market for "sensuous decoration and personal ornament" (p. 120). See pp. 110–20.
57. See also Mitchell Mattelart, "Notes on 'Modernity': A Way of Reading Women's Magazines," in *Communications and Class Struggle,* ed. Armand Mattelart and Seth Siegelaub (Paris: International General, 1979), 1:158–70. She argues that "change, in as much as it affects women, becomes synonymous with integration into the 'modern.' And it is the

For second-generation immigrant women, one step away from arranged marriage and family obligation, these new movies were manuals of desire, wishes, and dreams. What was remarkable about them was the combination of new ideas of romance and sexuality with practical guidelines for change. Out of DeMille's movies came a visual textbook to American culture, a blend of romantic ideology and practical tips for the presentation of self in the new marriage market of urban life. Here was guidance their mothers could not offer. By presenting an illusory world where "a shop girl can marry a millionaire,"[58] these movies evoked a vision of the American dream for women and the means to its feminine realization.

The appropriation of Americanized styles of dress, manners, and relations to the opposite sex were experienced as a gap between immigrant mothers and their daughters. In this sense, the imagery in the films—supported by the rapid growth of the ready-made clothing industries, the cosmetics industry, and new forms of advertising and display—made possible the liquidation of traditional culture. Maria Zambiello, who migrated here in 1903 and was the mother of three children, explained:

> I don't feel as good as the American women because I am old-fashioned, from the other side. . . . When I am with American women, I am afraid I don't talk good enough for them. Then sometimes they serve tea or coffee in nice cups and napkins—I feel ashamed . . . and they got different manners. We put the hands on the table, they don't. That's why I don't feel so good. But the young Italian girls, my daughters, they're up to date, just as good, just as polite like the Americans. They were born here, they go to school together, they see the same movies, *they know.*[59]

In other cases, an uneasy compromise between cultures developed. Maria Frazaetti articulated this possibility:

> There are no old country customs prevailing in our house. My children follow the American customs. I would like them to remember that the parents must be considered as an authority. I approve of allowing my children the freedom they desire; by doing so, they learn for themselves. My children misunderstand me when I advise them what style clothes they should wear. I blame styles and clothes on some of the stuff in magazines and the movies of

image of the happy woman, the woman dazzled by the desires and possibilities of consumption, and progress . . . which is the best publicity for modernity" (p. 160). See also Higashi, p. 142.

58. Hampton, p. 225; Higashi, pp. 102–4.

59. Interview with Maria Zambiello, January 1976.

this country. If I had my way, I would like my children to follow some of the old disciplinary laws of the old country.[60]

Filomena Ognibene measured her distance from American culture by contrasting her real life and style of dress with those she saw in the movies:

We dressed plainly. We wore long dresses that were different than the styles in the movies. I knew about flappers from the movies, but I never dressed that way. None of my friends dressed that way. There was a flapper in my building. I guess . . . it was her nature. She was Italian and went to speakeasies. Her mother was upset at her daughter's behavior, but she didn't bother anybody.[61]

With the change in content came a dramatic change in form. As the time of the nickelodeons passed, movie houses designed to win over "the steady patronage of a new class"[62] were built to hold their audiences in the dark somnambulism of celluloid fantasy. Starting with the construction of the Strand Theatre in New York in 1914, these palaces, in the words of one of their architects, were designed as "social safety valves in that the public can partake of the same luxuries as the rich."[63] Another critic commented that "the differences of cunning . . . and wealth that determine our outside lives are forgotten. . . . our democratic nation reserves its new democracy for the temple of daydreams."[64] The form itself was a demonstration of new content. If the old noisy neighborhood nickelodeons were an experience of community, the new palaces were a reprieve from community, a vision of wealth, a touch of royalty. If there was sexuality and romance inside the frame, the dark interiors, away from the watchful eyes of parents and neighbors, encouraged sexuality outside the frame, creating a new definition of a participatory audience. One critic observed: "In the dim auditorium which seems to float on the world of dreams . . . an American woman may spend her afternoon alone. . . . she can let her fantasies slip through the darkened atmosphere to the screen where they drift in rhapsodic amours with handsome stars. In the isolation of this twilight palace . . . the blue dusk of the deluxe house has dissolved the Puritan strictures she had absorbed as a child."[65] Some early films spoke sympathetically to the confused cultural experience of uprooted women—to the tasks of maintaining home and

60. Interview with Maria Frazaetti, March 1976.
61. Interview with Filomena Ognibene, March 1975.
62. Sklar, pp. 44–45; see Nye (n. 16), pp. 377–79, and Hampton, p. 172.
63. Cited in Nye, p. 378.
64. Lloyd Lewis, "The Deluxe Picture Palace," *New Republic* (March 1929), pp. 174–76, reprinted in George Mowry, *The Twenties* (New Jersey: Prentice-Hall, Inc., 1963), p. 59.
65. Lewis, in Mowry, p. 58.

community in a world threatening to tear them apart. They helped to unify generations caught up in the divisive experiences of urban life. To the daughters, also the children of cultural transformation, film spoke differently. As themes of traditional family and community began to fade, the cinema spoke increasingly in the idiom of an urban, individualized culture. At first, these films briefly revealed new archetypes of feminine possibility that bore a relationship to the dynamics of cultural change. Yet in reaffirming the daughters' break from the traditions of family life, these films also pointed, as teachers and guides, to a mode of existence predicated on a commitment to individual survival and satisfaction within the social relationships defined by the consumer marketplace.

The ability of film to speak, in various ways, to the experience of its audience provides us with a key to understanding its appeal and power. In the first instance, film as a component of mass culture became a mediation between an historic uprooting and an unknown and threatening urban society. In the second instance, film became a mediation between traditional culture and the emergent terms of modern life. Film as a part of mass culture has the power to act as a force of unity as well as, to quote Walter Benjamin, becoming an aspect of "the liquidation of the traditional value of the cultural heritage."[66]

For feminists, this aspect of liquidation has special significance. While some of the contents of early films reflected a trend toward the liberation of women from patriarchal constraints, the social order was able to utilize this new release for the construction of a new form of domination. As women moved from the constricted family-dominated culture to the more individualized values of modern urban society, the form and content of domination changed, but new authorities replaced the old. In the name of freedom from tradition, they trapped women in fresh forms of sexual objectification and bound them to the consumerized and sexualized household.

Nonetheless, moving pictures were the most universal form of cheap and satisfying entertainment in urban immigrant communities. As escape, education, or pleasure, they constituted a major source of new ideas and social experience. For immigrant women, motion pictures were a community-sanctioned form of urban mass culture, beguiling in its presentation of dress, manners, freedom, and sexual imagery. They provided an escape, but they also extended the world as a visual universe of magic and illusion.

Department of American Studies
State University of New York at Old Westbury

66. Walter Benjamin, "The Work of Art in the Age of Mechanical Reproduction," in *Illuminations,* ed. Hannah Arendt (New York: Harcourt, Brace & World, 1968), p. 223.

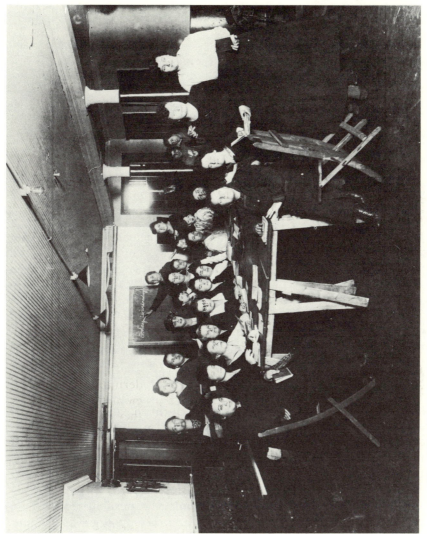

Class of immigrant mothers learning English ca. 1910 (Museum of the City of New York)

Changing Women's Roles in Political Volunteerism and Reform of the City

Marilyn Gittell and Teresa Shtob

Any description of women's political role in nineteenth- and twentieth-century America must begin with one major premise: in national and municipal electoral political organizations, the role of women has been marginal. Male politicians have dominated parties and machines in American cities, as the urban middle classes and financial and commercial elites charted the direction of urban growth—sometimes in conflict with each other, sometimes in unison. During that growth, cities developed different modes of urbanization in order to assimilate and control the poor and working-class populations that were their base. Unfortunately, the specificity of what role women did play in the politics of cities has been lost to us in two ways. Historians of the Progressive era, the high-water mark of women's urban reform activity, have tended to collapse women's contributions into the general category of urban reformers. Next, feminist historians have tended to focus on the suffragists' struggle for the acquisition of formal legal and political rights. In this essay, we wish to change that emphasis. Although excluded from the centers of urban power, women led urban reform movements. We are interested in describing and analyzing who participated in these movements, under what circumstances, and the strategies, tactics, and substantive issues they chose.

Women who could not participate directly in the political life of the city historically used the voluntary association as a channel for their interests and energies. Probably the earliest important role played by women in urban voluntary associations was as the "dedicated army of urban-morality foot soldiers"[1] fighting urban vice in the 1820s and

1. Paul Boyer, *Urban Masses and Moral Order in America* (Cambridge, Mass.: Harvard University Press, 1978), p. 15. Another view of nineteenth-century female reform may be found in Barbara Berg, *The Remembered Gate* (New York: Oxford University Press, 1978).

1830s. Middle-class women, the wives and daughters of the upwardly mobile entrepreneurial class, were not bound to domestic routine and became energetic supporters of the benevolent and moral reform societies. They were not the leaders of these groups; those positions were reserved for locally prominent men. The movement had a decided religious, even evangelical, thrust. Its primary targets were gambling, profanity, prostitution, and sabbath breaking. Open prostitution in the city was a particular concern; the first antiprostitution campaign began in New York City in the 1830s. In 1834, several New York City women founded the New York Female Moral Reform Society. In contrast to their male counterparts, they described the prostitutes as innocent victims of male lust, and focused on the male patron. In fact, they recommended that the names of men seen entering and leaving brothels be published. Similar groups were established in Boston and other New England cities.[2]

This generation of middle-class reformers assumed that poverty and vice were rooted in individual flaws, and therefore that the betterment of the city could be achieved through the moral reconstitution of families and individuals. The Association for the Improvement of the Poor, typically, hoped "not merely to alleviate wretchedness, but to reform character."[3] An ulterior motive of this mid-century organization was also to control the inherently explosive possibilities of urban poverty. By the end of the nineteenth century, however, an environmental analysis, which called for a restructuring of urban society, was emerging. Women's charitable and social service organizations were among the first organizations to reflect this change.

The Charity Organization Society (COS), headed by the wealthy Josephine Lowell, was the prototype of these organizations. It aimed to reconstitute the able-bodied poor by putting them in contact with a "friendly visitor," a middle-class female volunteer who tried to bring middle-class values into the immoral environment. Organizations like the COS stressed systematic investigation of slum life as well as moral uplift and involved thousands of young middle-class women. By 1890 over 4,000 friendly visitors were spreading moral rectitude among the poor people of Boston, New York, and Baltimore. Similarly, the National Council of Jewish Women developed a different analysis of the problems of urban life. Frustrated at attempts by male Jewish leaders to exclude them from national organizational work, Jewish women founded the council in 1893 with an orientation toward social work in the slums. Council members, for example, met immigrant women at Ellis Island, helped them find lodging, and "visited" them on a regular basis. For members of the council, "friendly visiting" was not simply the

2. Boyer, pp. 18–19.
3. Ibid., p. 90.

inculcation of moral standards among immigrant women, but vocational training and channeling into appropriate social and medical services.[4] Likewise, when they became concerned over the rising incidence of Jewish female prostitution and unwed mothers, it was with an eye toward the victimization of women.

Equally significant was the shift in the outlook of the General Federation of Women's Clubs (GFWC) in the 1890s. In its origins the club movement had represented a turn toward the world outside the home for middle-class urban women, but the activities had been limited to literary and cultural pursuits. From the 1890s on, however, the GFWC tended to see the mission of the clubs as urban service and reform. These reform activities were justified by the traditional "women's sphere" argument—that the moral superiority of women could be put to social use, and that women would constitute a purifying and stabilizing influence in urban life. Yet the GFWC, partly because of the broadness of its organization (as of 1911 it claimed a membership of 1 million through affiliated local clubs), was conservative and did not endorse women's suffrage until 1914.[5]

The Women's Christian Temperance Union (WCTU) was the first truly national women's organization. Founded in 1873, it had hundreds of thousands of members by the end of the century, with its greatest strength in the Midwest. Although its initial interest was in temperance alone, the WCTU eventually focused on the social conditions that produced the saloon and consequently affected the lives of women and children. Their campaigns included prison reform, child-labor laws, working women's protective legislation, women's suffrage, and the establishment of kindergartens. Their work was carried out primarily at the local level by over 10,000 branches. Frances Willard, the leader of the WCTU for twenty years, deepened its analysis of what was necessary to improve the lot of women and children. She justified these activities as part of women's special sphere; she wrote to Susan B. Anthony in 1898 that "men have made a dead failure of municipal government, just as they would have of housekeeping; and government is only housekeeping on the broadest scale."[6]

While the organizations so far discussed were engaged in a greater consideration of environmental conditions and urban poverty, the settlement-house movement decisively shifted the focus of public attention from the individual causes of poverty to the social and economic conditions producing it. Women were central to the settlement-house

    4. Charlotte Baum, Paula Hyman, and Sonya Michel, *The Jewish Woman in America* (New York: Dial Press, 1976).

    5. Carol Hymowitz and Michaele Weissman, *A History of Women in America* (New York: Bantam Books, 1978), pp. 221–22.

    6. Cited in Aileen Kraditor, *The Ideas of the Woman Suffrage Movement, 1890–1920* (New York: Times Books, 1968), p. 52.

movement. By 1910 there were 400 settlement houses in eastern and midwestern cities, and three-quarters of their residents were women. Half the settlement workers came directly from college, so that the houses served as field-based graduate schools for a generation of college-educated women.

The major innovation of the settlement house over previous voluntary associations in the city was the idea that volunteers would live in the neighborhood, using the house as a center of education and culture for the poor. Implicit in this notion was still the middle-class model of bringing culture to the masses, but it provided for a more intimate knowledge of working-class and immigrant life than had been possible for "friendly visitors." The settlements initially provided instruction in literature, art, American history, sewing, cooking, and music to neighborhood residents. But activities soon became geared more closely to the people's needs. Settlement workers, for instance, popularized the use of kindergartens as a service for women in their neighborhoods. They came to provide practical training in vocational skills. In contrast to the friendly visitors' emphasis on frugality, temperance, and moral rectitude, settlement-house workers focused on instruction in hygiene and child care in an attempt to inculcate what Sheila Rothman has called the "ideology of educated motherhood"[7] in immigrant women. This meant, for example, that model apartments were set up in tenements as examples of proper housekeeping, where cooking, cleaning, and child care according to the new principles of domestic science could be taught.

While these programs, in retrospect, seem burdened with middle-class bias and compulsion to transform immigrant life, they also reflect more awareness of the needs of these populations in their new urban setting than the moralistic antivice crusades of the previous generation. The women leaders of the settlement houses themselves were transformed by the experience, becoming what Allen David, the chief historian of the movement, has called "spearheads of reform"[8] in the Progressive era. Jane Addams, increasingly aware of the political dimension of social reform, launched a campaign against the local ward boss, Johnny Powers, in the late 1890s. Florence Kelley, also of Hull House, became interested in child-labor laws, and her efforts led to the establishment of the Children's Bureau in 1912. Mary Sayles, connected with the College Settlement Association, conducted the first systematic survey of housing conditions in Jersey City in 1902.[9] The first national conference on city planning, held in 1909, was organized by Lillian Wald, Florence Kelley, Mary Simkovitch, and others.

Women settlement-house leaders continued to justify their initiatives in social reform, and the involvement of all women in urban

7. Sheila Rothman, *Woman's Proper Place* (New York: Basic Books, 1978).

8. Allen Davis, *Spearheads for Reform* (New York: Oxford University Press, 1967).

9. Ibid., p. 66.

policymaking, as the special responsibility of women in a modern industrial society. As Jane Addams put it, "if woman would keep on with her old business of caring for her house and rearing her children she will have to have some conscience in regard to public affairs lying quite outside her immediate household."[10] Women settlement-house leaders enlisted working-class women in the ranks of the social reformers, arguing that "running New York is just a big housekeeping job, just like your own home, only a larger scale. Therefore you should be interested in city wide affairs."[11]

In the Progressive period, the settlement movement had close ties to labor. Unions frequently held meetings at Hull House in Chicago, Denison and South End Houses in Boston, and University and Henry Street Settlements in New York. Settlement-house funds were used to support neighbors who were on strike, and settlement residents supported unionization as a way to eradicate poverty. Mary McDowell, of the University of Chicago Settlement, helped organize women workers at the Chicago stockyards and helped to found the Women's Trade Union League (WTUL). The WTUL included settlement and union women and was responsible for much of the lobbying for federal investigations of women in industry, support of striking women workers, agitation for protective legislation for women, and the training of women as leaders. All of these efforts had a direct impact on the lives of women in American cities.

Their growing sense of women's political responsibilities in the cities led settlement-house figures, such as Florence Kelley and Jane Addams, to become ardent supporters of suffrage, and they were instrumental in winning over some working-class women to the side of suffrage. In the 1890s some suffrage leaders had argued that giving middle-class women the vote would counterbalance the votes of foreign men; with the increased participation of some middle-class women in settlement-house work, the vote was seen as a means to reform.

Yet, despite their awareness of the political implications of urban social problems, women in the reform movement shared the male Progressives' belief that the city's problems were amenable to nonpolitical solutions of urban and environmental planning. Their continued justification of political participation by the "special sphere" argument was partly a matter of expediency, but it also fit with the concept of rational administration in both household and city dear to all Progressives. Civic reform became to Progressives largely a "scientific" endeavor, analogous to scientific management in the factory. At the same time that women's special contribution was to some degree publically recognized, their role was being undermined by the increasing professionalization of social

10. Cited in Kraditor, p. 53.
11. Cited in Rothman, p. 117.

service work and the manipulation of urban issues by a new generation of civic experts who were primarily men. The ideological legacy of this era has been the perpetuation of a political analysis of the problems of cities which has insulated government officials from the demands of working-class and minority people. The political energies of Progressive reform, like those of the suffrage movement, were channeled into several directions during the 1920s. The League of Women Voters, for example, continued to lobby for such measures as equal pay, child-labor laws, and regulation of women's wages and working hours, while the Women's Party pushed for an Equal Rights Amendment. Many middle-class women entered the burgeoning profession of social work, while working-class women, when politically involved, participated in socialist or trade-union movements.

The New Deal period witnessed even more active political participation by women in city issues than the Progressive era. With the depression and the establishment of national social welfare programs, women social workers took positions in government agencies and the Democratic party. Mary Dewson of the National Consumers League took charge of "women's affairs" for the Democratic party and developed a "Reporter Plan" which sent female party workers door to door to inform the electorate about New Deal legislation. Fifteen thousand women reporters and 60,000 women precinct workers supported Roosevelt's 1936 campaign, the greatest political participation of women in party politics to that date. Increased participation was reflected on the national level of the party as well: female delegates to the 1936 Democratic convention were given equal power on the Program Committee. The number of women appointed to policymaking posts during the Roosevelt Administration increased, partly due to the influence of Eleanor Roosevelt, who was also instrumental in convincing many women social workers to involve themselves in politics and government. Unfortunately, local bases of power for women did not develop, and New Deal political activity, like that of the Progressive years, primarily involved middle-class women.

By the early 1960s, the small amount of social scientific literature on women that existed confirmed that the "traditional division of labor which assigns the political role to men rather than women has not vanished. The finding that men are more likely to participate in politics than women is one of the most thoroughly substantiated in social science."[12] Despite this assertion, there are very little data on the participation of women in voluntary associations dealing with political issues, although many case studies of organizations report comparative statistics on male and female membership. The consensus of sociology and political science in the 1960s was that women's participation in electoral politics was increasing, but was still well below male participation; that the only sig-

---

12. Lester Milbraith, *Political Participation* (Chicago: Random House, 1972), p. 135.

nificant area of women's participation was in charitable, philanthropic, and service organizations which avoided partisan political positions. Research findings report exclusively the activity of middle-class women; working-class women and lower-class women are presented as "nonjoiners" inextricably bound to the home and extended family. Classic sociological studies, such as Rainwater's *Workingman's Wife* and Komarovsky's *Blue Collar Marriage,* reiterate this theme. Yet even if we suspected a bias in the reporting of these data, it would undoubtedly be verifiable that women, and working-class women in particular, did not display a high level of political activism in the period between the end of World War II and the mid-1960s.

In reporting on women's participation, few social scientists questioned the reasons for low participation, attributing it to inherent female characteristics or offering no explanation at all. Few were aware of the political role of women in the urban political reforms of the Progressive era. Given this approach to research on women's political activity, many social scientists see the participation of middle-class and working-class women in activist community organizations in the 1960s and 1970s as a complete reversal of their "normal" behavior.

The contemporary period marks a decisive rupture with both the relative political inactivity of women in city politics between the wars and with the Progressive legacy of urban reform. In the 1960s and the 1970s, we see the first active participation of working-class women in community and neighborhood political organizations (with the important exceptions of the labor and socialist movements). Women are using these organizations to argue that the city is inherently political, and that access to political power is crucial to its reform. This period has also witnessed the development of grass-roots, urban, issue-oriented activist community organizations with female memberships and staffs.

Within the larger social history of the 1960s we find some keys to women's new activism. Growing out of the civil rights, antiwar, and women's movements of the 1960s were lower-class organizations and community organizations. Poor and working-class people organized for access to a power structure, and that challenge entailed a growing consciousness of the need for active political participation. The federal government admitted that the poor had been excluded from political participation in the cities and developed programs, such as antipoverty agencies, to increase their participation. The organizations formed during this period are generally considered to have had an extensive politicizing effect on the populations they served and represented. Lower-class groups began demanding systematic change in their own name and with their own voices, a break with the Progressive legacy of urban reform.

The civil rights movement in particular involved thousands of black and minority women in political organizing and created an activist ethos important for women's later political participation. With its tactics of grass-roots mobilization of large numbers of people, demonstrations, and public pressure, the civil rights movement served as a model for community organizations in the cities. The women's movement indirectly provided a social context for the increased political participation of working-class women in community organizations. Although many of the women in such organizations in the 1960s and 1970s would not call themselves feminists, the women's movement has meant that divergences from traditional sex roles by working-class women have been more readily accepted in their communities and families. It also provided a model of political efficacy not lost on the working-class women in new community organizations.

This general context favorable to increased women's participation first bore fruit in the mid-1960s when several communities organized to control government-sponsored "demonstration projects" were established to promote increased participation in education. In New York City, black women were particularly active when communities organized in Ocean Hill–Brownsville and in the neighborhood of Intermediate School 201. Similarly, attempts to achieve community control over health services, as with Lincoln Hospital in the Bronx, were activated by community residents demanding a real share in the administration of community services. Neighborhood associations and community-action councils have a high female involvement, according to all observers of the government-sponsored organizations (e.g., TAOs in San Diego, Community Action Agency neighborhood associations) and according to War on Poverty research studies.[13]

One of the major community organizations which arose in the 1960s, the Welfare Rights Organization (WRO), demonstrates the relation between increased women's activism in city politics and belief in their own political effectiveness. Although the National Welfare Rights Organization was established primarily by black male activists from the civil rights movement, the majority of its active membership came from grass-roots welfare recipients and welfare mothers' organizations formed prior to the national organization. The participation and militancy of working-class and black women were high in the period of the largest National Welfare Rights Organization membership (1967–69), when there were close to 500 groups nationally. The AFDC mothers staged hundreds of demonstrations, sit-ins, and confrontations at welfare offices. The demands included a thorough reform of the welfare system and a critique of the administrator-client relationship based on

13. Norman and Susan Fainstein, *Urban Political Movements* (Englewood Cliffs, N.J.: Prentice-Hall, Inc., 1974); Kathleen McCourt, *Working Class Women and Grassroots Politics* (Bloomington: Indiana University Press, 1977); Marilyn Gittell, *Citizen Organization: Citizen Participation in Educational Decisionmaking* (Boston: Institute for Responsive Education, 1979).

the powerlessness of the welfare recipient. These demands overturned the relationship between administrator and client established by the middle-class reformers of the Progressive period. A study of a local WRO in Minnesota[14] found that many welfare mothers were politicized by participation in the organization and saw themselves as politically more effective after participating. Additionally, the example of welfare mothers organizing was important for other women who did not participate. A HEW report on the WRO noted: "The number of AFDC women who reported they belong to WRO's was very small in cities. . . . These small percentages could lead however to false conclusions. . . . There was a strong inverse relationship between percentage of WRO members and numbers of recipients who felt helpless (the more WRO members in a city, the fewer the number of recipients who felt powerless)."[15]

During the 1970s, the process of women's entrance into political participation has accelerated, so that many activist grass-roots community organizations have now been initiated and led by women. Recent social science research has corroborated the tremendous change in working-class women's political participation, seeing in the "recruitment of women to urban movements a major deviation from the typical pattern in the United States."[16] A study conducted by Gittell on sixteen grass-roots voluntary community organizations in Boston, Atlanta, and Los Angeles found that female members outnumber male members in all the organizations, but, more significantly, the leadership pattern shows that women have hegemony over men.[17] Another study of minority community organizations in American cities by Norman and Susan Fainstein, *Urban Political Movements,* confirms these findings.[18]

The most thorough study to date of white working-class women's political behavior in the 1970s is the McCourt survey of women from eight "assertive" community organizations on Chicago's south side. The organizations were all community based and politically oriented, in the sense that they made demands on the political system by direct-action techniques modeled on both the welfare rights and feminist tactics. McCourt found a predominance of women in leadership roles in these organizations. White working-class women who had never been involved in the civil rights or feminist movements were drawn to them by their concern with the issues of educational quality, neighborhood preservation in the face of racial change, and competition with blacks for scarce resources. McCourt ties intensive involvement in a community organiza-

14. Susan Hertz, "The Politics of the Welfare Mothers Movement: A Case Study," *Signs: Journal of Women in Culture and Society* 2, no. 3 (Spring 1977): 600–611.

15. Cited in Frances Fox Piven and Richard Cloward, *Regulating the Poor* (New York: Pantheon Books, 1971), pp. 326–27.

16. Fainstein and Fainstein, p. 177.

17. Gittell.

18. Fainstein and Fainstein.

tion by working-class women to a "realistic assessment of minimal input into the political system as things are currently operating combined with a strong sense of potential power and a diminishing befuddlement with the complexities of government."[19] The women in these groups have become increasingly well informed about the social and political system and have developed feelings of political efficacy, a major shift from the traditional nonparticipation of working-class women.

Women in south-side Chicago tend to justify their political activity in terms of the argument that neighborhood issues are the particular province of women. Some working-class women's groups have echoed this older justification for their political work more often than activists in the women's movement would care to acknowledge. Given the recent proliferation of community organizations in which working-class women are active, it appears that it was their awareness that they lacked political efficacy rather than inherent characteristics that formerly discouraged women from participation in local organizations.

The Congress of Neighborhood Women illustrates this transformation. Founded in 1974 by Monsignor Baroni (then head of the National Center for Urban Ethnic Affairs), it is composed of working-class and lower-class ethnic white women. The organization has affiliate groups in over thirty cities; a typical chapter is the one in Greenpoint/Williamsburg in New York City. Increasingly, as they have developed political experience in local issues, its members have become aware of the national character of many of those issues. Consequently, they have begun campaigning and lobbying for legal and consumer rights, as well as organizing networks for social services and employment. They have recognized the necessity for working on both fronts.

The organizations now being formed by working-class women share certain characteristics, which appear most clearly when we compare them to the Progressive tradition of urban reform. Working-class women today are propelled into political organizing by the unsatisfactory and unresponsive functioning of their local government. The social services they encounter in their daily lives do not meet their needs. The main objective of these groups is to force the political and economic structure to address their interests and social needs. No longer is reform the province of the urban middle class attempting to spread its values to the lower-class population.

At the same time that working-class and minority women's political activism has increased, middle-class women, formerly associated exclusively with "volunteerism" in charitable, philanthropic, and service organizations, are showing signs of change. As professional work opportunities open for middle-class women, they are devoting less time to nonpolitical volunteer activity. One indication that even middle-class women

19. McCourt, p. 181.

are becoming politicized is the research finding that a traditional women's "civic" organization, such as the League of Women Voters, had a significant decline in membership between 1973 and 1978.[20] Ironically, at the same time that the feminist movement first called into question the value of volunteerism for women, the Nixon administration attempted to institutionalize voluntary service organizations by creating a cabinet-level committee on volunteerism, providing information and funds to local voluntary organizations through the Departments of Agriculture, Labor, and HEW. For middle-class women, the position of the women's movement on volunteer activity may have been an important influence in changing attitudes. The National Organization for Women took the position that: "(1) . . . volunteering is an extension of unpaid housework and of women's traditional roles in the home . . . which have been extended to the community. (2) . . . volunteering reinforces a woman's low self image by offering work which, because it is unpaid, confers little status. (3) . . . volunteerism has been society's solution for those including but not limited to women, for which there is little real employment choice."[21] That view is shared by increasing numbers of middle-class women.

As with working-class women's activism, middle-class women's participation in voluntary organizations now tends to be more political than in the past, and there is an attempt to acquire political power in order to confront vital urban issues of housing, education, and environment. Middle-class women are increasingly leaving the role of "foot soldier" and are exercising political power in the cities in their own name. One example is Women For, a voluntary issue-oriented organization established in Los Angeles in 1964 with a membership of over 2,000 primarily middle- to upper-income white women. The founders of the organization were motivated primarily by an interest in promoting political change by supporting liberal candidates, which continues to be one of Women For's major activities. In addition, the organization has participated actively in the movement to curtail the use of nuclear energy and in the local effort to carry out desegregation. The organization has also been active in education concerning women's rights. It has extensive connections with key decision makers at the city and state level and has a city-wide reputation for political effectiveness. Women For is encountering the same kind of problem as is the League of Women Voters in holding its voluntary membership. As more women begin to work professionally, the pool of unpaid time and labor, historically the mainstay of these organizations, will dry up.

20. Louise Napoli, "The Effect of Selected Social Trends and Women's Volunteer Activity" (research project, Department of Political Science, University of California, Long Beach, December 1978).

21. National Organization for Women, Task Force on Volunteerism, *Position Paper* (Washington, D.C.: National Organization for Women, November 1973).

The social movements of the 1960s, both the civil rights and the women's movements, provided a social context in which the urban reform spirit of the Progressive era, with its attempted social control of the poor, could no longer exist. The poor people's, minority, and women's groups are demanding not just political reform of cities and city services but self-determination and direct political participation. The activism of women today has involved community-based, or at least community-originating, issues. The preponderance of women in new forms of political organizing is a continuation of the Progressive and settlement-house concerns and activities. The issues traditionally addressed by women—education, health, housing, sanitation, the urban environment—have come increasingly to be viewed as the major issues of urban life in the 1970s and 1980s.

The participation of increasing numbers of women in political movements and organizations is a positive phenomenon. But we cannot simply applaud every such organization. As the McCourt study shows, increased women's participation can pit one group of working-class women against another. The greater participation of middle-class women in the existing political party structure can merely aim at formal equality. Ultimately, the evaluation of women's increased participation in political community organization must be based on an analysis of its purpose and of the distribution of power, resources, and services in American society.

Department of Political Science
Graduate Center, City University of New York (Gittell)

Department of Sociology
Graduate Center, City University of New York (Shtob)

Women in Urban Parks

Galen Cranz

American urban parks were a nineteenth-century attempt to right the imbalances of industrialization and urbanization. Unlike their European predecessors, American public parks have been intimately linked with urban problems. Park advocates have offered various types and styles of parks at different times as ways to solve those social difficulties and redress those imbalances. Each model has had implications for women's place in public life. Because "women" as a category have not been perceived as an urban problem, park policymakers have used females primarily to help ameliorate other problems which disrupted social order, such as alcoholism, prostitution, psychological anonymity, loss of community, physical degeneration due to lack of exercise, disease, delinquency, and the absence of a shared civic order.

The deployment of women has changed with specific historical perceptions of what was wrong with society and the city. The pleasure ground (1850–1900) was an antidote to the ills of the rapidly industrializing city, visually and programmatically its antithesis, with a curving, picturesque landscape and emphasis on mental refreshment. The standards of order, for both the physical environment and social intercourse, would help set common values for the diverse population. Women played a key role in that scenario.

The reform park (1900–1930) accepted industrial life and attempted to rationalize it by siting the park near working-class tenements and by stressing physical exercise, supervision, and organization, while minimizing the significance of fine art and nature appreciation. Physical degeneration and juvenile delinquency were prominent urban issues which the playground would help solve. Focus on these problems diverted attention to boys more than to girls.

The recreation facility (1930–65) rested on the claim that recreation had become a recognized municipal function necessary in its own right, independent of how much it contributed to the solution of urban problems. Standardization and efficiency were the watchwords of urban planners, who proceeded as if the city were a mechanical system which could be balanced by a proper distribution of the parts—parks, schools, hospitals, transit, housing, shopping centers, industrial sectors. In this unsentimental view females did not get as much treatment as a special class as they had before.

The open-space system (1965 to the present) returned to the belief that parks could be used to solve urban problems, particularly urban decay and riots. Making the city safe and attractive to middle-class women reemerged as a central concern.[1]

Women in the Pleasure Garden (1850–1900)

Nineteenth-century reformers worried about density, pollution, lack of space, psychological stress, and the commercialization of culture of the newly industrialized city. They believed that the family could cushion the individual from many of these stresses, yet they feared that the family itself was being undermined by alcoholism, prostitution, and boardinghouse living. Women's central role in the family meant that urban reform and women were often linked explicitly. The park commissioners, not wanting to compete with the home as the proper mechanism of moral reform, underscored the important ways in which the park would help reinforce the family unit. Charles Eliot, park advocate and president of Harvard University, claimed that parks could promote "a high standard of family life" since "the pleasures men share with their wives and children are apt to be safer pleasures than those they take by themselves."[2]

If the home was the fortress of morality, why should the woman be brought into the public sphere at all? Park advocates thought that a respectable setting where a woman could appear in public with her husband would contribute to a family's sense of itself. By going out with his family in a public setting, a man would see himself as others saw him: the head of a family, wife on arm, children in tow, all in Sunday best. Reformers reasoned that he would experience this as pleasurable and resolve to make it the mainstay of his life.[3]

1. This analysis is based on three major U.S. cities—New York, Chicago, and San Francisco. It is part of a larger, forthcoming study of American urban parks. This typology is presently available in Galen Cranz, "The Changing Roles of Urban Parks: From Pleasure Garden to Open-Space System," *Landscape* 22, no. 3 (Summer 1978): 9–18.

2. Charles Eliot, "Popular Utilization of Public Reservations," *American Park and Outdoor Art Association* 6 (July 1903): 14.

3. Women's presence would help stabilize the family and, conversely, the park would educate the entire family: "A park would educate him [the tired workman] and his family." Otherwise, "he and his" would be "educated into the ways of disease and vice . . ." (medical

Reformers were sure that women would set a tone which would demand high standards from everyone: "The respectable part of the community should establish a custom of behavior in the Park which will have a wholesome influence on all who resort to it. A large use of the Park by families, by good women and dutiful children, will accomplish this result. Nothing else will. No laws and no police force will do it."[4]

For a public setting to function in this way, it had to be a respectable setting for middle-class women, who were not supposed to go out alone. The literature is dotted with claims that the park must be made a safe resort for unprotected ladies, women, mothers, wives, and children. Since the park was for respectable women, prostitutes were automatically excluded from park life. In the 1880s the women of San Francisco petitioned the city to remove the prostitutes from a permanent city location to the relative isolation of St. Mary's Square, which was hidden by a row of business establishments. Respectability also dictated nonalcoholic refreshments, but the issue was touchy. Several ethnic traditions and the desire to attract people conflicted with temperance views. When ice skating became popular in New York City, and private farm ponds competed with Central Park, one of the advantages of Central Park was that it was a more orderly place, without the sale of intoxicating drink, so that women and girls could skate there alone with their friends "without fear of being annoyed by roughs."[5] The spa in Central Park was originally (1862) designed as a place for women to drink mineral water after strolling through the park. Two years later, the Casino was opened as a "Ladies' Refreshment Salon," a "place of light refreshment for ladies and young children." In 1873 it was enlarged as a restaurant serving alcoholic drinks, which it remained until 1934.[6] In the 1870s beer, wine, and cider were sold along with other refreshments to Central Park visitors, not at a socially dubious bar but, rather, at tables where men and women sat respectably together.[7]

Chicagoans found that their Retreat did not pay its own way, even though it was popular with women and children.[8] San Francisco was slow

---

doctor quoted in Thomas E. Will, "Park and Playgrounds: A Symposium," *Arena* 10, no. 56 [July 1894]: 277).

4. Boston City Council, *Documents for the City of Boston for the Year 1890*, document 15, Fifteenth Annual Report of the Board of Commissioners of the Department of Parks (Boston: Boston Public Library, 1890), p. 30.

5. "Central Park, Part Two," *Scribner's Monthly* 6, no. 5 (October 1873): 673–91.

6. William J. Tooley, "Concessions in New York City Parks," *Proceedings of the Second Annual Conference of Revenue-producing Facilities for Governmental Parks, Recreation, and Zoological Parks* (Wheeling, W. Va.: American Institute of Park Executives, 1962), p. 22.

7. Charles Doell, "Origin and Development of Parks," *Parks and Recreation* 35, no. 11 (November 1952): 10.

8. *Report of the South Park Commissioners to the Board of County Commissioners of Cook County from December 1, 1876 to December 1, 1877* (Chicago, 1877), p. 5. In Chicago three

in establishing a similar place of refreshment. One commissioner blamed the failure of San Francisco's first Casino not on alcohol per se but on some of the "vice" which surrounded it; according to him, "The place became too common." In the new Casino alcohol would be part of an elegant scene—a symphony of music, clinking goblets, dazzling lights, gay women, gallant men, Tahoe trout in egg crumbs, and terrapin patés.[9]

Women's ideal role was not as a user of facilities for games and sports but as a stabilizing presence. Nevertheless, women, especially young women, were responsible for much of the burgeoning interest in athletics. They began to play lawn tennis, croquet, and basketball and to ride bicycles in the 1890s. When girls, wives, and mothers diverged from their passive function—as they did almost immediately—commentators responded with disbelief and disdain.

Despite women's demonstrated ability to learn to skate, when bicycles became popular in the late nineteenth century, one male instructor announced, "Bicycle riding is like swimming. It requires confidence and courage, and because they lack those qualities, the majority of women will never do either well."[10] The *San Francisco Call* titillated its readers with mocking reports of women's activities: "The ladies have a new fad. They are learning to row on Stowe Lake, at Golden Gate Park. They have started gently with small biceps, and a wholesome fear of calloused places and blisters on their hands. They have progressed in skill aquatic, and have developed their muscle." The article was even more contemptuous of Chinese women, who did not ask "any instruction in rowing . . . such as the keeper of the boathouse imparts to the Caucasian ladies. Their idea appears to be to get afloat and then laugh as much as possible."[11]

Despite such psychological ambivalence and denial, reporters noted in the same breath that women used Golden Gate Park's Stowe Lake more than men did.[12] Newspapers confirmed that women enjoyed active sports on their own without the company of men: " 'You would be astonished,' said the guy in charge of boathouses and boats, 'what interest the ladies of this City are taking in boating. They come in the forenoon when the weather is clear and there is not much wind, and they have a glorious time.' "[13] Numerous women had owned and been driving their

---

major park commissions existed until their consolidation in 1934. The South Park Commissioners reports are longer, published more regularly, and describe the philosophy of park service more fully than the reports of the Lincoln and West Park Commissioners. (Hereafter South Park report titles are shortened to *Annual Report for* [the year].)

9. *San Francisco Examiner* (November 2, 1900).

10. *San Francisco Call* (September 9, 1885).

11. "San Francisco Belles Gain Health and Muscle on Stowe Lake," *San Francisco Call* (October 11, 1896).

12. Ibid.

13. *San Francisco Call* (July 20, 1896).

own trotters and racers for some time, and at the end of the 1800s a woman won the sleigh race on the first snow for the magnum of champagne traditionally offered at Tavern on the Green in Central Park.[14]

The artistic images of women's role in public parks were slow to acknowledge the reality of their active sports life. Artists, like park planners, confirmed the ideal that women would be tied to the family and their men, while extending a calming presence on the public scene. A lithograph of New York's Harlem Lane speed track shows only men driving rigs; the only evidence of women is a sign at the Casino that says "Women's Entrance," for women on foot.[15] Lithographs of skating in Central Park express the ideal of heterosexual civility. Men teach women to skate, but only men suffer the indignity of falling down. In the paintings, women are always linked with men on a one-to-one basis. In photographs of the same scene, the ideal is betrayed by reality: Women are in pairs teaching each other how to skate. Ideally, women are escorted by men, presumably their husbands, and learn from them; in practice women learned from each other and probably fell down, too. Similarly, the photographic evidence for Central Park shows that women fixed their own bicycles and equipment without men.[16]

Policymakers assumed that children's needs were satisfied by meeting the needs of their mothers and did not make distinctions between the needs of boys and girls until the next era. The needs of children and their caretakers before 1900 were best articulated in San Francisco in regard to the Children's Quarter. Senator William Sharon left a bequest to the Parks Department for large monumental entry gates to Golden Gate, but the commissioners convinced his heirs that the money would be more appropriately spent on something less showy and more in keeping with the social purposes and picturesque ideals of the park.

The Children's Quarter was a playground and building sited in the southeast corner of the park for ease of access and visual privacy. On the ground floor of the building children could buy snacks and wholesome refreshments adjacent to their playground. The second floor was reached by a ramp from the ground, which wrapped around the building and turned into a viewing gallery where coffee was served. Each child was supervised by her own parent or nurse; hence, the building, overlooking the playground, had to accommodate large numbers of adults. On the veranda they could be in the company of one another, drinking coffee, and yet have direct visual access to their charges.[17]

14. Martin Green, "Old-Timer Recalls Days When Race for That Magnum Counted," *New York Sun* (December 1933).

15. Currier and Ives, *Fast Trotters on Harlem Lane, New York,* lithograph.

16. "Central Park File—Photos and Lithos pre-1900," vertical files (New York: Museum of the City of New York).

17. The Children's Quarter must have become popular for women and their adult friends because when free days were instituted, the minutes specified that only children and their caretakers should be entertained free, not mothers and their friends (San Fran-

Inside the building were private rooms for nursing. A married couple lived in the peaked rooms of the third floor, available twenty-four hours a day for assistance.

The Sharon Building was just for mothers and their children, and this care to provide them with a safe and respectable environment had some unintended consequences. It kept fathers from taking a direct role in the care and supervision of their children. One indignant father complained to the editor of the *Examiner:* "That means that married men who have children at play in the ground must either get a lady to watch the little ones, or the man hides in the distance, or those men accompanying their wives may look at their family from the far road in order not to conflict with the Park Ordinance which reads, "This lawn reserved for ladies and children." This man suggested that the sign be altered to read, "This lawn reserved for children and their guardians." However, since his views were exceptional, no efforts were made to include men in the supervision of children until the reform park era.[18]

The initial rhetoric in favor of establishing parks within cities was built on boyhood images: The country boy had advantages that city youth also needed. Advocates would call upon adults to remember their own "boyhood" days, to remember why an urban park might be necessary.[19] Yet the planners of the Children's Quarters recognized that little girls in particular would benefit, since they "never have an opportunity of running races with each other or playing with a skipping rope, or giving their muscles exercise, or their lungs a chance to expand, just for want of such a place as this."[20] This plan to meet the needs of girls must have been popular, because by 1893 newspapers took for granted that girls were the major users. For example, referring to swings, "Girls, as a matter of course, were in the largest majority here. . . ."[21]

Sex-role differentiation was never as pronounced in pleasure garden days as it was to become in the years after 1900. Croquet, rolling hoop, and blindman's bluff were thought to attract older girls, while a good ball ground would meet the needs of boys.[22] Gymnastic equipment at the children's playground at the Sharon Building included a double

---

cisco Park Commission minutes, May 8, 1903 [McLaren Lodge, Golden Gate Park, San Francisco], p. 414).

18. *San Francisco Examiner* (August 22, 1893). The existence of a separate environment for children contradicted the idea of the family using the parks as a group. Most park systems simply offered benches for the exclusive use of women and children during the pleasure garden era. Consequently, the problem experienced by the father in Golden Gate Park usually did not arise.

19. One example of the boyhood language is in Alpheus Hyatt, "The Next Stage in the Development of Public Parks," *Atlantic Monthly* 67, no. 399 (1891): 215–24.

20. *San Francisco Call* (March 8, 1887).

21. *San Francisco Chronicle* (May 2, 1893).

22. San Francisco Park Commission, *Bi-Annual Report for 1872–73* (San Francisco, 1973).

slide, one for boys and the other for girls. Half of the horses on the carousel in Golden Gate Park had sidesaddles.

Women did use the parks as much as planned, even if more on their own and more actively than men envisaged. As early as 1871 in Central Park the proportion of women and girls estimated to have atttended the park on any fine day was about 40 percent.[23] Today the passivity of the nineteenth-century female has been exaggerated. Looking back at nineteenth-century photographs, some commentators have assumed that because the women wore "ankle-length skirts and voluminous sleeves," both sexes strolled about in "quiet contemplation." Conversely, because many people now wear sports clothes, shorts, or blue jeans, we assume that this "means, of course, that they can be and are far more active in outdoor sports than their progenitors."[24] On the contrary, a nineteenth-century newspaper commented that Chicken Point—a vantage point for viewing the parade of carriages in Golden Gate Park—was filled with its usual "Sunday load of families and young couples," and "no question of sex hinders the observers there from reclining on the grass. . . ."[25]

Women in the Reform Park (1900–1930)

Settlement-house workers wanted to bring wholesome recreational opportunities to the working class, especially to the "children and women of the wage-earning families," who had neither the time nor the money to travel to the outlying pleasure grounds. At the same time playground advocates wanted to insure that urban children got enough physical exercise in a safe setting, not the street. At the turn of the century, park and playground advocates successfully pressured for legislation to create the small park in the heart of the urban slum. The campaign for this new type of park was a part of the larger progressive era, and its purposes are succinctly summarized by the term, "reform" park. In New York its swings and sandheaps were well used during the summer heat, proving "to be godsends to the mothers of the tenement districts."[26] At the same time, child mortality was reduced.

Progressive park advocates also hoped to tackle the problems presented by the commercialization of culture and the unprecedented increase in leisure time. Wholesome sports would replace movies, dance halls, and saloons. Park advocates were happy to convert "by means of

23. C. E. Doell and G. B. Fitzgerald, "Origin and Development of Parks," *A Brief History of Parks and Recreation in the U.S.* (Chicago: Athletic Institute, 1954), p. 10.

24. Sidney N. Shurcliff, "Progress in Park Design during the Last Fifty Years," *Parks and Recreation* 31, no. 11 (November 1948): 623.

25. *San Francisco Chronicle* (July 30, 1894).

26. New York City, Department of Parks, *Report for 1903* (New York, 1904), p. 12.

tactful suggestion" a tired shopgirl's idea of amusement from a stuffy movie theater to a game of tennis.[27] Pleasure garden planners had excluded social dances from the parks. In the reform era, city fathers decided they had better accept the popularity of dances; so they sponsored and chaperoned them closely. The "open" public dance, defined as open to unattended girls or to anyone without qualification, was not permitted in the South Park field houses of Chicago. Only "natural groups," representing their "various strata" in society, were allowed to hold dances in the park field houses.[28]

Park promoters hoped to use the park to assimilate immigrants, reduce nervousness, and fight delinquency. Park planners devoted disproportionate attention to boys in trying to thwart their delinquency. Without a "legitimate outlet" for the "instinct" to distinguish themselves or their groups, planners thought, boys and young men form gangs for "antisocial acts of which every large city is all too conscious," and "distinguish themselves in ways which fill the juvenile courts and even jails. . . ."[29] The park departments all around the country took pride in the potential of the park movement to reduce juvenile delinquency. Since it was defined as a male problem, park administrators did not even collect statistics for girl offenders.[30]

Both women and girls began to use the parks for active sports in the pleasure garden era. Thus their increasing participation after 1900 was not the dramatic reversal claimed by reform park theorists but an acceleration and rationalization of a previously established behavior. Eventually the reform park philosophy caught up with this reality by treating women as users in their own right, not primarily as instruments through which to influence men's behavior.

The relationship between the sexes changed dramatically. The pleasure garden emphasis on the family unit entailed both age and sex integration; in contrast, the reform model turned age and sex segregation into virtues. The family would no longer use the park, but its individual members would use it as their time schedules, set by the rhythms of their schooling or work, permitted. The park organizers divided the day into sections and offered programming appropriate to the schoolchildren who would come before and after class, the mothers who would bring toddlers in the late morning, the working men who might take

27. Edna E. Wilson (YMCA), "World-wide Recreation for Girls," *Park International* 1, no. 2 (September 1920): 126.

28. Chicago South Park Commission, *Annual Report for 1911*, p. 44.

29. Chicago South Park Commission, *Annual Report for 1919*, p. 37.

30. Nevertheless, two park experts said that even though there were no statistics for girls, they knew that the "parks have helped them." The kinds of deviance that girls might be guilty of were generally not crimes against other persons but crimes without victims, such as prostitution (F. L. Olmsted and John Nolen, "Experts' Report on Civic Center," *Preliminary Reports on the City Planning Commission of the City of Milwaukee* [Milwaukee: Phoenix Printing Co., 1911], pp. 19–24).

lunch breaks there, and working boys and girls who could visit in the evening after work and dinner.[31] Each group was expected to use the park separately.

The theoretical justification was grounded in developmental theory: "The psychological, sociological, and physiological factors involved in the play interests of a group of sixteen-year-old boys differ from the interests of a group of seven-year-old boys, and the interests of a group of fourteen-year-old girls differ from both. Separate and distinct gymnasiums, therefore, with apparatus of the character, sizes, and heights adapted to these groups' interests were planned and installed."[32] A biological rationale ("dominant interests") for this division of play dotted the park literature.

If males and females or different age groups happened to use the park at the same time of day, they used different parts of it. The outdoor gymnastic equipment for men and women was located at opposite ends of the park, with a building or trees, shrubbery, and lawns in between. A fence enclosed the women's area and was in turn concealed by shrubbery.[33] (In accordance with today's preoccupation with safety, rather than propriety, this screen of shrubbery would have been eliminated and the area prominently lit in order to increase surveillance.) The designers and administrators of the reform park specified that every park should have a separate building for the toilet for men and for women and that each sex should have separate showers as well as separate gyms.[34] Elaborating the separate-benches theme were wide porches on field houses facing the park, with comfortable (but unpadded) wide-armed rocking chairs, again for the exclusive use of women accompanied by small children. This popular feature was called "mothers' corner."[35]

Boys and girls were also segregated. The girls' section contained swings, seesaws, maypoles, basketball, volleyball, croquet, and tennis.

31. Gymnasium classes offered in the evening for married men and women were popular (Chicago South Park Commission, *Annual Report for 1905*).

32. Gym Director's Report, in ibid., p. 46. In 1905 and 1906, two years after the new philosophy was instated in Chicago, the number of references to women in the Chicago South Park Commission's annual reports increased. Both male and female instructors were specified, and the pronouns of reference did not rely on the universalistic "him" or "himself," but, rather, they were specified "his" or "her" or "himself" or "herself." Furthermore, park statisticians analyzed data on park users by sex in the reform park era (e.g., see New York City, Department of Parks, *Annual Report for 1915*, p. 70, list of proposed tables).

33. Clarence Elmer Rainwater, *The Play Movement in the United States: A Study of Community Recreation* (Chicago: University of Chicago Press, 1922), p. 73. Almost invariably the children's play area was adjacent to women's spatial arrangements, reflecting the assumption that mothers, not fathers, would be primarily responsible for child care (see, e.g., *Chicago South Park Commission, Annual Report for 1906*, pp. 24–25; and ibid. for 1916, pp. 64–65).

34. New York City, Department of Parks, *Annual Report for 1901*, p. 13.

35. New York City, Department of Parks, *Annual Report for 1904*, p. 19. Note the similarity to the Sharon Building's observation gallery.

Boys had facilities for basketball, baseball, handball, track and field, and an "apparatus frame" (today's monkey bars).[36] The spaces, the equipment, the games, and the rules of the games all reflected sex-role differentiation. For example, team games had special "girls' rules," and the "dashes" in which the girls were permitted to participate were shorter than those for boys.[37] An outdoor gymnasium was shared by boys and girls under ten years of age, but two separate ones were created for boys and girls over ten.[38] Generally, time and space were trade-offs. With separate gyms the department could accommodate both boys and girls simultaneously, whereas with only one they had to divide the day temporally.[39]

Park planners thought that segregation promoted safety (although today urban planners believe that only mixed use attracts enough people to public places to make them safe). For example, in the 1920s a recreation worker's survey of San Francisco's southside district discovered that a group of boys, loafers and loungers, had made a playground at a school their headquarters, thereby depriving girls of a place just for themselves where they could "play unsubjected to scrutiny and disturbance of hard balls." She recommended, among other things, that the loafers and loungers be prohibited and that a section of the playground be set aside for girls.[40] A recurrent specification in park reports and other literature throughout this entire era was that areas of a park, and especially benches, should be reserved exclusively for the "use of women and their children."[41]

The reform park contained public baths, initially a sanitation measure but immediately popular as recreation. Soon "provision was also made for their use by women during certain restricted periods."[42] Generally, women had two days and nights each week, whereas boys and men had three days and nights.[43] The protective attitude toward girls

36. Rainwater, p. 105.
37. Ibid., p. 254.
38. Chicago South Park Commission, *Annual Report for 1908*, p. 115.
39. Chicago South Park Commission, *Annual Report for 1911*, p. 32.
40. C. H. Meeds, "Should Playgrounds Be Landscaped?" *Parks and Recreation* 7, no. 1 (September–October 1923): 74.
41. A small park might be divided by a fence, within which women and girls and little children would be allowed, while boys and men would be seated outside (New York City, Department of Parks, *Annual Report for 1913*, p. 7). As late as 1922, the San Francisco Park Commission received a request for more benches in Huntington Square with signs to read, "These Benches and This Part of This Square Is Hereby Reserved for Ladies and Children." The motion passed (San Francisco Park Commission minutes, April 1922, p. 620). In 1926, the Department of Health similarly requested that a portion of Columbia Square be fenced or roped off for the use of women and children, and again the park commission complied. Only in the 1930s did this kind of protective segregation wane.
42. New York City, Department of Parks, *Annual Report for 1904*, p. 19.
43. Chicago South Park Commission, *Annual Report for 1904*, p. 34; and ibid. for 1908, p. 119.

sometimes required that the municipality assume responsibility for escorting girls to the bathhouses for swimming.[44] On one of the few occasions where black children are mentioned, they, too, were segregated by sex.[45] Mixed bathing had been traditionally permitted on the beaches. In the 1920s, when mixed bathing was also allowed in pools, attendance increased.[46]

Sexual segregation, sex-role stereotyping, and unequal treatment to the point of discrimination are closely linked. The theory for separating boys and girls assumed that they were different and at the same time guaranteed that treatment of the sexes would not be equal. In the early days, for example, before theorists assumed that girls would like to participate in athletic competitions, boys' playgrounds hosted city-wide athletic championships, whereas girls' playgrounds might accommodate a festival.[47] The boys often had a larger playground than the girls, and administrators allocated children's vegetable gardens unevenly.[48]

On one hand, the park programming reinforced stereotypes; on the other, it threatened them. The sheer fact of accommodating females, separate or not, suggested that women's needs for recreation were similar to males. Furthermore, the vigor with which females pursued activities must have laid many ideals about female passivity to rest. The varied reactions to female sport left a zigzag trail of pronouncements throughout park records. The prevailing cultural attitudes toward women's ultimate goals as wives and mothers meant that athletic activity for women and girls had to be justified in terms of motherhood. Chicago's *Annual Report for 1906* assured the public: "It is a biological law that 'kind begets kind'; hence the value and economy" of a "playground that assists in the preparation of the girls of the community for the best type of motherhood."[49] Even when the public record acknowledged that girls have a competitive spirit and might like to join in athletic contests, their tournaments still had to be held under special conditions because of the widespread opinion that respectable girls could not appear in public without supervision: "Girls are as much interested in athletic contests as are boys. It is improper, however, from a physical and social point of view, for girls to travel about the city for inter-institutional athletic con-

44. San Francisco Playground Commission minutes, June 6, 1923 (McLaren Lodge, Golden Gate Park, San Francisco).

45. The activities on playgrounds included "one colored group of boys and one colored group of girls are also served" (San Francisco Playground Commission minutes, January 23, 1924).

46. P. Horace, "Park Architecture: Bathing Establishments," *Park International* 1, no. 1 (July 1920): 25–34.

47. E.g., Report of the Bureau of Recreation in New York, pt. 1 (New York City, Department of Parks, *Annual Report of 1911*, p. 5).

48. E.g., at De Witt Clinton Playground in New York, 215 plots were allocated to girls, 243 for boys (New York City, Department of Parks, *Annual Report for 1905*, p. 138).

49. Chicago South Park Commission, *Annual Report for 1906*, p. 47.

tests."[50] A moderate position was that female competitions should be conducted like "a play party [rather] than a contest between rivals," in order to avoid "the undesirable masculine tendencies so commonly seen in match games between girls' teams."[51]

Occasionally park planners recognized that girls needed more. The director of recreation in Chicago, immediately after World War I, said that the restricted programming for girls regarding athletics would have to be relaxed.[52] In 1919 the San Francisco Playground Commission also began the expansion of its athletic programming for girls by hosting the first swimming meet for high school girls. Chicago girls were included in athletic tournaments in 1921.

The new emphasis on women did not mean that men were ignored. Men still petitioned commissioners for athletic fields for their sports, and, like others before him, President Teddy Roosevelt relied heavily upon masculine imagery ("liberal ideas, manly independence, and appeal on behalf of manly character in public and private life")[53] in promoting park activities. The masculine symbolism of San Francisco's McLaren Lodge, especially the commissioners' meeting room, is thorough: handsome wood and leather-covered table, chairs, and walls, all decorated with metal studs.

Women in the Recreation Facility (1930–65)

The paternalistic concern with working-class women and girls declined, just as the emphasis on class disappeared generally throughout this era. Although administrators made no special claim to meet the needs of the working class, they differentiated the target population of women into types—"junior girls, adult women, and industrial women." This categorization had been in effect since the reform era and continued well into the 1950s.[54] Industrial recreation organized employees into leagues of softball players, tennis, table tennis, basketball, folk dancing, golf, field days and picnics, and indoor bowling. The San Francisco Recreation Commission hinted only obliquely that it met the needs of lower-middle-class clerical workers in the caption under a photograph of two women who "left their clattering typewriters to join other downtown workers in enjoying a touch of spring at St. Mary's Square."[55]

50. Chicago South Park Commission, *Annual Report for 1907,* p. 69.
51. Chicago South Park Commission, *Annual Report for 1906,* pp. 50–52.
52. Chicago South Park Commission, *Annual Report for 1918,* pp. 67–69.
53. San Francisco Park Commission minutes, May 8, 1903, p. 419.
54. E.g., San Francisco Park and Recreation Department, *Annual Report for 1950* (San Francisco, 1951).
55. San Francisco Park Commission minutes, March 14, 1947.

Sex-role segregation, although still practiced, began to wane in the era of the recreation facility. The practice of designing special sections of the park, playground, or beach for females dwindled.[56] Planners included more types of females in more types of activities. Special classes for women's activities continued into the mid-thirties, but segregation reached its limits. Park departments concluded that "co-recreation parties had greater appeal than when segregation of the sexes is enforced."[57] The pragmatic impetus toward sexual integration was that park departments wanted to increase their attendance figures, but ideology was soon hot on the trail. The emphasis in the 1950s was on family togetherness and the idea that "Mom, Pop, and the kids must do things as a group,"[58] a return by a different route to pleasure garden attitudes toward the family. In direct opposition to reform park ideology, the recreation theorists said that a recreation program should be directed to "keeping the family together instead of separating it into skill and age groups."[59]

One of the consequences of age and sex segregation of the reform era had been that mothers were no longer the only supervisors of their children. Once beyond the toddler stage, children played together under the supervision of a trained leader. This separation of parenthood from supervision led logically to the possibility of the park services' providing day care. In San Francisco in 1926 a representative of the Golden Gate Kindergarten Association asked the playground commission to consider the purchase of property near Mission Playground which their group could use for a nursery kindergarten to take care of small children whose mothers had to work during the morning. In the afternoon it would be used by the playground department. The commissioners balked at this suggestion of providing day care: "The consensus of opinion was that the matter be held in abeyance."[60] In 1943, the recreation commission requested funds from the Lanham Act for day care after school hours from three to seven in the evening.[61] The service lasted only a year. In the 1950s the idea was implicitly rejected through the emphasis on family togetherness.[62]

The philosophy behind the recreation facility deemphasized sex-

56. The last example of a special area for women and children on a San Francisco beach was mentioned in May 1934 in the minutes of the San Francisco Park Commission.

57. Chicago South Park Commission, *Annual Report for 1939*, p. 150.

58. Charles A. Boucher, "Family Recreation: Foe of Juvenile Delinquency," *Recreation* 50, no. 2 (February 1957): 46.

59. Ben Solomon, "Preventive Recreation," *Recreation* 44, no. 10 (March 1951): 566.

60. San Francisco Playground Commission minutes, December 29, 1926.

61. San Francisco Recreation Commission minutes, January 7, 1943 (McLaren Lodge, Golden Gate Park, San Francisco).

62. Ideology notwithstanding, parents never again could be counted on for full-time supervision.

role segregation for girls. A woman professional in the National Recreational Association described all-girls programming as a stepping-stone to sexually integrated recreation:

> The scene has changed greatly since the early '30s, when there was so much discussion of "girls' " athletics, boys' rules versus girls' rules, and the fight against exploitation. Now we know that no recreation program is complete unless it carries a carefully planned program for the girls themselves—a program which will give them social confidence and personality development, so that they are ready to share activities with boys. They need to be brought into things in such a natural way that they are ready for the next step—co-recreation activities.[63]

As females became less distinctive and less in need of protection, the literature no longer insisted that women should not go out alone in public. But apparently objective conditions did not change, for complaints regarding "offenses against women" became more frequent.[64] The protective attitude toward girls took longer to erode than it did toward adult women. One impact on recruitment to local parks was that girls typically traveled a shorter distance than boys to attend a park.[65]

Despite the decrease in sexual segregation, sex-role stereotyping did not decline. By the end of the war, public relations stunts had reached a peak and programming a nadir, epitomized by Chicago's "Easter hat parade." Women were invited to craft groups in the field houses, where they learned to design and make their own Easter hats.[66] The public relations division turned this into a media event. In order to combat the image of women as workers, as they had been during World War II, park publicity introduced photographs of women in sexually alluring poses.

Sex-role stereotyping was perpetuated through children's activities. Toys for building and construction were most popular among the boys, whereas toys for mimic housekeeping were the most used by the girls.[67] Park programmers recommended that cooking be offered during vacations for those recalcitrant girls who did not enjoy the subject and re-

63. Helen M. Doncey, "In the Field: Helen M. Doncey," *Recreation* 42, no. 11 (February 1949): 517.

64. San Francisco Park Commission minutes, November 6–7, 1941.

65. Chicago South Park Commission, *Annual Report for 1939,* p. 151. Since then, observers have linked the increase in offenses to a decline in public order. I believe that abuse against women has been constant over time despite changes in rate. In a hierarchical, anonymous, sexist society, one alternative to high rates of offenses against women is to keep unaccompanied women off the streets. The preferred solution would be simultaneously to resocialize both sexes and restructure social relations to remove females from the status of victim.

66. Chicago South Park Commission, *Annual Report for 1947,* p. 18.

67. Chicago South Park Commission, *Annual Report for 1938,* p. 147.

garded it as "hard work or a bore," so that it would be perceived as recreation and they could benefit from the surreptitious instruction.[68]

Women in the Open-Space System (1965 to the Present)

The central goal of the open-space system was to help revitalize the inner city visually, economically, and socially. The new attitude toward open space was that it was valuable wherever found. Planners abandoned previous standards regarding size, shape, topography, and location. Consequently, park departments picked sites as small as a lot for both the adult "vest pocket" park and the children's totlot and adventure playground. Designers believed that the value of all unbuilt space—streets, sidewalks, plazas, parks, and playgrounds—would be enhanced if linked together into a network. Accordingly, street tree planting, street furniture, and attention to surfaces would help make streets and other open spaces seem continuous. Programming reinforced the idea by organizing events ("happenings") which moved from one place to another in and through the streets.

Implicitly, the goal of central-city revitalization focused on middle-class users—the businessmen and women on their lunch breaks from downtown offices—and the upper-middle-class suburban shoppers being courted back to the central business district.[69] Thus the needs of middle-class women for a safe and attractive urban environment have directed park planning for adults. Paley Park in New York City is an example of an environment designed for the relief of the shopper and white-collar worker: It is tucked between two buildings and the sheet of falling water at its back muffles traffic noise.

The concern for riot control in the late 1960s meant that ghetto youth were also a target population for the park department. Cultural programming was updated to include elements of popular and hip culture—rock concerts, be-ins, experiential celebrations, dancemobiles. Keeping swimming pools open at night was credited with having directly helped keep New York City "cool" while other cities erupted in riot. Planners seldom needed to explain that "ghetto youth" were black adolescent males; girls' recreational needs have not been enunciated clearly in this era. Women's athletic needs have been acknowledged by maintaining separate programs in volleyball, basketball, and softball, while adding belly dancing and yoga classes. Nevertheless, park programming has remained predominantly male oriented.

68. "Recreation in U.S. Office of Education," *Recreation* 40, no. 11 (February 1947): 616–17). The same article noted that interscholastic and intercollegiate sports were still not recommended for high school girls and college women, who should have, instead, an intramural organization emphasizing mass participation.

69. John V. Lindsay, "Parks and Recreation," mimeographed (New York, 1965).

Summary and Directions for the Future

The plans made for women's use of the parks involve them primarily as means to an end rather than as ends in themselves. Park leaders have used women to help solve contemporary urban problems. They designed females' roles in parks to help protect and stabilize the family, to improve the physical fitness of the working-class population, to keep up morale during the Depression, to keep recreational and other municipal agencies running during the world wars, and to keep cash flowing through the department stores of the central business districts. Seldom have women advocated the kind of service they wanted for themselves in their own interests. In the absence of a mandate from female users to female park promoters, women park commissioners, philanthropists, volunteers, professionals, and staff have fit into the organizational apparatus established by their male counterparts and have seldom acted as advocates on behalf of a female constituency. Because women citizens allowed themselves to be passive regarding their recreational needs, they have not been a ready and logical constituency for female policymakers. Conversely, the female leaders have not made an effort to stimulate women's awareness of urban parks as a potential agency for meeting women's needs in cities.

Because women have not constituted a "social problem," few people, including women themselves, have realized that they might have distinctive urban needs. Yet their need for mental stimulation, both educational and entertaining, has not always been overlooked by park designers. Frederick Law Olmsted, the nation's first professional park designer (beginning with Central Park in 1853), said that cities were more attractive than the countryside, especially to women, because of the cultural advantages—schools, libraries, music, and fine art: "The greatest wealth can hardly command as much of these in the country as the poorest work-girl is offered . . . in Boston at the mere cost of a walk for a short distance over a good, firm, clean pathway, lighted at night and made interesting to her by shop fronts and a variety of people passing."[70] More recently, in *The City Is the Frontier,* Charles Abrams has emphasized the potential advantages of urban life, especially for single females looking for mates, as well as for mothers needing child-care support.[71] His recommendations fly in the face of the patriarchal controls that established strong prohibitions against prostitution, dances, and unchaperoned trysting places in parks. Most recently, feminists have begun to write and confer about the issue of women's need of cities and how women must come to see urban planning issues as women's issues.[72]

70. F. L. Olmsted, "Public Parks and the Enlargment of Towns," *Journal of Social Sciences: Containing the Transactions of the American Association,* no. 3 (1871), p. 6.

71. Charles Abrams, *The City Is the Frontier* (New York: Harper & Row, 1965).

72. E.g., conference on Planning for a Nonsexist Society, University of California, Los

Nothing in the definition or practice of park service suggests that the women's movement could not turn around the old image of women as unathletic and make full use of the athletic facilities that are partially neglected during fiscal crises. Existing facilities are currently over-crowded by women of all ages who increasingly understand the value of exercise for their appearance, physical health, and mental well-being, especially since most of their jobs are sedentary. They should organize to demand better and more extensive hours for swimming pools and gym-nasiums, for example. Parks could be turned to the purposes of the human potential movement, since so many women are struggling with self-actualization and fulfillment. Compatible with this direction, parks could become holistic health centers and sense centers with saunas and whirlpools.

Community gardens, so popular with both sexes during both world wars, should be reestablished. Vegetable and flower gardening offers activities which people of all ages have enjoyed. Such gardens are also educational for children. When park departments have issued permits for allotment gardens, the demand has always been greater than the spaces allocated.

One of the most pressing needs of this society is for a rational process for raising children. Parks could become a setting for private and governmental experimentation with different types and styles of day-care centers. Parks are an ideal site for this activity because they are near neighborhoods but not within them, so that the noise of such cen-ters would not disturb local residents. The architecture is there, the landscape is there; what is needed is money for staffing and the attitude that child rearing is a social, not only an individual or a family, function.

The role of women in public places is still as problematic as it was in the nineteenth century. In trying to change the status of women in the social structure, we must not overlook the function of the physical envi-ronment in reinforcing the desired social changes.

Department of Architecture
University of California, Berkeley

Angeles, Spring 1979; Gerda R. Wekerle, Rebecca Paterson, David Morley, eds., *New Space for Women* (Boulder, Colo.: Westview Press, 1980); Gerda Wekerle and David Popenoe, chairpersons, "Spatial Inequality in American Life: Consequences for Women" (paper session at the annual meeting of the American Sociological Association, San Francisco, August 1978); Gerda Wekerle, "Review Essay: Women in the Urban Environment" (this volume, pp. S188–S214).

Masculine Cities and Feminine Suburbs: Polarized Ideas, Contradictory Realities

Susan Saegert

"Cities" and "suburbs," "men" and "women," are names of categories that encompass individual entities which are, in many ways, as different from each other as they are similar. Yet, because the commonalities that do exist are, for various reasons, important to us, we find the labels meaningful. In this paper, I will try to deal with three related uses of the words "women," "men," "suburbs," and "cities." First, they are symbols that our culture has construed as polar opposites: the city against the suburb, men against women. We have gone on to link the city with men, the suburbs with women. Next, they are both symbols and actual events in the lives of contemporary Americans who talk about themselves. Finally, they are the subjects of statistical descriptions of the distribution of people of various racial and socioeconomic groups in different residential locations, household types, and jobs. The pictures that emerge from each type of data—the cultural, the introspective self-report, and the demographic—have a certain apparent consistency. Yet, taken together, contradictions between symbols, lived experience, and demographic description become obvious.

Symbolic Dichotomies

I would argue that a wide range of symbolic associations attach to women and suburbs versus men and cities, although it is not possible to document this fully in this essay. Urban life and men tend to be thought

This paper extends some of the themes developed in an earlier work I coauthored with Gary Winkel entitled, "The Home: A Critical Problem for Changing Sex Roles," to appear in *New Space for Women,* ed. Gerda Wekerle, Rebecca Peterson, and David Morley (Boulder, Colo.: Westview Press, 1980). Our research and that of Mackintosh, Olsen, and Wentworth was supported by NIMH grant MH 124795-02.

of as more aggressive, assertive, definers of important world events, intellectual, powerful, active, and sometimes dangerous. Women and suburbs share domesticity, repose, closeness to nature, lack of seriousness, mindlessness, and safety. Figuratively, women and suburbs tend to be more conservative about political and moral issues and norms. In his essay on the meaning of suburbs as a sociological concept, Barry Schwartz clearly recognizes our symbolic structuring of female/suburban and male/urban: "No wonder that male and female symbolism should distinguish city and suburb with such decisiveness. Not only to the gender of the daytime population does suburbia owe its essential femininity, but also to the domesticity which is its very *raison d'être,* and to its corresponding alienation from the 'serious' work which has always taken place within the masculine province of the city. . . . The suburbs, in this sense, conform to the Freudian conception of femininity: passive, intellectually void, instinctually distractive. . . ."[1] When Paul Davidoff took Schwartz to task for "showing no signs of raised consciousness" in this statement, he was quite right. He was also, I think, responding from a phase of "raised consciousness" that is now giving way to a more complex analysis.[2]

That analysis suggests that just as the female symbolism Schwartz evokes is too narrow to comprehend the real lives of women, so the suburban-urban dichotomy is too clean, too fictional, to describe their sociological, economic, and ecological actuality. Unfortunately, some of the pain and alienation women and men feel may well be engendered by the gap between the symbolic and the lived experience. Yet, these culturally bifurcated conceptions have power. They help to give rise to organizations of space and time that make real choices between domestic, private activities and public, productive ones difficult. Further, the symbolic dichotomy of female/male and suburban/urban may reinforce and reflect a variation of an actual segregation of much private life from public, socially organized productive life that perpetuates inequalities.

Identification of Women with the Home[3]

Working as an anthropologist, Michelle Z. Rosaldo framed the hypothesis that women's status will be lowest in conditions of sharp sep-

1. Barry Schwartz, "Images of Suburbia: Some Revisionist Comments," in *The Changing Face of the Suburbs,* ed. Barry Schwartz (Chicago: University of Chicago Press, 1976), pp. 334–35.

2. Paul Davidoff, "Review of Barry Schwartz (ed.), *The Changing Face of the Suburbs,*" *Journal of the American Institute of Planners* 43 (January 1977): 88–90.

3. Throughout this section I draw on data that have been analyzed by various statistical methods, all of which assess group tendencies and ignore individual responses. Reports of such analyses tend to reify the group, i.e., "women do *X* and men do *Y*." I have tried to minimize this problem by using qualifiers like "many women do more *X*." Nonetheless, it is important to read statements based on group differences as such and not as sweeping

aration of domestic life and the public sphere of activity and of isolation from each other in homes belonging to men. Egalitarian societies will be ones in which men participate in domestic activities and women in important public events. She saw American society as marked by "a radical distance between private and public, domestic and social, female and male." Women, defined as domestic, are held back from employment, while men inhabit the public working world. From this point of view, the separation of work and home characteristic of suburban residents confirms her characterization of American life. Indeed, Sylvia Fava's critique of suburban life for women provides numerous examples of how opportunities for combining domestic and public activities are limited by such suburban characteristics as low density, lack of public transportation and public services, and limited provision of housing alternatives.[4]

Inseparable from our profound associations of women, the domestic, and the suburban is our psychic, economic, and cultural sense of home and of "the home." Homes, like women, are most likely to be private property. The suburban homes themselves are more spacious than urban ones and offer more privacy. Indeed, the home is so intimately tied to the definition of men's and women's roles that one might even say it exists as a cultural symbol primarily through these roles. Evidence for this assertion can be drawn from the images of women presented in the various media as well as from behavioral and interview studies concerning the home-related attitudes and activities of women and men. Numerous sociological investigations continue to document the symbolic and real identification of women's roles with the making of a home, even when women pursue other activities. In 1951, A. Rose found that most of the college women he studied expected to work full time, volunteer for church and community work, entertain, and raise a large family. Most time-use studies reveal that the majority of women who work outside the home simply add it on to other tasks.[5] While this taking on of additional roles may be physically tiring, it could more cheerfully be taken as representative of many women's progress in achieving fuller lives. However, studies of very different sample populations reveal at least two sources of conflict. One arises from the assump-

generalizations about all women and all men everywhere forever. A second caution is also advisable. All of the data on enjoyment, satisfaction, meaning, expectations, etc., are verbal statements of internal states. They may not be "real" in any ultimate sense. They may be self-conscious misrepresentations of what people feel, unconscious distortions, or simply partially successful efforts to express the ineffable.

4. Michelle Zimbalist Rosaldo, "Women, Culture, and Society: A Theoretical Overview," in *Women, Culture, and Society*, ed. Michelle Zimbalist Rosaldo and Louise Lamphere (Stanford, Calif.: Stanford University Press, 1974), pp. 17–42; Sylvia Fava, "Women's Place in the New Suburbia," in Wekerle et al.

5. A. Rose, "The Adequacy of Women's Expectations for Adult Roles," *Social Forces* 5 (1951): 69–77; A. Szalai, *The Use of Time* (The Hague: Mouton & Co., 1972); Joann Vanek, "The New Family Equality: Myth or Reality?" (paper presented at the annual meeting of the American Sociological Association, Chicago, September 8, 1977).

tion that, for women, the home must come first, regardless of their other involvements. The second stems from cultural ambivalence toward, and at times devaluation of, homemaking activities and the homemaker role. Thus women are, on the one hand, committing themselves to and taking responsibility for the home, and, on the other, being denigrated when they are "nothing but a housewife." They may be providing an alternative to the pressures of the individualistic, achievement-oriented public world, but they are both being judged negatively by the criteria of that world and widely expected to continue to manage the home.

A large number of the Ivy League male college students in Mirra Komarovsky's study of male sex-role dilemmas clearly evidence this ambivalent attitude. One senior states: "I believe that it is good for mothers to return to full-time work when the children are grown provided the work is important and worthwhile. Otherwise, housewives get hung up on tranquilizers, because they have no outlet for their abilities. Of course it would be difficult if a wife becomes successful in her own right. A woman should want her husband's career more than he should want hers. . . . For example, if he is transferred, his wife should follow—and not vice versa." Similarly, Bernard's review of data on the attitudes of female adolescents shows that most expect to combine work and domestic life. Most of these young women, however, expect more out of their husbands than Komarovsky's respondents see as ideal. These attitudes and expectations make the social and physical ecology of home and work even more critical. They are realistic reflections of existing patterns, but not of existing policies, support systems, and physical planning.[6]

In these circumstances, the options and constraints presented by the sociophysical environment are likely to have a significant effect on the feasibility of being involved both in the private world of the home and the world beyond. Two aspects of women's lives affect importantly their ability to combine home-related activities and values with pursuits and fulfillments in other domains. The first is the degree of sharing of household tasks with a partner. Even though overall men may not be taking on much of the work of homemaking, individual variation would be expected to influence women's opportunities to commit themselves to goals outside the home and the equality of the psychological investment of the man and woman in the home. A suburban residence, with its reduction of time spent by husbands at home because of commuting, might be expected to reduce a husband's help.

Second, the accessibility of other pursuits in her physical environment helps to shape a woman's potential involvement outside the home. This hypothesis is suggested by data from several sources. Looking at white middle-class couples in northern California over a forty-year time

6. Mirra Komarovsky, "Cultural Contradictions and Sex Roles: The Masculine Case," *American Journal of Sociology* 78, no. 4 (January 1973): 873–84; Jesse Bernard, *Women, Wives, Mothers: Values and Options* (Chicago: Aldine Publishing Co., 1975).

span, H. Maas and J. Kuyper found that the adult life-styles of women in their sample were more affected by the accessibility to sources of satisfactions in the sociophysical environment than were those of men. Further, more women who, in older age, were described as most poorly adjusted and unhappy lived in remote suburban or rural locations. They focused most of their activities around home and family. The well-being and interests of the men in the sample were apparently little influenced by the location of their homes.[7] We can perhaps understand women's dependency on the environment more clearly when we look at the concrete opportunities women have for pursuits outside the home. R. Palm and A. Pred, for example, concluded that distances to activities outside the home, lack of transportation, and time schedules imposed by household duties and child care made involvement in pursuits outside the home difficult, if not impossible, for many women.[8] While most of the data they drew on were gathered in northern California prior to 1970, their conclusions seem likely to be valid in many places today. Indeed, both cutbacks in financial support of public services and increased deconcentration of the population have probably exacerbated these constraints. Simultaneously, inflation and unemployment have reduced many women's ability to buy needed services on the private market.

Suburban-Urban Differences in the Use and Meaning of Homes

In American society, the home is a place where most people spend large amounts of time. A number of significant human activities take place there. It is a setting that provides the boundary between public on-stage activities and private, interpersonal as well as solitary pursuits. Beyond that, the home affords opportunities for some measure of control over how one's time is spent, what activities are pursued, the types and qualities of relationships that may be developed, and the ways in which personal fulfillment may be sought. Gary Winkel and I discovered some interesting suburban and urban differences in the use and meaning of the home in the lives of married couples we interviewed.[9] Our sample included 110 couples in an upper-middle-class section in Stamford, Connecticut, and 106 couples in an upper-middle-class residential area of New York City.

We found that while women in both locations did vastly more of the household chores, the differences between men and women's domestic contributions were smaller in the city. In addition, suburbanites re-

7. H. S. Maas and J. M. Kuper, *From Thirty to Seventy* (San Francisco: Jossey-Bass, 1974).

8. R. Palm and A. Pred, "A Time-geographic Perspective on Problems of Inequality for Women," unpublished manuscript (Berkeley: University of California, n.d.).

9. S. Saegert and G. Winkel, "The Home: A Critical Problem for Changing Sex Roles," in Wekerle et al.

ported doing more housework, even though our respondents in both areas were similar. About a third of the wives were working, most having one or two children. The average family income was more than $40,000 a year. Reflecting the areas sampled, most of the couples we interviewed were white; the number of black women and men in both places was small. In both the cities and the suburbs, more women thought it was important for the home to express their personalities than did most men. Many of these women also placed more significance on the home as a place for social relationships, for being alone, for relaxing, and for displaying things. More women were also more satisfied with their homes for these purposes than were the majority of men. When Winkel and I looked at ratings of satisfaction with the home and the importance of various uses of it, we found no instances in which the average male responses indicated more satisfaction with the home or a greater sense of its importance than the average for female responses.

More women in both locations reported feeling that a number of specific uses of the home were more important than most men did. However, the average female and male suburbanite reported being better satisfied than the urbanite with their homes on these ratings: the home as a place to raise children; a place to do work you enjoy; a place to have fun; a space to use freely; and a setting for a chosen kind of life. The suburban sample also found certain aspects of the home more important and more satisfactory than did the urban sample. This pattern was revealed in questions about home as a place for intimate relationships; a place to have fun; a place to be alone; and a space you can use any way you want.

These data have a number of implications for assessing change in sex roles. The first, of course, is to point out once again that, on the average, women bear the responsibility for the overwhelming majority of household chores. Second, more women in our study seemed to care more about the home and to gain more satisfactions from it. Other conclusions to be drawn from the differences among urban and suburban men and women are more complex. Apparently, while more urban couples report less sex-stereotyping of household tasks, differences in attitudes toward the home are greater among them than for the average suburban couple. However, it would be too simple to conclude that, despite potentially greater responsibility for housework, urban women might be happier in a suburban setting. Our data show that the urban women commonly place a much higher value on working outside the home (whether or not they are currently employed). In this, they are similar to their average male counterpart. Most suburban men in our sample also valued their work highly; most suburban women did not. Throughout our data, it is clear that, as one might expect, the urban sample is generally more involved in work-related and cultural pursuits. The suburban group is primarily family-centered. However, it appears that more women in the city and more men in the suburbs tend to value both areas more equally, whereas the majority of urban men emphasize work and the average suburban woman focuses primarily on the home.

For the sample that Winkel and I studied, the city does not seem to provide as satisfactory a set of residential environments, even though the area is considered one of the best residential neighborhoods in New York City. The urbanites report more times that they are dissatisfied with their homes, in part because of the smaller average size of dwelling units in the city and because of a sense of lack of safety—especially among women. One might speculate that inadequacies of the residential environments often affect women more than men since they spend more time at home and seem to see the home as a more important place for many aspects of life.

Thus far I have reported similarities and differences among urban and suburban men's and women's use and evaluation of their homes based on analysis of variance. This technique does not tell us about correlations among items. For example, there might be no group differences on a particular measure of specific home satisfaction but that item might correlate with rated general enjoyment of home for urban women but not for urban men or for suburbanites. We could infer from this analysis that the two items were probably contingent for urban women and unrelated for other groups.

The patterns of correlation that emerged for all four groups were substantially similar with a few notable exceptions. The urban sample tended to be either satisfied or dissatisfied with their homes for all purposes, while the suburbanites generally discriminated between being satisfied with their homes for adult purposes as opposed to child-related purposes. Enjoyment of the time at home depended on adult satisfactions for most of the suburban men and women. For urban women, enjoyment of time at home frequently accompanied satisfaction with the home for social, family, and personal activities. These satisfactions also formed a single dimension for urban men but were unrelated to reports of enjoyment time at home.

Frequently suburban women were more dissatisfied at home when they would have liked to be free to leave the home and when they did not see the home as a satisfying setting for their particular life-style. Probably this pattern characterizes women who, while living in the home-centered suburban environment, would prefer other sources of satisfaction and activities. Understanding the role of the home as a retreat for urban couples appears from our data to be especially crucial. Generally, the home as retreat and as a place to be alone seems to be more important in the city, for both women and men. However, the effects of satisfying this value tend to be opposite for urban men and women. Many urban men enjoyed their homes only to the extent that they served as retreats from the external world. Many urban women who reported that it was important that their homes serve as a retreat and that it did so satisfactorily also said that many times they were dissatisfied with being at home. This theme also emerged in interviews conducted by Betty Mackintosh and her colleagues.[10] They found that the men in their urban sample were more likely to stress the role that the home played in providing them with a retreat from the stresses of urban living. Many urban men felt that suburban living was much more likely to provide a desirable degree of separation between home life and work life. Urban women, on the other hand, frequently made comments regarding the importance of the city to their aspirations, which often involved either part-time work or full-time work. Even if these urban women were not employed, they felt that they were not cut off from the activities and options presented by the city as they would be if they moved to the suburbs.[11]

Locational Trade-offs for Women and Men

If we relate the patterns of evaluation that characterize the various groups to differences in importance of and satisfaction with particular uses of the home, some interesting implications appear. For three of the four groups we have looked at, the very uses of the home that are most related to its enjoyment are ones with which they are less satisfied than other groups. Urban men were frequently less satisfied than most urban women with the home as a retreat, yet when urban men were satisfied they tended to enjoy their homes. Those urban women who were satisfied with their homes as retreats were the very ones who generally felt otherwise dissatisfied at home. Many urban women placed more importance on the home as a place to raise children than did their spouses, while on the average both reported less satisfaction with the home for this purpose than did suburban couples. This dissatisfaction may not matter too much to many urban men, since it did not strongly influence their overall enjoyment of home. However, for large numbers of urban women it is part of the complex of child- and family-centered uses of home that were significant in overall satisfaction.

The case is less clear for suburban women. Yet it generally appears that often their overall enjoyment of the home is most related to adult activities and the satisfactory definition of a life-style in the home setting. Here the suburban woman must frequently depend on the resources of her own family and self, being somewhat cut off from activities outside the

10. E. Mackintosh, R. Olsen, and W. Wentworth, "The Attitudes and Experiences of the Middle-Income Family in an Urban High-Rise Complex and in the Suburbs" (New York: Center for Human Environments, City University of New York, Graduate Center, 1977).

11. Ibid.

home. On the average, only the suburban man seems well-situated to achieve his home values most successfully. His two environments, perhaps plus the commitment of his wife to household tasks, provide both options for adult activities and a satisfying family-centered environment.

Certainly our data are not unequivocal enough to make this argument strongly. However, Michelson's findings and Fava's work on the problems of women in the suburbs support the idea. In addition, the research by Mackintosh and her colleagues indicates that urban environments generally offer more options for women but expose them to many difficulties in child rearing, safety, and inadequate space in the dwelling unit. Most men seem to favor suburban living.[12] Mackintosh, West, and Olson began by asking a question that was not explicitly focused on sex roles. They were interested in the experience of raising children in an urban high-rise development, an environment usually thought of as bad for that activity. They chose for study a building that has a reputation as an unusually good family setting. In preliminary interviews, many respondents indicated their intentions to move to the suburbs in the near future. Therefore the investigators decided to add a comparison group of respondents who had moved from the development to suburban housing.

Fifteen urban and fifteen suburban couples participated in an open-ended, in-depth interview in which each partner was interviewed separately by a same-sex interviewer. While respondents were extremely concerned about the problems of assuring children's safety and good schooling in the city, a second conflict also seemed to exist—between the attachment of many wives to the cultural and social opportunities of the city and the desire of many husbands for the relaxation and status of a suburban home. Of these couples, 48 percent reported a greater desire on the part of the husband to move to the suburbs than the wife. The wife was more positive in only 14 percent of the cases. When the move to the suburbs was agreed on, or anticipated, women expressed more worry. Typical remarks included statements like, "I was afraid of isolation, intellectual stagnation, and boredom." Husbands expressed no such fears; instead, they looked forward to a more relaxed life and more outdoor activities. Women also tended to place less value on owning a detached, single-family home.

After moving to the suburbs, half of the women felt they suffered from lack of stimulation. They often stated that they themselves had become more boring. In contrast, one-third of the suburban men (and no suburban women) said they enjoyed leaving the hectic pace of the

12. Ibid.; Fava (n. 4 above); W. Michelson, "The Place of Time in Longitudinal Evaluation of Spatial Structures by Women," University of Toronto Center for Urban and Community Studies Research Paper no. 61 (Toronto, 1973).

city. Many women also expressed discouragement about the possibility of getting a job. They saw fewer options available in the suburbs, yet the commute to the city was ruled out because of family obligations. In this urban site women particularly valued their friendships with other mothers of young children. Over half of them listed other residents of the developments as their closest friends. Only two husbands did so. Urban women commented on their enjoyment of casual socializing and indeed, time-use diaries showed them spending almost two hours less alone per weekday than suburban women. Of those women who had moved to the suburbs, a third reported feeling lonely, missing their old patterns of socializing. Suburban women who located in more dense suburbs, or near already established friends, experienced less difficulty with isolation.

Fathers frequently talked of the values of the suburban experience for their children. They especially emphasized outdoor play and a more natural environment. In contrast, women committed to urban living saw the city as providing advantages to children by giving them more varied experiences. Overall, women seemed less positive to suburban living than men. Of all groups, suburban men reported the greatest satisfaction with their residences—again confirming Canadian findings.[13] However, despite women's generally more favorable attitude toward city living, the urban residence also had some negative impact on them. The small size of apartments and the necessity of supervising children closely to protect their safety were seen as problems. Urban mothers, who spent almost three hours a day more with their children than suburban mothers, reported very great concern about allowing their children outside alone. Urban women also spent more time in the apartment with the children than their husbands did and may, therefore, have experienced more tension due to lack of privacy in the apartment. Both urban and suburban women felt that children could be allowed more freedom in the suburbs, a conviction again confirmed in the time-budget data.

The relations between husbands and wives were complexly affected by the different place urban and suburban homes had in their lives. Almost half of the suburban residents thought family dynamics improved after the move. One suburban woman said, "My husband does not have to be as intimately involved in the children's activities and affairs. . . . I think that has lessened for us potential tensions. In the city, I very strongly felt that one day during the weekend, it was necessary for me to be totally alone. Which would mean I would have to leave the apartment and do something outside or he would go with the children. Here, there is more freedom for each of us to do what we want." Generally, suburban men seemed to find the time they spent with their families more relaxing than it had been in the city. The increase in commuting

13. Michelson.

time was viewed negatively, but only three suburban respondents said commuting decreased the time they spent with their family. Overall, however, time-use diaries showed that suburban men did spend significantly less time with their families as well as less time with their children alone and with their wives alone.

In summary, husbands and wives evaluated their residential choices quite differently. The retreat and recreation in the home were generally more satisfying for men in the suburban setting. In addition, suburban homes were seen as generally better for children, as a financial investment, and as a source of status. Many wives in this situation appear to be caught in a difficult set of choices. On the one hand, they value their children's independence and well-being very highly, as well as their husbands' enjoyment of the home. However, women often seem to rely on the city to provide them with stimulation, opportunity for activities outside the home, and rewarding social relationships. While the majority of men maintain their involvement in urban life after moving to the suburbs by continuing to work in the city, women frequently feel a great loss of options after the move. Sometimes this loss of options, combined with loneliness, led to feelings of depression and stagnation. Once again, we see many women in the suburbs being forced to choose between the private world of the home and the outside world. For men the range of home-related satisfactions is broadened in the suburbs without as great a loss of other opportunities.

The Mackintosh study and mine with Winkel are limited in themselves since they concern relatively small samples of middle- to upper-income couples. Yet the work of other researchers tends to confirm such conclusions. A large, economically stratified sample of Canadian families were studied as they moved to either center city or suburban homes and apartments. While the investigator had only incidental interest in the differences in men's and women's experiences, he did report that many suburban women found isolation to be a problem despite their greater amount of visiting and entertaining. Suburban women generally were the least satisfied with their residential locations, their husbands the most satisfied.

Research on blue-collar couples in the suburbs presents a similar picture. More women in blue-collar families who move from cities to suburbs displayed feelings of anomie, social isolation, and marital tension than women moving within cities. Men as a group showed the opposite pattern. Many working-class women lost their close ties to friends and relatives when they located in a suburb and did not find others to replace them. This was part of a shift from more sex-segregated social relationships, characteristic of urban couples, to the greater sharing and reliance on spouses among suburbanites. In this trade, many men reported more ability to share problems with another person—their wives. Thus many working-class urban men did not find as much openness to communication about problems among male friends and relatives as many suburban men achieved with their wives. Working-class suburban men also scored lower on measures of anomie that did urban men.[14]

Changing Demographic Trends

The discussion thus far has focused on evidence suggesting that suburban residences tend to isolate women from involvement outside the home, thus unhappily reinforcing the real and symbolic distinctions between the private, domestic female world and the public, productive male world. Yet the demographic shifts in the location of residences and workplaces, as well as the great increase in female labor force participation in the last decade, suggest that at least on some levels, this separation is breaking down. Both the nature of women's lives and the physical and social characteristics of cities and suburbs are rapidly changing. The simple imagery of female-domestic and male-public is also increasingly inaccurate. Statistics on women's labor force participation amply document this change. Suburban women as well as city women are increasingly employed outside the home. While employment rates for women remain higher in central cities than in suburbs, the rates for suburban women in 1970 exceeded labor force participation of central city women in 1960. This is true even for married women and women with children under six.

As the accuracy of the exclusively domestic image of women rapidly erodes, the same appears true for the exclusively residential quality of suburbs. In the decade between 1960 and 1970 the number of jobs in metropolitan areas has increased more outside of central cities than in them. Suburbs are increasingly heterogeneous with respect to household composition and age. While suburbs continue to be less open to black residents, other socioeconomic characteristics of suburbs vary greatly.[15] J. D. Kasarda describes these shifts in occupational structure with the growth of administrative, professional, and specialized business services in the central cities and the concomitant increase in residential population, manufacturing, and the provision of standard goods and services in suburbs. This distribution has meant a mismatch of jobs requiring higher educational attainment with a less educated resident population in central cities, while job opportunities for the less educated expand in those suburbs with the better-educated populations.

These changes in labor force participation of women, and in the locations of residences and workplaces, may well lead to a complex inter-

---

14. Ibid.; I. Tallman, "Working-Class Wives in Suburbia: Fulfillment or Crisis," *Journal of Marriage and the Family* (February 1969), pp. 65–72.

15. Vanek (n. 5 above); Larry Long and Paul C. Glick, "Family Patterns in Suburban Areas: Recent Trends," in Schwartz (n. 1 above), pp. 39–68.

relationship of sex-, race-, and class-related occupational and residential patterns. Kasarda has provided evidence of suburban increases in blue- and white-collar jobs. However, while more people began both to live and work in suburban areas between 1960 and 1970, this decade also was marked by an increased percent of both blue- and white-collar workers who commuted between workplaces and homes in different metropolitan regions. These data also reveal that blacks have disproportionately been required to commute from central-city residences to suburban employment.[16]

Like the majority of blacks, many women have low-paying jobs, with black women falling into the lowest paid group of all. This conglomeration of changes suggests a number of questions. First, are the low-paying jobs that are being redistributed from central city to suburban locations going disproportionately to white suburban women? Second, are the new white-collar jobs in the city favoring female employment, as is likely if these are mainly clerical? Would this redistribution then be related both to a lowering of wages for women and an increase in unemployment for blacks as well as a decline in black wages related to increased competition for jobs? How does this redistribution affect black women?

Another set of questions concerns the way women are experiencing and responding to the shifts in employment and residential patterns. For example, are many women willing to take lower-paying jobs in suburbs, rather than commute to higher-paying city jobs, in order to be nearer their homes? It would be interesting to replicate Kasarda's comparison of occupational and residential patterns for blacks and whites, including sex and household composition as variables. Would mothers of young children be most likely to make this compromise? If so, then how do they cope with the lesser availability of child care, public transportation, and other services in suburban areas? How do women trade off these difficulties against the acknowledged benefits of suburban living for children: better schools, greater access to out-of-doors, greater safety, more spacious housing? Kreps and Leaper state that recently women have tended to withdraw from the labor market rather than to engage in prolonged search in an unfavorable location in these times of high unemployment. Perhaps women's increased employment roles and low wages suggest that women are settling for whatever jobs they can get that are accessible. Are difficulties in providing adequate household services in suburban locations related to this tendency? What impact does inflation and the increased number of female-headed households have on this tendency to withdraw? How are these factors related to women's needs in residential environments?

16. J. D. Kasarda, "The Changing Occupational Structure of the American Metropolis: Apropos the Urban Problem," in Schwartz (n. 1 above), pp. 113–36.

Employment patterns are not the only demographic changes. More people are living in the suburbs now than ever before, especially if they are white. In 1970, 58 percent of the white population in standard metropolitan areas lived in suburbs, while 18 percent of the black population was located outside the central city. Not only are more people living in suburbs, but also the composition of the populations of cities and suburbs are becoming more similar, with suburbs having increasingly more singles, fewer married couples, more working wives, and more working mothers.[17] Clearly, then, demographic data show a breaking down of the dichotomy of female/private/suburban versus male/public/urban. How then are these changes being experienced? The previously reported data on sex differences in attitudes and behavior of males and females in cities and suburbs were gathered during the mid-sixties to mid-seventies. While they are less comprehensive than demographic statistics, they nonetheless suggest that the demographic resolution of the polarization has not led to a complete dissolution of the dichotomy in people's minds and daily activities.

Two recent volumes of research on suburban life both present the view that while more and more people live in suburbia, the zoning and development of suburban areas reflect and perpetuate the concept of suburbia as a place populated by middle-class, intact nuclear families. The same restrictions and policies that keep minority members out of suburbia also discriminate against female-headed households and single women. Both have in common lower average incomes, needs for cheap multifamily housing, and more social services. For example, Carol Brown's study of divorced women in the Boston area shows that after divorce the detached single-family housing occupied by many of these women no longer met their needs or their income.[18]

Contradictions, Constraints, and the Future

The growth of suburban populations during a time of increased female labor force participation can be added to a list of contradictory trends in this era that place rather greater demands on women. Many now have two roles—work outside the home and responsibility for domestic life. As Kamerman has pointed out, in many European countries this situation has led to the development of family policies to

17. J. M. Kreps and R. J. Leaper, "Home Work, Market Work and the Allocation on Time," in *Women and the American Economy: A Look to the 1980s,* ed. J. M. Kreps (Englewood Cliffs, N.J.: Prentice-Hall, Inc., 1976), pp. 61–81.

18. Carol Brown, "Housing Needs of Divorced Women" (paper presented at the annual meeting of the American Sociological Association, San Francisco, September, 1978).

ameliorate women's burdens but not in the United States.[19] The public services that might help women manage have been subject to funding cuts at city, state, and federal levels. The cities, hurt by heavy financial deficits, cannot provide as many of these services as they have in the past while suburbs, operating under the myth of the housewife in an effort to preserve class and racial exclusiveness, do not give priority to those services. Lower-income suburbs cannot afford them.

Current research suggests that higher density, mixed-use residential environments give women more options. The residential choices of the samples studied force couples to choose either small apartments and social and physical environmental conditions they consider nonoptimal for child rearing (high crime, pollution, lack of nature, unsatisfactory schools) or the loss of social and cultural opportunities, especially for the wife. Thus I concur with Michelson on the desirability of maintaining and developing satisfactory residential environments in the city. Improved public transportation in suburban areas is also a potential way of ameliorating some of these problems. A second implication of these data does not lead to such clear-cut suggestions. It may even raise doubts about the successfulness of the urban housing alternative. Many urban men appear to be less emotionally invested in the home than their wives. For the majority of women in all samples, the home is closely linked to women's identities and provides some very significant satisfactions. Men frequently seem to be happier and more psychologically invested in suburban homes. Where does this leave women who value their homes, who want them to be meaningful centers of the family, *and* who want to expand their roles outside the home? Looking at the same issue from the male point of view, it appears that men prefer residential environments that reinforce the public-private distinction. This may be an inadvertent consequence of the bonuses of suburban life—retreat, outdoor activities, homeownership, relief from the pace of the city—or it may be partially motivated by the perhaps unconscious desire in many men to assure that their home will be taken care of by a woman with few other options.

Several major obstacles appear to limit the availability of a diversity of roles and satisfactions, and these seem to particularly affect women. The time schedule and reward structure of most work is clearly one of the strongest pressures against the combination of physical and psychological investment in the home and outside. The geographic segregation of residential environments from public life reinforces the cultural choice of work or home, especially for women, who do not have the luxury of a wife. Women who invest energy in work outside the home cannot assume that anyone else will compensate. By the same token, women who commit themselves primarily to home-related goals generally do not gain a second meaningful environment through their hus-

19. Sheila B. Kamerman, "Work and Family in Industrialized Societies," *Signs: Journal of Women in Culture and Society* 4, no. 4 (Summer 1979): 632–50.

bands' work, whereas men working outside the home usually do gain this from marriage. In addition, the many women who are financially required to work, especially sole heads of household, must juggle both sets of demands and goals in a context that supports commitment to one or the other, but not to both.

The idealized opposition of female, domestic, private, often suburban worlds and male, productive, public, usually urban worlds does not really describe the lives of many people. Moreover, the convergence of changes in residential and occupational distribution and in female employment and family compositions suggests that a strong and intimate link, not a gap, exists between the domestic and the public spheres. Women's cheap labor, relative good manners, and educational distribution may presently make them desirable as workers from an employer's point of view, compared to the employer's image of unskilled, unruly minority workers in the city.[20] Women, by accepting both low wages and major responsibility for domestic life, are a bargain. Here cultural and personal understandings of women and of domestic life become critical. Research shows that many women, even when they work, think of themselves first as homemakers.[21] The vast majority of both men and women value the male work role more than the female domestic role for men. This continuing devaluation of domestic private life, and its assignment to women in the context of policies and environments, make the handling of both difficult indeed.

The segregation of public and private, male and female domains appears strongest as a guiding fiction, yet one that finds its way into public policy and planning and into women's and men's sense of who they are. This fiction places a burden of a kind of dual reality on many women: double duty at home and work, split loyalties, and too scanty a recognition of achievement in either sphere. Women's energy must go to holding together the necessary areas of life that are organized temporally and spatially to create separation. Existing separations are difficult for individuals to overcome on their own, even if they aim toward a new identity. Collective visions of an integrated life of domestic work, productive work, and leisure must inform public policy and physical planning in order to bring forth an organization of time and space in which that integration is fostered.

Department of Environmental Psychology
Graduate Center, City University of New York

20. Kasarda, pp. 126–27.
21. H. Z. Lopata, *Occupation: Housewife* (London: Oxford University Press, 1971); A. Oakley, *The Sociology of Housework* (New York: Random House, 1974).

The Health Careers of Urban Women: A Study in East Harlem

Marsha Hurst and Ruth E. Zambrana

Women and their families in East Harlem, a low-income urban minority area, have special health needs and problems that merit, but do not receive, special attention. Both the birthrate and the infant mortality rate are higher in East Harlem than in Manhattan as a whole.[1] The residents of East Harlem recognize the critical role of good health in their lives, and Puerto Rican women in particular have indicated in a 1970 survey that they feel their health is poorer than that of women of other racial or ethnic groups (Italian and black).[2] They face multiple barriers both in understanding their health needs and in obtaining and using health services. Their lower income and educational status make it difficult for them to become educated health consumers; linguistic and cultural barriers further impede equal access to information and care. Finally, like other women, they face sexual barriers in the male-dominated medical system.

The intent of this paper is to explore the relationship between the low-income—and particularly the Puerto Rican—woman and the health-care system. The pilot study on which this work is based examines the "health careers" of a random selection of women registered at the Neighborhood Health Center (NHC), a primary-care facility in East Harlem (*El Barrio*), New York City. The health and health care of these

A version of this paper was presented at the Women and Society Symposium, St. Michael's College, Winooski, Vermont, March 23–25, 1979. It appears here with the permission of St. Michael's College.

1. Health Systems Agency of New York City, *The Communities of Harlem: A Plan for Health Care,* Data Book (New York: Health Systems Agency, 1978).

2. L. Johnson, *East Harlem Community Health Study* (New York: City University of New York, Mount Sinai School of Medicine, Department of Community Medicine, 1972).

women in East Harlem must be viewed first in the perspective of their position in the larger society as females, as poor Americans, and as members of minority groups. Further, health care is a relationship between provider and consumer. Not only are the characteristics of the consumer determinant of the character and quality of the relationship, but so are the characteristics of the provider. Together, consumer and provider are part of an interdependent patterned interaction, which in various manifestations has been remarkably stable.

Background

Woman's role in society has been defined in terms of her relation to the means of reproduction. Historically, poor and minority women have labored under a double burden. Their bodies have been considered sick, and their persons, because they are poor, have been considered objects for others' use.[3] In recent years, women have begun to examine and to understand more clearly their position and role in society. One result of this process has been a focus on women's role as clients within the health-care system, a role that provides critical clues to the understanding of woman's past and present situation in the larger society.[4] Since society has defined woman's social role in terms of her relationship to the means of reproduction, women have frequently initiated the process of political and social assertion by striving to understand and control their own reproductive health.[5] Poor women's relationship to the health-care system has been mainly as passive recipients of medical interventions, generally playing dependent patients to the dominant providers in a system in which they have no bargaining power.[6] Poor women have also been the reserve labor force of the health-care system, not only providing the bottom layer of work force for the least skilled hospital jobs, but

3. L. Gordon, *Woman's Body, Woman's Right* (New York: Penguin Books, 1977); B. Ehrenreich and D. English, *Complaints and Disorders* (Old Westbury, N.Y.: Feminist Press, 1973).

4. G. Corea, *The Hidden Malpractice* (New York: William Morrow & Co., 1977); B. Seaman, *Free and Female* (New York: Coward, McCann & Geoghegan, 1972); E. Frankfort, *Vaginal Politics* (New York: Quadrangle Books, 1972); M. T. Notman and C. C. Nadelson, eds., *The Woman Patient* (New York: Plenum Publishers, 1978), vol. 1.

5. Boston Women's Health Collective, *Our Bodies, Ourselves* (New York: Simon & Schuster, 1976); A. Rossi, "Children and Work in the Lives of Women" (paper delivered at the University of Arizona, Tucson, February 7, 1976); R. Dunbar, "Female Liberation as a Basis for Social Revolution," in *Sisterhood Is Powerful*, ed. R. Morgan (New York: Random House, 1970), pp. 477–92; E. Boulding, "Familial Constraints on Women's Work Roles," International Women's Year Studies on Women, paper no. 5, mimeographed (Boulder, Colo.: Institute of Behavioral Science, May 1975).

6. M. T. Notman and C. C. Nadelson, "The Woman Patient," in Notman and Nadelson, eds.

providing the bodies on which physicians train, research, and practice.[7] As is characteristic of reserve labor, the inclusion or exclusion of poor women from the care-giving arenas has been dependent on the needs of society's institutions rather than on the needs of the laborers themselves.

Poor women have historically paid for their penury with their privacy.[8] Not only are they essential for teaching and practice, but they are used to test medical technology—chemical, procedural, or mechanical. The random assignment of clinic patients to treatment groups to teach medical students and to test drugs or procedures is accepted as basis of sound pedagogy and critical evaluation in medicine.[9]

Many studies correlate low socioeconomic status, low educational level, and poor degree of social integration with receipt of medical care that is poor in both quantity and quality.[10] A critical outcome of these interrelationships is the "underutilization" of medical and health services by the poor. The use of health services by poor populations has not been well understood. Patterns of utilization are complex and must be examined in categories which encompass cultural as well as socioenvironmental variables.[11] Utilization by definition includes consumer choices that are determined by personal attitudes, cultural context, and

7. B. Ehrenreich and J. Ehrenreich, "Health Care and Social Control," *Social Policy* 5, no. 1 (May–June 1974): 26–40.

8. N. S. Shaw, *Forced Labor: Maternity Care in the United States* (New York: Pergamon Press, 1974).

9. K. Rosenberg, "Human Experimentation," *Health/PAC Bulletin,* nos. 81–82 (1979), pp. 2, 43–47; Women's Project, U.S. Commission on Civil Rights, "Medical Experimentation on Women and the Role of the FDA" (Washington, D.C.: Government Printing Office, n.d.).

10. W. C. Richardson, "Poverty, Illness, and the Use of Health Services in the United States," in *Patients, Physicians and Illness,* ed. E. Gartly Jaco (New York: Free Press, 1972), pp. 240–49; P. Moody and R. Gray, "Social Class, Social Integration and the Use of Preventive Health Services," in Jaco, ed., pp. 250–61; R. Anderson and O. W. Anderson, *A Decade of Health Services* (Chicago: University of Chicago Press, 1967); E. A. Suchman, "Social Patterns of Illness and Medical Care," in Jaco, ed., pp. 262–79; chapter entitled "Social Structure and Dynamic Process: The Case of Modern Medical Practice," in Talcott Parsons's *The Social System* (New York: Free Press, 1964); Jerry L. Weaver, *National Health Policy and the Underserved: Ethnic Minorities, Women and the Elderly* (St. Louis, Mo.: C. V. Mosby Co., 1976); M. L. Lefcowitz, "Poverty and Health: A Re-examination," *Inquiry* 10 (March 1973): 3–13.

11. R. Geertsen et al., "A Re-examination of Suchman's Views on Social Factors in Health Care Utilization," *Journal of Health and Social Behavior* 16, no. 2 (1975): 226–37; W. C. Normand, J. Iglesias, and S. Payn, "Brief Group Therapy to Facilitate Utilization of Mental Health Services by Spanish-speaking Patients," *American Journal of Orthopsychiatry* 44, no. 1 (1974): 37–42; J. G. Bruhn and R. G. Fuentes, Jr., "Cultural Factors Affecting Utilization of Services by Mexican Americans," *Psychiatric Annals* 7, no. 12 (1977): 20–29; S. K. Hoppe and P. L. Heller, "Alienation, Familism and Utilization of Health Services by Mexican Americans," *Journal of Health and Social Behavior* 16, no. 3 (1975): 304–14; G. M. Queseda, "Language and Communication Barriers for Health Delivery to a Minority Group," *Social Science and Medicine* 10, no. 6 (1976): 323–27.

structural and financial points of access to the system. Systemic barriers are the most significant variables to examine because institutionalized health-care delivery systems maintain the distance between the insiders, those most closely identifiable with the system, and the outsiders, those most different from the principal actors in the system. Thus it has become increasingly important to discuss and analyze both the exclusionary and the inclusionary strategies of all dominant institutions regarding the poor.[12]

Part of the difficulty of gaining a broader understanding of the health problems of Hispanic women in particular is that their complaints and illnesses do not fit into the prediagnosed categories which have been devised as the norms for the population; or, if they do, they are inappropriately labeled.[13] Although some steps are being taken to revise these narrow conceptions,[14] providers have generally not addressed the priorities and problems of Hispanic women. The health problems most commonly identified by these women are closely tied to their own roles, as women and as primary caretakers of their families. In New York City, this family responsibility is particularly striking given the increase of Hispanic families headed by women and their disproportionately lower rate of labor-force participation.[15] Spanish-speaking women are at a greater disadvantage than the men or women of other ethnic groups in terms of education, ability to speak the language, health status, and earning power.[16]

A recent sociological analysis of this issue[17] focused on three types of explanation that have dominated interpretations of low utilization rates: first, a financial explanation emphasizing the inadequate financial resources or health insurance coverage of poor people; second, a cultural explanation focusing on attitudinal traits resulting from their economic and social situation; and third, a systemic explanation that focuses on barriers in the health-care delivery system itself, rather than on charac-

12. Ehrenreich and Ehrenreich.
13. A. M. Padilla, R. A. Ruiz, and R. Alvarez, "Community Mental Health Services for Spanish-speaking Surnamed Population," *American Psychologist* 30, no. 9 (1975): 892–905.
14. Normand et al.; E. J. Coller and M. H. Centro, "Group and Hispanic Prenatal Patient," *American Journal of Orthopsychiatry* 47, no. 4 (1977): 689–700; P. Ruiz, "Culture and Mental Health: Hispanic Perspective," *Journal of Contemporary Psychotherapy* 9, no. 1 (1976): 24–27.
15. U.S. Department of Labor, Bureau of Labor Statistics, "A Socio-Economic Profile of Puerto Rican New Yorkers," Middle Atlantic Regional Office, Regional Report 46 (New York: U.S. Department of Labor Statistics, July 1975); N. Gerard and M. McCormick, "The Impact of Women on the Economy of New York City," study prepared for Women United for New York, mimeographed (New York: Barnard College, 1978).
16. L. R. Marcos et al., "Language Barrier in Evaluating Spanish-American Patients," *Archives of General Psychiatry* 29, no. 5 (1973): 655–59.
17. D. Dutton, "Explaining the Low Use of Health Services by the Poor: Costs, Attitudes, or Delivery Systems?" *American Journal of Sociology* 43 (June 1978): 348–68.

teristics of the populations it serves. The author's analysis showed that systemic barriers of access, and public channels of care which are dehumanizing, discontinuous, and disease-oriented, accounted for more of the low utilization among a poor population than other explanations.

Setting

East Harlem is a low-income residential community in New York City with a population of approximately 135,000.[18] The bulk of the population consist of migrants, mainly Puerto Rican (48 percent) and black (35 percent), and white ethnics (17 percent), mainly Italian. The median East Harlem family income in 1972 was $5,895, and the percentage of families earning less than $5,000 per year was almost double that for New York City. One out of every three families in East Harlem is below the poverty level. Public assistance is common in this community, with 44 percent of the population dependent upon it for survival.

Almost 30 percent of the women in East Harlem are between the ages of fifteen and forty-four. The health status of this group has serious implications for the health-care delivery system. Data show that women in East Harlem have more children than women elsewhere, at a younger age, and more frequently without being married. In 1970 the rate of live births per 1,000 females in New York City was 81.5, in Manhattan 65.5, and in East Harlem 82.9. Among the Puerto Rican women in East Harlem, this rate jumped to 96.6. The percentage of births out of wedlock was significantly higher in East Harlem (52.1 percent) than in Manhattan (37.3 percent) in 1976. Although recent data show that infant mortality has been declining in all areas of the city, the infant mortality rate of 23.5 deaths per 1,000 live births in East Harlem remains quite high compared to the rate of 19.3 in New York City as a whole. In 1976, 12.1 percent of births in East Harlem were premature or low birth weight (defined as those infants born weighing less than 2,501 grams) compared with 9.5 percent citywide.

East Harlem has many health resources, although they are misused and underutilized. Within the area, at the time of the study, there were four general-service hospitals, five child-health stations, a district health center operated by the city, and a community-based neighborhood health center which opened in June 1975. Although drugstores are few within the area, *botanicas,* which sell medicinal herbs favored by many Puerto Rican people, are available. Few private physicians practice in East Harlem. "Medicaid mills," however, abound, with roughly twenty operating at any one time. The principal sources of ambulatory care are

---

18. Statistics in the following discussion are derived from Johnson (see n. 2 above) and Health Systems Agency of New York City (see n. 1 above.).

the outpatient and emergency departments of the several hospitals serving the community. The organization of these facilities follows traditional lines and is not designed to deliver well-integrated, comprehensive care for the individual and the family. Typically, these departments are overburdened and do not meet the minimum standards of amenity conducive to patient dignity and effective medical care.

Method

The exploratory nature of our inquiry was geared to examine two major areas: the utilization patterns of women in East Harlem, and the women's own health needs and health behaviors. Two major methods were used to explore these areas: an extensive open-ended questionnaire administered to twenty-six women; and an open-ended interview schedule, used with personnel of the community-based NHC. Unpublished reports and studies conducted at the NHC and documents of the agency, particularly proposals, were also used.

Extensive interviews were conducted with twenty-six women who came to the pediatric or family-planning clinics of the NHC. Preliminary meetings were held with the pediatricians, the nurse-practitioner, the physician associate, and the community health workers to explain the nature of our study and to enlist their cooperation. These health professionals briefly explained the nature of our interview to the women they saw in consultation and then referred the women to us. Interviews with the women lasted approximately two and a half hours and were conducted in either Spanish or English, depending on the preference of the interviewee. Formal interviews were conducted with the nurse-practitioner and physician associate, and informal interviews were conducted with three other health-related professionals of the NHC. Mothers' health education groups conducted by the NHC director, but initiated by mothers themselves, were also attended to obtain a sense of the nature of the problems which might not normally be brought to the attention of health-care providers.

Although our study sample was not representative of all East Harlem women,[19] in this pilot study we were concerned with exploring the experiences and utilization behaviors and patterns of women who are relatively self-conscious consumers of health-care delivery services. The

19. The limitations of our methodology included pro-NHC respondent bias because the interviews were conducted on-site, and self-selection problems generated by choosing women who were registered at and users of a primary-care center. We attempted to minimize other biases by identifying ourselves as women who were interested in health but did not work at NHC, by attending morning, evening, and weekend sessions to conduct interviews, and by interviewing both walk-in patients and patients with prior appointments.

sample population was selected on the basis of urban residence, lower socioeconomic status, and minority-group membership. Our focus was to identify the shared experiences of these women, all of whom had at least one hospitalization for childbirth, in their use of health services in the New York City area. In this respect, their intra- and intercultural differences do not represent a major focus of our inquiry and analysis.

Results and Discussion

Description of Sample Population

The great majority of the women (twenty-one of the twenty-six interviewed) were between the ages of twenty and forty. Most of the women were Hispanic (nineteen), predominantly Puerto Rican; the remaining seven were black American. Sixteen out of twenty-six women had two to three children, and fourteen of the women had a maximum of five individuals in the household. Only eight of the women were working. The rest were either on public assistance programs and/or the husband's income. The majority of women were on Medicaid; only a few were on the NHC fee scale indicating some working income for the family. Of the eight women who did work, most were in lower-level white-collar occupations based in the community, such as teacher's aide, community worker, and community health workers.

Use of Services

Utilization behavior among the women in the sample showed a clear understanding of the types of facilities available. Also, the women's patterns of use were very much related to previous experience, time available, seriousness of problem, and lay referral network.[20] The mean number of facilities used regularly by the patients for both their needs and the health care of their children was five facilities per family. The utilization range over the past few years was from two to nine facilities. The most frequently used facilities in East Harlem were the municipal hospital and the medical center. Over half of the women used both of them during any given period. Although the NHC was visited on a continuous basis for the pediatric care of the children, including follow-up care, the other facilities were used for emergency, routine, or particularly acute problems of the women themselves, and/or emergency problems of the children which occurred when the NHC was closed. For prenatal care, a number of women went to the district health station, which provided prenatal care connected to the obstetrical service of one

20. E. Friedson, *Patients' Views of Medical Practice* (New York: Russell Sage Foundation, 1961); R. I. Ailinger, "Illness Referral System of Latin-American Immigrant Families" (Ph.D. diss., Catholic University of America, 1974).

of the teaching hospitals and also provided food coupons for the women under the Maternal, Infant and Child Program (MIC). A small number of women (six) used facilities in Central Harlem. Fourteen women reported going to other types of facilities, which were described as group practices or Medicaid mills.

Although some studies have implied that the consumer, particularly the Hispanic consumer, does not really have knowledge of the existing facilities and "shops around" without criteria, our results indicate that rational utilization patterns do exist that would not be understood by a survey-type study. One explicit reason for "shopping around" behavior relates to a sense of the need for "second opinions": "I don't want to take my kids to the municipal hospital because you don't know if they are telling you the truth. . . . I like to shop around to get different opinions and the truth. You read all the time in the newspaper and TV that doctors are doing bad things and giving people wrong diagnosis."

Inquiry into the reasons for use of multiple facilities yielded some interesting results. The high residential mobility among many of the women who had moved into the different boroughs and back into East Harlem accounted for the use of twenty-five hospitals in other boroughs and services in Central Harlem. In addition, several women had had some of their children in Puerto Rico or in the South, and one bore her third child in Germany during her husband's military service. Another reason given by the sample population for using many health-care delivery services was an awareness of the waiting period for the different facilities. There was a consensus among the women that if their children were sick and the NHC was open, they would usually walk into the clinic and be seen by a physician within a reasonable amount of time. However, if their time was limited, and particularly if their own health rather than their children's were involved, they would usually use a group practice or a Medicaid mill. In these centers they were seen quite rapidly and medication was dispensed rather easily. For emergencies for either themselves or their children, they usually chose either the emergency room in the municipal hospital or the medical center, depending on their previous experiences in these centers. Respondents tended to go to the emergency room, particularly during hours when other facilities were not open.

Contrary to the popular assumptions of health-care providers, consumer utilization patterns, however random they may initially appear, are based upon sophisticated analysis. The woman must respond to the primary and preventive health needs of herself and her family using a white, male, affluent health-care delivery system oriented toward tertiary care. At each step of the way she is faced with complex responsibilities and multiple barriers. First, she is responsible for maintaining health and preventing illness for her family in a situation in which the socioeconomic conditions of life encourage mental and physical illness. Second, she must sort out which of her health concerns are most appropriately dealt with through traditional support, information, and assistance from family and community, and which are best served by modern medicine and institutional providers. Third, she must learn how the health-care system is organized, where to seek appropriate care, and how to translate her concerns, often both linguistically and culturally, into information that will be meaningful to health professionals. Fourth, she must make her way to and through the appropriate health-care institutions and personnel. Fifth, she bears the burden of evaluating prescribed treatment, both in modern medical-risk terms and in terms of congruence with her own resources, culture, and life-style. The nature of these tasks, the perceived seriousness of the illness or complaint, and the member of the family needing treatment combine to determine a rational if complicated pattern of service utilization.

The use of Medicaid mills, for example, was perceived by the respondents as constituting private care, the nearest equivalent to the idealized direct fee-for-service private physician–patient relationship. A respondent who transferred from outpatient care at a local voluntary hospital to care by a physician at a Medicaid "clinic" when she found she had a cyst that needed removal emphasized the personal benefits of the private hospital with which the new physician was affiliated: "The staff was nice and I had my own room too, and earphones which I enjoyed." More frequently, the respondents visited Medicaid mills for what they felt were relatively simple health problems, such as common colds or flus, chronic but nonserious conditions, or simple refill of prescriptions. Rarely were Medicaid mills chosen for pediatric care or for adult care that the respondent felt would require hospital follow-up. Women frequently commented that doctors at Medicaid mills were poorly qualified and "robbed you blind," but they felt that for certain routine care, particularly for themselves, the benefits outweighed the risks. Even the woman who had transferred to the Medicaid mill physician for her own care emphasized that care of her child was a different matter: "I take my baby to the Neighborhood Health Center if she is not really sick, but when she is really sick I take her to the [large specialized] hospital." Given the limited hours of most health-care services and the difficulties of registering for and attending appropriate outpatient department services (there are 102 specialty clinics in one East Harlem hospital), respondents' use of Medicaid mills appears entirely appropriate.

A complaint perceived as serious required the respondent to use larger, more traditional health-care delivery systems, and thus to overcome barriers to access that included cultural[21] and language differences of consumers[22] and attributes and attitudes of professional health-care

---

21. Hoppe and Heller (see n. 11 above); Padilla et al. (see n. 13 above).
22. Marcos et al.

providers.[23] The lack of bilingual professionals and/or bilingual facilitators often posed a formidable barrier. Materials for registration, health information, or consent forms are occasionally written in technical Spanish, but this is not an institutionalized or widely accepted procedure.

Our results indicated that for many women and their families, even under optimum conditions, general communication with staff and lack of information still represented major barriers to obtaining health-care services. Frequently women used services reluctantly, or stopped using them because of neglectful or abusive treatment by staff. One twenty-eight-year-old respondent stopped using a local hospital because "women are treated like nobodies." This feeling was prevalent enough in the unit that the women decided to write a letter to the administration asking for the removal of the offending staff.

In seeking obstetrical care, the women were very much aware of the attitudes of staff, both nurses and doctors, in the hospital. This information was usually obtained from previous experience or by asking others about their experiences. Many women described instances where they were "cursed out" by the doctor for screaming while in labor, or where they were simply ignored. The outcome of these experiences provided some criteria for their use of facilities and a basis for recommending, or not recommending, a facility for obstetrical care to a friend or relative. Some verbal abuse, however, was more subtly degrading: "The nurses encouraged me to keep my baby. They stated, 'If you enjoyed making it, keep it.' Later when the doctor was examining me, he stated, 'This isn't going to hurt you any more than when you were doing it.'" Sexist remarks by physicians or snide comments by nurses that made the patient uncomfortable were considered almost routine. However, the women usually would not generalize specific instances of abuse to the institution unless abuse was widespread and continual among the staff, as, for example, the nursing staff at the local municipal hospital. Commonly described situations were those in which women had responded actively and had been either threatened ("cursed out") or ignored. One woman said that, while in labor with her first child, she did not know anything and was screaming. Her doctors kept "cursing" at her, threatening to leave her unless she kept quiet. Another respondent who repeatedly questioned a report of abnormal cells on her pap smear said no one would explain what abnormal meant and "I got the feeling that I should stop bugging them."

Except for cases of extreme abuse or obvious medical negligence, however, the women in our sample, like most poor women, took their

23. I. Murillo-Rohde, "Family Life among Mainland Puerto Ricans in New York City," *Perspectives in Psychiatric Care* 14 (1976): 174–79; B. A. Baldwin, H. Hugh Floyd, Jr., and D. R. Seveney, "Status Inconsistency and Psychiatric Diagnosis: A Structural Approach to Labeling Theory," *Journal of Health and Social Behavior* 16, no. 3 (1975): 257–67.

own object status for granted. These women in East Harlem did not consider that their privacy or dignity was rightfully part of their patient status. They thus did not make decisions about the use of facilities based on the human quality of care received, but on their perception of the staff's technical expertise, understood as "curing ability," as it applied to their physical health and that of their infants.

Even sexual abuse was often accepted as a routine part of care. One of the few consistent complaints mentioned concerned the numbers of students who participated in the internal examinations of laboring women. A female medical student on a gynecology rotation told us how, in a not unusual situation,[24] one female clinic patient was internally examined at least seven times by three medical students, an intern, and a resident so that all could feel a particular kind of cyst. One young woman became so accustomed to being examined by different doctors in training that it took her a number of nocturnal visits to realize that the man who woke her up in the middle of each night to give her an internal and ask her sexual questions while she was in the hospital for an appendectomy was sexually assaulting her.

Municipal hospital encounters, particularly if they involved a child, evoked many of the strongest reactions: "Forget about it! That hospital [municipal] stinks. They should tear it down." The woman continued with an account of the incident that turned her permanently away from municipal hospital care: "When my oldest child was four, we went there. We waited for fifteen hours and then they told me he had a cold. When we got home, he went into convulsions. I took him to a private hospital and he had to stay overnight because they told me he had scarlet fever." These incidents, of course, were not confined to the municipal hospital. Problems in the voluntary hospitals were reported frequently relating to the use of students and semiskilled residents on clinic patients. A twenty-five-year-old Hispanic woman who went to the outpatient department of the local large voluntary hospital because she had not menstruated for a long time, reported being seen by a "student" who did a vaginal biopsy to determine the source of her problem. When the woman started to bleed profusely, an attending physician was called in and diagnosed her as being in the fourth month of a pregnancy. Because of the unnecessary biopsy, however, she was hospitalized to keep her from losing the baby. Another woman of about the same age who had been using a private physician also reported that a biopsy had been improperly done for diagnosis of a suspicious pap smear result, causing her to hemorrhage and to be hospitalized.

A combination of pragmatic access factors and a search for some control of the health-care delivery process appeared, in our sample, to be more significant than financial considerations. In fact, it is not at all

24. Ehrenreich and Ehrenreich, p. 17 (see n. 7 above).

unreasonable that since these low-income women felt that they had little or no control over the medical encounter itself in terms of choosing a physician, gaining information, deciding among alternative therapies, and so forth, they exerted their control during the initial process of selecting a provider. Consumers whose pocketbook limits their shopping choices must pay even more attention to shopping with their feet. Unfortunately, the consequent use of multiple facilities results in fragmented care. (Interestingly enough, one physician at the NHC attributed "shopping around" to avoidance of bad debt records by patients unable or unwilling to pay. Other professionals at the Center, however, hypothesized that the lack of communication with health professionals and the resulting lack of control in the doctor-patient encounter were more significant causes of multiple use of resources.)

Health Problems and Health-seeking Behaviors

Most women in our sample were conscious of the importance of early and regular prenatal care. This is particularly significant since many of these women experienced nutrition-related complications, commonly found among poor women. Most of the women had not been prepared for the birth experience and lacked information on birth procedures. Only one woman attended childbirth classes. The most common attitude toward childbirth-education classes was expressed clearly by one woman who said, "I am chicken and am not interested in childbirth classes because I don't want natural childbirth." Although the women interviewed mentioned several complications, such as high blood pressure, and water retention and swelling (preeclampsia), they did not understand their implications. It was difficult to determine if this lack of knowledge was due to communication barriers, cultural inhibitions regarding the discussion of sexuality, and/or the negative attitudes of the health-care providers. Possibly a combination of all three factors fostered these women's unpreparedness for the birth experience. They expected childbirth to be unbearably painful; they did not expect, and in many instances did not want, their male partners to participate in the birth experience. Often they sought help or solace from their mothers during labor and delivery. Unfortunately, their fears were reinforced by the disapproving attitude of the health-care providers, and tension probably made the births more difficult.

There are two outstanding attitudes on the part of the professionals which emerged from the interviews and presented barriers to addressing the needs of these women. The health-care providers frequently expressed the sentiment that no painkillers should be given to them because they deserved pain, presumably because of their alleged promiscuity; or that they should be "knocked out," presumably because of their lower-class status or their reported exaggeration of and inability to tolerate pain. These attitudes not only reinforce provider control and consumer passivity but also prevent meaningful communication and informative dialogue that would lead to a better understanding of the health needs of poor women and thus to better health services. Although the descriptions of these women's birth experiences would be judged by many as negative, our respondents had no expectation of being able to alter the experience of giving birth.

Sometimes the inability of the low-income women interviewed to demand to take advantage of options within the health-care delivery system used by private patients may be more related to the women's perception of their own lack of resources than to objective conditions. Many respondents, when questioned about breast-feeding practices, said that they decided not to breast-feed because they were told they had to eat well in order for their breast milk to be healthy for their babies, and they did not feel they could afford nutritious eating habits. Only two women in our sample breast-fed. In fact, the vast majority of the women were not informed of the advantages of breast-feeding or encouraged to breast-feed by the physicians or nurses. For example, one thirty-six-year-old woman said about her fourth and last infant, "I couldn't breast-feed because my glucose tolerance test showed some diabetes." She was uncertain why diabetes would affect her milk and was unable to obtain clarification. Another woman, thirty-two, with a twenty-two-month-old child, stated that she had tried breast-feeding "but it was too painful." There are, in fact, recent indications that although increased information and advice have caused more women to consider breast-feeding, they have no effect on whether women ultimately choose to breast-feed or not. Women who receive advice and information regarding breast-feeding from grandmothers or other significant female figures are more likely to give breast-feeding full consideration than those who are informed or advised by medical personnel, but were still unlikely to change their behavior.[25]

Breast-feeding is related to postpartum mother-child bonding, but again, most of the women knew nothing about bonding, and passively acquiesced in the institutional practice of separating mother and infant. The majority of women did not hold their baby until several hours after birth, and a few not for several days after birth. The women did not question this practice unless after a few days they felt that the baby was ill and information about their child was being kept from them.

Family-planning services were frequently used to discuss health complaints unrelated to family planning. The major presenting complaints included infections, predominantly vaginal, cervical, and urinary

25. L. M. Esteves, "Proposal for a Nutrition Education Program for Women Receiving Prenatal Care at the Dr. Martin Luther King, Jr. Health Center, Bronx, New York," mimeographed (New York: City University of New York, Mount Sinai School of Medicine, July 1978).

tract inflammations; menstrual irregularity and cramps; hypertension and headaches; dizziness; and nervousness and depression. In fact, many of their manifested health problems, including asthma, obesity, and headaches, seemed to be stress-induced. These somatic symptoms and psychologically related health problems have been noted in other studies as being common to Puerto Rican women, and related to stressses of conflicting cultures and norms[26] and/or culturally patterned responses to the same stresses faced by other population groups.[27]

In terms of type of contraception, a significantly large number of women (42.3 percent) had had a tubal ligation or hysterectomy. These operations in many instances were performed on the recommendation of the doctor. One woman was sterilized in Puerto Rico and now regrets it, and another woman told us that she had had her tubes "temporarily tied" until she wanted more children. The patient was a twenty-seven-year-old Hispanic woman who after her second child wanted her tubes tied for five years. She first went to a Catholic hospital downtown, which would not perform the procedure. A friend then recommended a municipal hospital uptown. The doctor who performed the operation told her that "any doctor could untie her tubes when she wanted to." Six women were not using any contraceptives; three used the pill, three the IUD, and two the diaphragm. Three reported that their husbands used prophylactics. The majority of women were informed about different contraceptive methods and were particularly conscious of the dangers of the pill. However, due to religious or personal ambivalence about fertility control and family size, women often came for contraception only after deciding to have an abortion for an unwanted pregnancy.

The sample population was very conscious of the need for regular health care. Most women reported that they did not take care of their health very well, although they did have regular pap smears and breast examinations at the NHC. Their expressions of inadequate self-care appeared to be based on acknowledged failure to eat well, exercise, and generally adhere to healthy practices.

Among low-income women, repeated experiences with the health-care system that reinforce the passive-patient role, the lack of exposure and familiarity with the advantages of alternatives in obstetrical care and services for health maintenance, and the absence of a personal "gatekeeper" (private physician) all contribute to a pattern of care in which the woman has no participatory role. Options, even when formally offered, are meaningless within an institutional setting which sees no active involvement for these women.

26. C. Torres Matrullo, "Acculturation and Psychopathology among Puerto Rican Women in Mainland United States," *American Journal of Orthopsychiatry* 47, no. 4 (1976): 710–19.

27. P. W. Haberman, "Psychiatric Symptoms among Puerto Ricans in Puerto Rico and New York City," *Ethnicity* 3, no. 2 (1976): 133–44.

Conclusion

In many respects, the health needs of the women in East Harlem are universal in the sense that they represent the needs of all women, particularly poor women. Three major health areas in which the poor minority urban woman has special needs are: stress-related symptomatology that may be related either to actual illness or to socioenvironmental problems; knowledge of birth process and early childhood development, particularly important in a culture that emphasizes family bonding; and knowledge about bodily functions and appropriate self-care, particularly in the area of nutrition and common female problems.

Despite systemic barriers, poor minority women do seek and receive health care. Knowing how they function as consumers should be important to health planners and providers. An important step in the identification and service of poor women's health needs and priorities is reorganizing not only specific delivery services but the planning process itself, so that it is based on population needs rather than on the holistic and specialized needs of the current health-care system.

Current moves toward regionalization of health services may have the planned effect of increasing accessibility, but, by eliminating duplication of services, they may also eliminate choice of alternatives. If health planners eliminate the choices inherent in "shopping around," they are also eliminating an important part of the control low-income women have obtained over one aspect of their lives.

Department of Government
John Jay College of Criminal Justice, City University of New York
and
Department of Community Medicine
Mount Sinai School of Medicine (Hurst)

Department of Community Medicine
Mount Sinai School of Medicine (Zambrana)

Older Women in the City

Elizabeth W. Markson and Beth B. Hess

The particular vulnerabilities of women and the vicissitudes of aging[1] combine to isolate the older woman. This situation, which urban settings often exacerbate, is our concern here. Because so many older women live in cities, often in great difficulty, our subject is hardly a trivial one. Despite this, and despite ruminations about the "graying of America," old women have received surprisingly little scholarly attention.

Until relatively recently, large numbers of old women in the city or elsewhere were scarce. In 1900 the average life expectancy at birth for white women was 48.7, for nonwhite women 33.5. However, in 1976, the average life expectancy at birth was 77.3 for white, 72.6 for nonwhite females. The proportion of women reaching age 65 has also changed dramatically. By 1973, 82.2 percent of all white and 68.1 percent of all nonwhite women could expect to reach age 65. Obviously changes in these mortality patterns have had marked effects on the demographic

---

1. For relevant interdisciplinary comment about attitudes toward aging, see Florine Livson, "Cultural Faces of Eve: Images of Women" (paper presented at the annual meeting of the American Psychological Association, San Francisco, August 1977); Leo Simmons, *The Role of the Aged in Primitive Society* (New Haven, Conn.: Yale University Press, 1945); Tom Sheehan, "Senior Esteem as a Factor of Socio-Economic Complexity," *Gerontologist* 16 (1976): 433–40; David Guttman, "The Cross-cultural Perspective: Notes toward a Comparative Psychology of Aging," in *The Handbook of the Psychology of Aging*, ed. J. E. Birren and K. W. Schaie (New York: Van Nostrand Reinhold Co., 1977); Barbara Turner, "The Self-Concepts of Older Women" (paper presented at the annual meeting of the American Psychological Association, San Francisco, 1977); Robert LeVine, "Witchcraft and Sorcery in a Gusii Community," in *Witchcraft and Sorcery in East Africa*, ed. J. Middleton and E. Winter (London: Routledge & Kegan Paul, 1963); M. Fortes, *The Web of Clanship among the Tallensi* (London: Oxford University Press, 1962); E. Westermarck, *Ritual and Belief in Morocco* (London: Kegan Paul, 1926); Susan Sontag, "The Double Standard of Aging," *Saturday Review* 23 (September 23, 1972): 29; Valerie I. Fennel, "Age Relations and Rapid Change in a Small Town," *Gerontologist* 17 (October 1977): 405–11.

"shape" of our population as well as that of most other industrialized nations. In 1900, the ratio of women 65+ to men 65+ was only 98 to every 100. By 1970, this pattern had reversed to 138 women 65+ for every 100 men. By the year 2000, given current age adjusted mortality rates, there will be 154 women to every 100 men 65+.

A fiction persists that the majority of the old live in nonmetropolitan areas or in retirement communities. Yet 63.6 percent of all women 65+ and 60.5 percent of all men 65+ resided in metropolitan areas in the United States in 1978. The city is home to 65.3 percent of the black female elderly and to 87.1 percent of the Hispanic female elderly, a little more than half of whom (52.7 percent of the black and 56.6 percent of the Hispanic women) live in the inner city.[2] Numerically, 8.4 million of the 13.3 million women 65+ and 5.5 million of the 9.1 million men 65+ live in urban areas. About one half of these reside within central cities rather than on the urban fringe. Old women are concentrated in the center of cities because they have "aged in place"; their children have moved to the suburbs on the urban fringe.[3] These large numbers are extremely diverse. The older female population in urban centers, like the older population in general, is composed of many subgroups. Contrary to the public belief that people become more homogeneous as they grow older, the opposite actually occurs. In the major cities— Chicago, New York, San Francisco, Boston, and Los Angeles, for example—one can find both wealthy widows (the source of the myth that women own most of the wealth of America) and women whose resources can be carried about in a shopping bag.

Despite such diversities, older women in the city share structural and psychological hazards. In a set of essays in the early 1960s, Irving Rosow saw the condition of America's aged as a "moral dilemma for an affluent society."[4] Paradoxically, our very success as a modern industrial nation has created special problems for the elderly. The old suffer not only from low incomes and poor health in comparison to younger people, but from a more pernicious deprivation—loss of function and status. Rosow listed seven factors that predict the social worth of old people: control over resources required by younger people for their success as adults; possession of needed skills and strategic knowledge that must be transmitted directly from seniors to juniors; importance as links to the past and as persons nearest in time to becoming ancestors;

---

2. Administration on Aging, Special Tabulation, "Women 60+ and 65+ Years Old by Metropolitan–Non-Metropolitan Residence, Race, and Spanish Origin," photocopied (Washington, D.C.: Department of Health, Education, and Welfare, March 1978).

3. Donald O. Cowgill, "Residential Segregation by Age in American Metropolitan Areas," *Journal of Gerontology* 33 (May 1978): 446–53.

4. Irving Rosow, "And Then We Were Old," *Trans-Action/Society* 2 (January–February 1965): 20–26, and "Old Age: One Moral Dilemma of an Affluent Society," *Gerontologist* 2 (December 1962): 182–91.

membership in an extended family bound by mutual obligations; membership in stable, small communities with sacred values, in which one interacts with the same group of people in a variety of roles; participation in an economy characterized by *low* productivity, so that the contribution of any productive members is relatively important; and embeddedness in groups based on reciprocity, where mutual dependencies assure that all will be taken care of as a matter of duty. Little has been published since that would lead us to challenge the essential correctness of Rosow's formulation. A return to some presumed "golden age" of family life is neither possible nor desirable for women, on many counts. Nonetheless, if we apply Rosow's categories to the older population, women are more disadvantaged than men; among old women, those in central cities are in many respects most deprived. Let us take each category in turn.

Control over resources.—In general, old people in urbanized societies are relatively powerless to decide their children's occupational and marital fates. Achieved statuses replace ascribed ones; young people do not have to wait for a parent's death or generosity in order to secure land, jobs, or spouses. In any event, these kinds of resources were held by men, not women. Old women have had to bargain for care through their influence on their husbands, or, as widows, through claims on reciprocity from their children. Incomes are lowest, and the incidence of poverty greatest, among the black and Hispanic populations of the inner cities. For black, female, unrelated individuals 65+, over 68 percent have incomes below the poverty level. The comparable figure for white women 65+ is about 30 percent; for males, 44 percent and 24 percent, respectively.

Possession of needed skills and strategic knowledge.—There is not much of a market for the skills and knowledge possessed by either men or women 65+. New technologies and the higher educational levels of successive birth cohorts make it difficult for an old person to claim superior knowledge. No doubt a fund of wisdom resides in the elderly, but few appreciate it. Among the elderly of the inner city, in addition to those whom we typically think of as minority women, are the remnant of white ethnic immigrants of the years before the restrictive legislation of the 1920s. Many of these women never relinquished their "old-country" expectations of family support nor fully accepted the ways of American women. Relatively unsophisticated, with minimal schooling, they have few personal resources to call upon when coping with the normal losses of age—the death of their husbands especially.[5] Minority women, however, can and do maintain the family in the absence of men. The majority of black grandmothers still provide care for their daughters and their grandchildren.

5. Helena Znaniecki Lopata, *Widowhood in an American City* (Cambridge, Mass.: Schenckman Publishing Co., 1973).

Links to the past and nearness to God.—Few Americans truly consider the elderly graced by their nearness to the next world. Where such beliefs should remain strong—in Asian-American communities—there are clear signs of weakening of traditional norms. Thousands of aged Oriental women live in isolation and poverty in the major cities of America.[6] As for the past, that can be read in history books; no need remains for an oral tradition. Perhaps the current interest in genealogy will make older family members valuable sources of information, but this is a far cry from social value by virtue of strategic knowledge. Since females are generally less likely than males to be considered "experts" (even on child rearing), their deficit in knowledge is compounded.

Membership in extended family groups.—The young adults who streamed to the suburbs from 1945 on, did so as nuclear units, leaving parents, siblings, and other relatives. The extended family mystique, a set of obligations to blood kin, is diluted by achievement values and the companionate marriage style. Conjugality replaces consanguine responsibility. The urban elderly fall outside the magic circle of domesticity. The exception, again, is the urban black grandmother who maintains an extended household, less intentionally than forced by circumstances. The urban Hispanic grandmother is in a very different situation; when widowed she is likely to make her home with an adult child, but to be given minimal family tasks. She is more the guest in the child's home than the vital and necessary family member that the black grandmother has become.

In fact, living with an adult child is the least popular residential choice for most old people, especially if this entails moving from a familiar neighborhood. Most who eventually do make their home in the house of offspring are very old women, widowed, often physically unable to maintain a separate residence. Only one in ten old men, and two in ten old women, reside with offspring today. The figure has been steadily declining as Social Security increases have permitted old people to remain independent. The problem of the elderly who do live with children is a woman's problem. A daughter is expected to maintain kinkeeping tasks, and subsequently to make a home for an ailing or widowed parent. Most old people who live with offspring are mothers in the home of a daughter.

The inner city does, however, contain large numbers of elderly women with "extended expectations."[7] They are usually white ethnic

6. Frances Carp and Eunice Katoaka, "Health Care Problems of the Elderly of San Francisco's Chinatown," *Gerontologist* 16 (February 1976): 30–38.

7. Wayne C. Seelbach and William J. Sauer, "Filial Responsibility Expectations and Morale among Aged Parents," *Gerontologist* 17 (December 1977): 492–99. See also Bernard J. Cosneck, "Family Patterns of Older Widowed Jewish People," *Family Coordinator* 19 (1970): 368–73; Elizabeth W. Markson, "Factors in Institutionalization of the Ethnic Aged," in *Ethnicity and Aging*, ed. Donald E. Gelfand and Alfred J. Kutzik (New York: Springer Publishing Co., 1979).

women who have not relinquished the extended family values of their early socialization. Resentful of children who have not done their duty, offended when their children treat them as guests in their homes, these women have, in a real sense, been abandoned by time.

Membership in small, stable communities.—When children left for the suburbs, most parents preferred to remain in familiar urban neighborhoods—re-creations of village life which were ethnically distinct, protective, and supportive. There, older residents probably were respected and honored: they held strategic knowledge for dealing with the outside; they were the first to organize the resources of the community; and they could still call on family members for displays of power and authority. As times changed, the elders' control of resources declined, other types of people began to invade the territory, shops closed, friends died, buildings changed in their ethnic and racial composition. Indeed, the old neighborhood could become quite frightening. Whatever local power derived from the stable neighborhood is now all but lost to the elderly in the inner city. Since this power typically resided in the males, the loss of authority is not such a problem for the women, but they are no longer protected by those who were powerful. Yet to move out of the known city neighborhood has its dangers. Choices are not simple, and often there is no choice.

Participation in a low-productivity economy.—High levels of productivity, automation, and a large reserve labor force all render the economic contribution of urban old women unnecessary or valueless. Most old people, regardless of locale, may not want to work; the age of voluntary retirement has been declining steadily, and not many old people are expected to take advantage of the recent legislation extending the age of mandatory retirement. The reasons that old people—except those with prestigious occupations and high levels of education—would have for continuing to work are a need for money and for the social network of friends that most employment provides.[8] But neither old men nor old women are essential to the economy.

The status of retired persons is that of "dependents." The Bureau of the Census compiles a dependency ratio—the number of nonworkers (children and old people) to active workers. Over this century and projected through the first third of the next century, the dependency ratio has steadily grown; that is, there are increasingly more dependents for each worker. Being officially designated a dependent and relying on Social Security for income (a transfer payment from current workers to former ones and their survivors), the old person is not only an unimportant part of the urban economy but might even be perceived as a cause of lowered incomes for younger families. Again, this is especially

8. Matilda White Riley and Anne Foner, *Aging and Society*, vol. 1, *An Inventory of Research Findings* (New York: Russell Sage Foundation, 1968).

true for old women. Only 8.2 percent of women as compared to 21.1 percent of men 65+ were classified as "in the labor force" in 1974,[9] the major reason for which was that they were "keeping house"; men, on the other hand, were more likely to be out of the labor force due to retirement.

Since men have worked throughout their adult life, they can at least maintain the fiction of having paid for their own retirement through their contributions into the Social Security system (although, in fact, they will take out many times more than they put in). Most women can have no such protective belief. Those women—one thinks primarily of inner-city white ethnic elderly—who had fulfilled family roles to the exclusion of all else will be most likely to be defined as useless. Actually, they may have so considered themselves from the onset of menopause.[10] If older women are objects of contempt and ridicule because they evoke infantile fears of annihilation by the all-embracing mother, they are now much more vulnerable. The very basis on which they can exercise a claim for care—the reciprocity owed one who has devoted all to others in their periods of need—is precisely the argument most likely to produce anxiety on the part of their children.

Embeddedness in mutually dependent groups.—This factor may be redundant for women. The two groups in which they are most embedded are family and community, both of which have been discussed above. In summary, elderly urban women are without the supports generated in these two milieux. The contemporary white urban elderly female is especially deprived of the attributes of functionality and high status.

Compounding the poor showing on Rosow's factors are four specific contemporary problems associated with being old and female in the city. The first, a major concern of the elderly, is crime. Contrary to popular opinion, the National Crime Survey has repeatedly shown that people 65+ are victims of personal crime, whether involving violence or theft, at *lower* rates than younger people.[11] For example, data from surveys in twenty-seven major U.S. cities indicate that age is inversely related to victimization in crimes of violence such as rape, assault, murder, and theft. In 1976, for example, the rate per 1,000 for crimes of violence was 59.0 among those 12–24 years old, 40.8 among those 25–34, 20.0 for 35–49, 12.2 for 50–64, and 7.6 among those 65+.[12] Burglary, household

9. U.S. Bureau of the Census, *Current Population Reports* (Washington, D.C.: Government Printing Office, 1975). Unless otherwise cited, all statistics given in this paper are from current published federal government reports.

10. See, e.g., Pauline Bart, "Portnoy's Mother's Complaint," *Trans-Action/Society* 8 (1970): 69–74.

11. U.S. Bureau of the Census, *Current Population Reports*, Series P-23; *Social and Economic Characteristics of the Older Population, 1974* (Washington, D.C.: Government Printing Office, 1975); U.S. Department of Justice, Law Enforcement Assistance Administration, *Myths and Realities about Crime* (Washington, D.C.: Government Printing Office, 1978).

12. U.S. Department of Justice, Law Enforcement Assistance Administration.

larceny, and automobile theft display the same pattern. The single area in which the elderly, especially elderly women, are most likely to be victimized is "larceny with contact"—most often purse snatching. While generally not considered a serious crime by police, purse snatching often imposes economic hardship and may also result in serious physical injuries—as well as psychological insult—to the victims.[13] From a variety of studies,[14] a composite picture of the elderly urban woman victim emerges. First, more women are victimized than men. This is due to the greater number of women in the population; rates per 1,000 population show men at greater *proportional* risk than women. Second, the victim of crime is most likely to be living alone, and, if female, to be a widow. The majority of elderly crime victims are poor as well (in Kansas City their median income was less than $3,000 per year), live on a fixed income, and have lived in the same house or apartment for ten or more years. Often physically handicapped (as were 22 percent of elderly Kansas City victims), they are frequently members of racial minority groups. In the Kansas City study, for example, 22 percent of the elderly victims were black—a significantly higher percentage than the proportion of black people over 50 in the population of that city.

From the offenders' perspective, the elderly, while relatively easy marks, are not particularly attractive victims; they are too poor. In Kansas City,[15] interviews with offenders indicated that greed, fear, and speed were the main factors governing choice of victim. All other factors being equal, offenders indicated they would prefer younger, more affluent victims. A 1977 study of crime against the elderly in New York City found that the criminal who preys on the elderly has a model age of about 16 years, with those who victimize old women younger than those who victimize men![16] As many as half the inner-city urban women, it has been estimated, live alone in areas with high rates of adolescent truancy; unemployment—particularly among males 16–20 years old; with higher than average concentrations of people; declining property values; and significant breakdowns of traditional business and retail

13. James B. Richardson, "Purse Snatch—Robbery's Ugly Stepchild," in *Crime and the Elderly*, ed. Jack Goldsmith (Lexington, Mass.: Lexington Books, 1976). See also John Tighe, "A Survey of Crimes against the Elderly," *Police Chief* 44 (February 1977): 18–19.

14. Midwest Research Institute, *Crimes against Aging Americans: The Kansas City Study* (Kansas City: Midwest Research Institute, 1976); D. A. Grossman, *Reducing the Impact of Crime against the Elderly—a Survey and Appraisal of Existing and Potential Programs* (New York: Florence V. Burden Foundation, 1977); J. E. Burkhardt, *Crime and the Elderly—Their Perceptions and Their Reactions* (Rockville, Md.: National Criminal Justice Reference Service Microfiche Program, 1977).

15. Midwest Research Institute, chaps. 2, 3, 4, 5.

16. Grossman, pp. 1–42.

patterns.[17] The suburban elderly of either sex are unlikely to be victimized. Although they may have more property to steal, the areas in which they live are generally more affluent and police surveillance more thorough.

The amount of crime against the old of either sex has been grossly exaggerated by the media. Indeed, the mass media perpetuate the notion of the powerlessness of older women. A survey of TV violence in 1976—a bloody year for television with an average of 9.5 violent episodes per hour—demonstrated that the most frequent victims were children, old women, nonwhite women, and lower-class women. While killers were most often men, murder victims were most frequently old, poor urban women. Among heavy television viewers, a greater sense of personal risk of victimization was observed. Old women's already empirically grounded fear is thereby exacerbated.[18] Taught throughout their lives to be less assertive, less physically active, and more yielding than men, women are more fearful precisely because they perceive themselves as potentially being overpowered by others.

According to a 1974 survey by Louis Harris et al.,[19] fear of crime varies markedly with both age and sex. Although men at any age are more frequent crime victims, among men 18–54 years old only 9 percent expressed concern about crime as a "serious problem." The pattern for women is different; at *every* age, women have a greater fear of crime than do men (20 percent of all women as opposed to 11 percent of all men). This fear increases with age—from 10 percent among women 18–54 years old to 18 percent among those 55–64 years old, and 28 percent among those 65+. Most fearful of crime, according to one recent study, are elderly women with limited education who live alone—especially in apartments. Most of these women are particularly frightened of going out at night and indicated that they are forced to curtail their social activities accordingly.[20]

A 1977 study by Patterson[21] indicated that elderly women have a far greater fear of being robbed or assaulted than do men. Part of this fear relates to marital and family status. It is interesting to note that women who lived with others were only slightly more fearful than men, while women living alone were highly fearful. Territoriality, that is, the extent to which older people of either sex marked their dwelling spaces as their

17. Midwest Research Institute; U.S. Bureau of the Census (see n. 11).

18. G. Gerbner and M. F. Eleey, "TV Violence Profile Number 8—the Highlights," *Journal of Communication* 27 (Spring 1977): 171–80.

19. Louis Harris and Associates, Inc., *The Myth and Reality of Aging in America: A Study for the National Council on the Aging* (Washington, D.C.: National Council on the Aging, 1975).

20. Burkhardt.

21. Arthur Patterson, "Territorial Behavior and Fear of Crime in the Elderly," *Police Chief* 44 (February 1977): 26–29.

own through use of protective surveillance devices, fences, signs, or welcome mats and initials on doors or chimneys, was a mitigating factor for men but not for women. While men in general were more "territorial" than women, men who were high on territoriality were significantly less fearful than were nonterritorial men. For women, however, high or low territoriality was relatively unimportant in reducing fear.

Both income and race are significant factors in fear of crime as well. Only 21 percent of whites 65+ as compared to 43 percent blacks[22] stated that fear of crime was a serious problem. The greater fear of blacks is related to their generally lower socioeconomic position. For both races, fear of being robbed or attacked on the street was associated with income; 27 percent of those 65+ with incomes of less than $7,000, 17 percent of the 65+ with incomes between $7,000–$14,999, and 15 percent of the 65+ with incomes of $15,000 or more saw the danger of being robbed or attacked on the street as a serious problem.[23] Clearly, minority group status, low income, and being female interact to produce a high level of anxiety about crime. If partially unwarranted by the statistics, this anxiety is very real to those who have been dislocated by urban change.

Measures of societal intervention—such as personalized transportation;[24] escort services;[25] within-neighborhood relocation from buildings with vacant apartments and inadequate lighting into well-lit, more heavily traveled areas;[26] and increased police protection[27]—have been proposed. The majority of cities have not implemented these suggestions. Rather, such individual solutions as educational programs targeted at the elderly, have received more publicity and, of course, consumed fewer urban resources. It offends that even one old woman should be attacked, and even more that so many should live in fear of attack. Nor is it any boon to race relations in America that the most publicized cases—again, despite substantial evidence to the contrary—involve black assailants and white victims. Elderly female black victims are not nearly as "newsworthy."

The second contemporary problem that haunts the urban aging woman is widowhood. Because of the increased life expectancy of women, the majority can expect to spend some portion of their last years as widows. While the vast majority of men 65+ are married and living with spouse (over 75 percent), it is a minority (37.6 percent) of women who are married and living with a spouse. About 52.5 percent of the

22. Harris, p. 133.
23. Ibid., pp. 130–32.
24. Burkhardt.
25. Grossman.
26. Ibid.
27. Burkhardt.

women 65+ in 1975 were widowed, 2.6 percent were divorced, another 5.8 percent were single, and the remainder were separated or had an absent spouse. This difference becomes more marked with age: among those 75+, 68.2 percent of men as compared to 22.3 percent of the women were living with their spouses. Even among the very old, this difference persists; among men 85+, only slightly over two-fifths are widowed, while almost four-fifths of women of that age are widows.[28]

Over one-half of elderly widows live alone or with nonrelatives. Elderly widows are among the most poverty stricken of all people, with the smallest budget for housing and other services. Yet, like all old people, widows are a diverse lot. The inner-city widow deserves special note. In poverty areas of New York City, for example—areas that also have the highest incidence of crime, greatest number of welfare recipients, and largest amount of deteriorated housing—the highest incidence of single person households is found among the most frail segment of the white population, that is, older people in their 70s and 80s, many of whom are widows.[29] Then, too, most of the elderly in public housing are widowed women; old men who are alone drift to hotels and rooming houses. Apparently, older women are more used to caring for themselves, preparing their own meals and maintaining their own households; men prefer the convenience of restaurants and hotels—and the absence of old women![30] Ethnic minorities of either sex are underrepresented among the elderly in public housing.[31] Whether this is a result of different familial practices, of discrimination, or of a combination of the two is, however, uncertain. Another factor may be reluctance to claim entitlements or lack of skills in negotiating bureaucracies.

At special risk are Hispanic old women. In New York City, they live in the worst housing conditions, have the smallest incomes, the least education, and the most health problems.[32] Asian-Americans, who have far less visibility in the city than do members of other minority groups, may be even worse off; used to a lifetime of ghettoization, they are unable to manipulate the existing power structure to obtain needed services. Fear and mistrust of the dominant society also retard their ability to obtain that which is theirs under existing social legislation provisions.[33] The white ethnic widow is also at a disadvantage.[34] Like other

28. U.S. Bureau of the Census, *Current Population Reports*, Series P-20, nos. 33, 105, 255, and 287; Series P-25, no. 607.

29. Marjorie Cantor, *Study of the Inner-City Elderly* (New York: Office of the Aging, 1978).

30. Frances Carp, *Patterns of Living and Housing of Middle Aged and Older Adults* (Washington, D.C.: Government Printing Office, 1966).

31. Ibid.

32. Cantor.

33. Richard A. Kalish and Sam Yuen, "Americans of East Asian Ancestry: Aging and the Aged," *Gerontologist* 11 (Spring 1971): 36–47.

34. Lopata.

aged and poor isolates, she is afraid of her living environment. A special such environment for approximately 600,000 old people is the "single room occupancy" (SRO) dwellings, most often hotels and rooming houses. While predominantly male, the inhabitants of these units share many of the characteristics of urban women living alone in the inner city. They are often physically sicker, psychologically more disadvantaged, poorer and more lonely than most of their age peers.[35]

The third contemporary problem of the urban elderly woman is her relationship with her children. This is linked to, and modifies, Rosow's category of the extended family. Despite periodic warnings that the family is dead and that the old are forgotten isolates left behind by their upwardly mobile children, data from various surveys are strikingly similar in proving the contrary. Over 80 percent of those 65+ have living children or grandchildren, and about 80 percent of these see one of their children at least once a week. The same proportion live within a day's travel from one or more offspring. Expectations for filial responsibility differ for men and women. For example, among the inner city, predominantly black elderly in Philadelphia, old women were significantly more likely than men to feel that children should take care of parents who were physically dependent or who did not desire to live alone. Yet three-fourths of both sexes felt that financial support of aged parents was the responsibility of government, not of children. Nor did either sex feel that a major reason for having children was to ensure one's own support and care in old age.[36]

Helping patterns and the exchange of goods and services vary, as one would expect, according to the needs and resources of family members. Among the inner-city elderly of New York City, for example, more than three-fourths of old people reported giving help to their children while 87 percent reported receiving some form of assistance such as gifts, crisis intervention, or help with chores from their children.[37] In this sample, those of lowest social status were most likely to rely on their children. The more disabled, too, received more help than did the healthier. While blacks and whites showed similar helping patterns, Hispanic aged were most likely to see, telephone, and help their children and to receive help in return. Compared to less than two-fifths of the elderly blacks and whites, almost half of the Hispanic aged relied solely on kin for their support networks. National data provided by Louis Harris indicates a generally high level of assistance from parents to

35. Joyce Stephens, *Loners, Losers and Lovers: A Sociological Study of the Aged Tenants of a Slum Hotel* (Seattle: University of Washington Press, 1977).

36. Wayne C. Seelbach, "Gender Differences in Expectations for Filial Responsibility," *Gerontologist* 17 (October 1977): 421–25.

37. Marjorie Cantor, "The Configuration and Intensity of the Informal Support System in a New York City Elderly Population" (paper presented at the annual meeting of the Gerontological Society, New York, November 1976).

children: three-quarters of the blacks and nine in ten of whites reported that they gave their children or grandchildren gifts; somewhat more than six in ten of both races indicated that they helped out when someone was ill, and about half said they take care of grandchildren. More pronounced differences exist among blacks and whites on giving general advice or specific counsel on bringing up children or running a home or jobs—black old people are much more likely to act in these advisory capacities than are whites. Older widowed females of either race are more likely to be receiving rather than giving gifts of money; the flow in these exchanges is generally from the less to the more needy family members.

Expectations of support from adult children vary not only by income but by characteristics such as ethnicity and religion, as we said earlier. For urban and nonurban women, the preferred pattern of relationships with one's children and grandchildren appears to be "intimacy at a distance."[38] Parents and children are likely to be unhappy when they are forced into contact with one another; they are also more likely to have high morale when intergenerational contacts and exchanges are freely chosen rather than imposed.[39]

Finally, a fourth contemporary problem for the older woman in the city is her erratic access to urban virtues. To be sure, the city has better transportation, more social and health services, more recreational and cultural facilities than nonmetropolitan areas.[40] However, not all urban women are able to enjoy such advantages. Low income elderly, for example, are more bothered by the costs of buses or subways than are people of higher incomes.[41] Not all public routes go where one wants to; cabs must be used. Subway stairs are long and steep, and the connecting tunnels can be fear-inducing. Lack of public transportation is also viewed differentially according to socioeconomic status: 17 percent of the elderly with incomes of less than $7,000, 11 percent of those with incomes of between $7,000 and $14,999, and 3 percent of those with incomes of $15,000 or more felt that lack of public transportation was a major problem.[42] The convenience of facilities, such as transportation, is determined by many factors other than physical location. Economic and

38. Ethel Shanas, "Family Kin Network and Aging: A Cross-Cultural Perspective," *Journal of Marriage and the Family* 35 (1973): 505–11.

39. Beth B. Hess and Joan M. Waring, "Parent and Child in Later Life: Rethinking the Relationship," in *Child Influences on Marital and Family Interaction,* ed. Richard M. Lerner and Graham B. Spanier (New York: Academic Press, 1978).

40. See, e.g., E. G. Youmans, *Aging Patterns in a Rural and Urban Area of Kentucky* (Lexington: University of Kentucky, Agricultural Experimental Station, 1963); C. I. Phihlblad and H. A. Rosencranz, *The Health of Older People in the Small Town* (Columbia: University of Missouri, 1967).

41. Harris, p. 143.

42. Ibid., p. 145.

physical mobility and education are key elements for the old that dictate the perceived convenience of the amenities of the city.[43] The inner-city woman, in midst of riches of resources, will experience paucity.

Benefits of the Urban Setting

Yet, for all the disadvantages of urban life in old age, there is even greater isolation among the rural elderly and those in suburbia.[44] If nothing else, cities do have mass transportation facilities, which, in fact, are more accessible than those in suburbia. The old woman in the suburb or small town will have greater difficulty than her urban counterpart in securing social services that are typically located in areas with high concentrations of elderly. In rural areas, transportation to services or of service to the client is a major problem.[45] Meals-on-wheels, for example, cannot operate over great distances, vans providing medical services must travel hundreds of miles for a few patients. In the suburbs, the older woman who can no longer drive is dependent on the assistance of relatives or the goodwill of volunteers. However, in the city, psychological and physical barriers may be present even though the service is there.

City life also permits a flexibility not afforded by suburbs or small towns. The very surplus of the city permits highly individualistic lifestyles, the most notable of which, perhaps, is the shopping-bag lady. Living in the interstices of the city off the surpluses of the metropolis, she has no fixed place of residence and carries all her belongings in one or more shopping bags.[46] While their lives are hard, uncomfortable, and certainly "deviant," they are able to survive precisely because of the abundance of the city whose garbage is their riches.

Old people, as do persons of any age, prefer to be with their peers. Their common age speaks of a lifetime of shared experiences, of similar socialization to a disappearing world, and of mutual concerns in the present.[47] Even though one's own type of young people has left and a different set moved in, other old people have remained. Old women are

43. Ibid., pp. 174–99.

44. See, e.g., U.S. Congress, Senate, Special Committee on Aging, *Older Americans in Rural Areas: Hearings before the Special Committee on Aging*, 95th Cong., 2d sess., 1977.

45. U.S. Congress, House, Select Committee on Aging, *Problems of Maine's Rural Elderly: Hearing before the Subcommittee on Health and Long-Term Care*, 94th Cong., 2d sess., 1976.

46. Jennifer Hand, "Shopping-Bag Ladies in Urban Areas" (paper presented at the annual meeting of the Society for the Study of Social Problems, New York, September 1976).

47. Beth B. Hess, "Friendship," in *Aging and Society*, vol. 3, *A Sociology of Age Stratification*, ed. Matilda White Riley, Marilyn E. Johnson, and Anne Foner (New York: Russell Sage Foundation, 1972).

more likely than old men to have intimate friends, confidants who provide assistance, solace, and understanding. The urban setting is in many ways conducive to friendship; there are more people to choose as friends, distance is minimized, and the opportunities to share excursions are enhanced. Rural and small-town life moves at a relatively slow pace, prized by those accustomed to it but frustrating to people imbued with a more selective and segmented system of social relationships.[48] The peculiar compartmentalization of friendships and social contacts that characterizes many relationships in the city permits one to enjoy people with specific shared interests, a luxury often not possible in a suburban or rural setting in which one must make do with those life-long acquaintances who are at hand.

For housing project dwellers, slum tenants, and other old people residing in the inner city, isolation is not as complete as it appears. There *are* social networks, though they may seem limited in scope and duration. This aspect of urban life—a kind of organized social segregation—has been viewed as yet another indication of "shallowness" by the more romantic commentators on the urban scene. However, it is undoubtedly related to the general characteristics of urban social life, to the "blasé attitude" that Georg Simmel saw, in which people seek interaction for specific, and reasonable, purposes.[49] Too much social contact, especially with people unlike one's self in ethnicity, education, race, income, and preferences, may be intrusive.

Finally, the majority of old people value independence. Urban women are no exception. The late Margaret Blenkner, who organized and studied the effects of protective service projects on the urban elderly, commented succinctly: "If an old person wants to stay out of an institution, he/she should stay away from friends and family."[50] The selective social interaction of many of the inner-city elderly could thus represent a continued drive to do just that—to remain at liberty, however, circumscribed.

*　*　*

We have written more about the hazards of the urban elderly woman than about her pleasures, more about her problems than her solutions, more about her suffering than her survival. Yet, such women are resilient, even heroic. Powerless and denigrated though they may be, frightened by crime and neighborhood change though they are, they cope; they fight back. Their lives offer us a contradictory picture of

48. Fennel (n. 1 above), pp. 405–11.
49. Georg Simmel, "The Metropolis and Mental Life," in *The Sociology of Georg Simmel,* ed. Kurt Wolff (New York: Free Press, 1964).
50. Personal communication (1968).

loneliness and freedom, of abandonment and community. We hope that we have given those who want to better those lives, through public and private action, the materials to see more clearly the troubles they might remedy, and the strengths they might nurture.

Gerontology Center and Department of Sociology
Boston University (Markson)

Department of Social Sciences
County College of Morris (Hess)

Photograph by Mel Rosenthal

Courtesy of Spring 3100, New York City Police Department

Crime, Women, and the Quality of Urban Life

Margaret T. Gordon, Stephanie Riger, Robert K. LeBailly, and Linda Heath

Although crime and the fear of crime affect both the men and women who live in cities, women are especially affected. In numerous studies they express significantly higher levels of fear than men. For example, according to a 1972 national poll,[1] over half the women surveyed, compared with 20 percent of the men, said they were afraid to walk in their neighborhoods at night. The proportion of women reporting such feelings has grown in recent years.[2] Accompanying this fear may be an increased use of certain safety precautions, such as staying home at night or avoiding certain parts of the city. This results in what Biderman[3] has called "foregone opportunities." Beyond serving as means of protection for women, such restrictions may serve as instruments of social control. Feminist analyses of one crime, rape, have made this point eloquently:

Gordon and Riger are coprincipal investigators of a research project at the Center for Urban Affairs, 2040 Sheridan Road, Evanston, Illinois 60201. The project is partially supported by grant no. 1R01MH29629-01 from the National Center for the Prevention and Control of Rape (NIMH). LeBailly and Heath are project associates. Requests for reprints should be addressed to Gordon at the Center for Urban Affairs.

1. Hazel Erskine, "The Polls: Fear of Violence and Crime," *Public Opinion Quarterly* 38 (Spring 1974): 131–45.

2. Arthur L. Stinchcombe, Carol Heiner, Rebecca A. Iliff, Kim Scheppel, Tom W. Smith, and Garth E. Taylor, "Trends in Public Opinion about Crime and Punishment," in "Crime and Punishment in Public Opinion: 1948–1974," mimeographed (Chicago: National Opinion Research Center, 1977).

3. Albert D. Biderman, Louise Johnson, Jennie McIntyre, and Adrianne Weir, *Report on a Pilot Study in the District of Columbia on Victimization and Attitude toward Law Enforcement,* prepared for the President's Commission on Law Enforcement and Administration of Justice, Field Surveys 1 (Washington, D.C.: Government Printing Office, Bureau of Social Science Research, 1967).

"The fear of rape keeps women off the streets at night. Keeps women at home. Keeps women passive and modest for fear that they be thought provocative."[4]

In an earlier paper,[5] we explored a variety of explanations for the finding that women's reported fear of crime is greater than men's. Sex role socialization may encourage timidity in women and a reluctance in men to admit to fear. Sex differences in strength and speed may cause women to feel more vulnerable to attack. Finally, and of critical importance, while women, for most crimes, are less frequently victimized than men, women are almost exclusively the victims of one crime—rape. Brownmiller has called rape "a conscious process of intimidation by which *all* men keep *all* women in a state of fear."[6] The extent of urban women's fear, the relationship between fear and the risk of rape victimization, and the consequences of crime and fear of crime for both women's and men's lives in cities have not previously been examined on a large scale. They are the subjects of this paper.

Sample

We explore these issues with data collected from in-depth interviews with women from six neighborhoods in Chicago, Philadelphia, and San Francisco. We chose these sites because extensive groundwork on the incidence and reactions to crime in them had already been done by other researchers.[7] The 299 women and sixty-eight men who were interviewed for our research were self-selected from the 5,000 people in these cities who had participated in a telephone survey concerning reactions to crime. A comparison of the sample of 367 persons who were interviewed in person with the randomly selected telephone sample in each city indicated no statistically significant differences between the samples in their area of residence or race.[8] However, more women in the in-person sample than in the telephone sample reported having been raped or sexually assaulted (11 percent compared with 2 percent), and the in-

4. Susan Griffin, "Rape: The All-American Crime," in *Forcible Rape: The Crime, the Victim, and the Offender,* ed. Duncan Chappell, Robley Geis, and Gilbert Geis (New York: Columbia University Press, 1977), p. 66.

5. Stephanie Riger, Margaret Gordon, and Robert LeBailly, "Women's Fear of Crime: From Blaming to Restricting the Victim," *Victimology* 3 (1978): 285–96.

6. Susan Brownmiller, *Against Our Will: Men, Women, and Rape* (New York: Simon & Schuster, 1975), p. 15.

7. Albert Hunter, "A Methodological Review of the RTC Project," mimeographed (Evanston, Ill.: Northwestern University, Center for Urban Affairs, 1979).

8. Robert K. LeBailly, "Method Artifacts in Telephone and In-Person Interviews: An Examination of Bias and Consistency," mimeographed (Evanston, Ill.: Northwestern University, Center for Urban Affairs, 1979).

person respondents were younger, better educated, and wealthier than the randomly selected telephone sample. We deliberately oversampled women so that we could investigate in depth the sources and consequences of women's fear of crime.

Measures of the Fear of Crime and Related Attitudes

Previous studies of crime-related attitudes have produced ambiguous results, in part because of the use of overlapping concepts: fear, concern, worry, and risk.[9] The most relevant distinction here is that between fear, or an emotional response to the possibility of victimization, and assessments of risk or one's subjective estimate of the likelihood of victimization. Therefore, we asked separate questions to tap each of these dimensions.

Fear.—The most widely used measure of fear by researchers in this field[10] has been the question: "How safe do you feel being out alone in your neighborhood at night: very safe, reasonably safe, somewhat unsafe, or very unsafe?" In order further to explore our respondents' perceptions of their local safety, we asked them to indicate (on a zero to ten scale) the extent to which they worried when they were alone at night in their neighborhoods in a series of twelve situations (e.g., at home, using public transportation, going to the laundromat). Many of these activities people must do, at least occasionally, in order to work or otherwise to participate in community life. Others, such as going to movies or bars, represent more choice. To examine whether fear levels are related to beliefs about physical vulnerability, we also asked our respondents to indicate whether or not they thought they could successfully defend themselves against attack and to assess their own strength and speed relative to other women and to men. A physical vulnerability index was created from these items.[11]

Risk of rape.—To assess perceptions about the risks of being raped, women were asked to estimate, on a scale from zero to ten, their chances of being raped or sexually assaulted in their neighborhoods. Men estimated the chances that this would happen to a woman.

9. Floyd J. Fowler and Thomas W. Mangione, "The Nature of Fear," mimeographed (Boston: Survey Research Program, University of Massachusetts, and the Joint Center for Urban Studies of M.I.T. and Harvard, 1974), available from authors; Frank Clemente and Michael B. Kleiman, "Fear of Crime in the U.S.: A Multivariate Analysis," *Social Forces* 56 (December 1977): 519–31.

10. Fowler and Mangione.

11. The four items in which respondents assessed their own speed relative to the average man and woman and their own strength relative to the average man and woman were used for this index.

Measures of Self-protective Behavior

A multitude of behaviors may be employed as self-defense strategies. They range from barricading oneself inside one's home to taking self-defense lessons to carrying a weapon for protection. One category is precautionary behaviors. Respondents were asked what they do to protect themselves in cities: "Sometimes when people live in the city they have ways of trying to prevent uncomfortable situations from happening. There are certain things they do to avoid unpleasant or dangerous situations. I would like you to tell me what things you do to avoid dangerous situations." To specify more precisely what precautions people take, we also asked our respondents to indicate how often they engaged in a series of protective behaviors: all the time, most of the time, occasionally, and never. The behaviors are ones commonly used at home (e.g., checking to see who is there before opening the door), on the street (e.g., crossing over to avoid someone suspicious looking), or when using a car (e.g., locking it when parking). Another category is that of potentially dangerous behaviors. As noted above, we also wanted our respondents to say how much they worried when alone at night in twelve situations. After assessing their worry about each, we asked them how often they found themselves in each of those situations. For example, we asked how worried they were that someone would try to harm them when they were home alone after dark; then we asked them how often they actually were home alone after dark.

Results

Our data strongly support the assertion that women report more fear than men, $F(1,332) = 38.5, p \leq .001$ (see table 1). Forty-nine percent of women in our sample indicated that they felt "very unsafe" or "somewhat unsafe" when out alone in their neighborhoods at night; only 7.5 percent of the men responded this way. The persistence of this feeling is evident in the finding that 48 percent of the women, compared with 25 percent of the men, reported "thinking of their own safety all or most of the time" or "fairly often." Women also said they worried more than men that someone might try to harm them while they were engaged in a variety of day-to-day activities, $F(1,363) = 68.9, p \leq .001$. In addition to sex differences in fear, we found differences in women's fear levels within cities by neighborhood. In Chicago and Philadelphia there were significant differences between neighborhoods, with women living in racially mixed, working-class neighborhoods expressing more fear than those living in ethnically homogenous or middle-class neighborhoods. To examine the relationship of demographic variables, we conducted

Table 1

Mean Scores on Fear, Worry, and Rape Risk by Sex and Neighborhood

	Fear (1=Very Safe, 4=Very Unsafe)	Worry (0=No Worry at All, 10= Very Worried)	Woman's Risk of Rape (0=Not Likely, 10=Very Likely)
Sex:			
Males (67)	1.8	3.2	4.4
Females (267)	2.5	5.9	4.3
Significance of ANOVA	$p<.0001$	$p<.0001$	N.S.
Variance explained	$\eta^2=.104$	$\eta^2=.160$	. . .
Neighborhood:			
Philadelphia:			
West Philadelphia (47)	2.5	5.7	4.6
South Philadelphia (37)	2.1	4.6	2.8
Significance of ANOVA	$p=.021$	$p=.0255$	$p=.0034$
Variance explained	$\eta^2=.066$	$\eta^2=.0542$	$\eta^2=.089$
Chicago:			
Lincoln Park (53)	2.2	5.3	3.5
Wicker Park (32)	2.9	7.3	5.5
Significance of ANOVA	$p=.0002$	$p<.0001$	$p=.0009$
Variance explained	$\eta^2=.150$	$\eta^2=.181$	$\eta^2=.114$
San Francisco:			
Sunset (50)	2.6	5.7	4.2
Visitacion Valley (48)	2.8	7.1	5.3
Significance of ANOVA	N.S.	$p=.0082$	$p=.071$
Variance explained	. . .	$\eta^2=.063$	$\eta^2=.030$

NOTE.—N's in parentheses indicate number of cases; they vary because of missing values.

regression analyses with fear (i.e., assessment of neighborhood safety) as the dependent variable, and age, sex, race, neighborhood, education, and number of children as the predictor variables. While sex and neighborhood were the only demographic variables that explained statistically significant proportions of variance, all the demographic variables combined explained 21.4 percent variance (see table 2).

The significant relationship between neighborhood and fear suggests that fear may be a function of the amount of crime in the area. While official crime statistics tend to underestimate the actual levels of the incidence of crime, such data are fairly reliable for establishing rank orderings of the incidence of crime among cities and neighborhoods within cities.[12] Therefore, we plotted the rate of rape per 1,000 residents (male and female) for neighborhoods (as determined by police data) against perceptions of risk of rape. Figure 1 indicates that, according to police statistics, the reported rape rates of South Philadelphians (working-class, ethnic neighborhood) and the Sunset (white, middle-class neighborhood in San Francisco) are the lowest, while the rates of Lincoln Park (white, middle-class neighborhood in Chicago) and Visita-

12. Wesley G. Skogan, "The Validity of Official Crime Statistics: An Empirical Investigation," *Social Science Quarterly* 55 (June 1974): 25–38.

Table 2

Results of Regression Analyses with Fear as Dependent and
Demographic Variables as Predictors

	Change Relative to Reference Group (β)	Significance of Effect
Women more fearful than men	+.68	.001
S. Philadelphians less fearful than Visitacion Valley residents..	−.76	.001
Lincoln Park residents less fearful than Visitacion Valley residents	−.46	.004
W. Philadelphians less fearful than Visitacion Valley residents..	−.25	.124
People with children more fearful than without	+.13	.216
Fear decreases with education	−.02	.469
Fear increases with age	+.005	.231
Sunset residents less fearful than Visitacion Valley residents..	−.16	.339
White respondents more fearful than nonwhite in same neighborhood...................................	+.11	.374
Fear decreases as income increases	−.02	.395
Wicker Park residents more fearful than Visitacion Valley residents	+.05	.764

NOTE.—Multiple R^2 = .214.

cion Valley (working-class, ethnically mixed neighborhood in San Francisco) are highest. It plots a regression line estimating the perceived risk of rape of women in each neighborhood, given the actual (police data) rate of rape for the neighborhoods. Sunset women as a group quite accurately estimate their risks, but South Philadelphians and Lincoln Park residents vastly underestimate theirs, while Wicker Park (ethnically mixed, working-class neighborhood in Chicago) women and Visitacion Valley women markedly overestimate theirs. Thus, the actual rates of rape (according to police data) are quite imperfectly related to perceived risks when the data are aggregated at the neighborhood level. Further, women's estimates of their own risk and men's estimates of risk for a woman in their neighborhood were quite similar.

Other Factors Contributing to Women's Fear

Women in our sample are less likely than men to believe they could successfully defend themselves against attack, $F(1,296) = 13.06$, $p \leq$ .001, and most women assess themselves as more physically vulnerable (that is, slower and weaker) than both the average man and the average woman, $F(1,365) = 214.46$, $p \leq .001$. Previous analyses suggest that these perceptions of physical vulnerability, combined with rape risk, contribute to women's fear. To test this assertion, we examined the impact on fear scores of statistically controlling for perceptions of rape risk and vulnerability.

As a first step, the mean fear scores for each sex were plotted (see fig. 2). A multiple regression was used to generate an equation that predicts women's fear scores, given a specified level of perceived risk of rape. That equation predicts a greatly diminished fear score for women when risk is statistically set to zero, which is plotted in figure 2 as point *C*. The resulting equation for men when risk is set to zero also predicts a diminished fear score, which is labeled *D*. The gap between women's and men's fear score controlling for risk of rape (*C-D*) is of approximately the same magnitude as the original fear scores (*A-B*).

We performed a similar analysis setting perceptions of physical vulnerability to zero. The resulting equations show that women's fear scores decrease substantially, whereas men's fear scores decrease only slightly (see fig. 2). (The *E-F* gap is smaller than either the *A-B* or the *C-D* gap.)

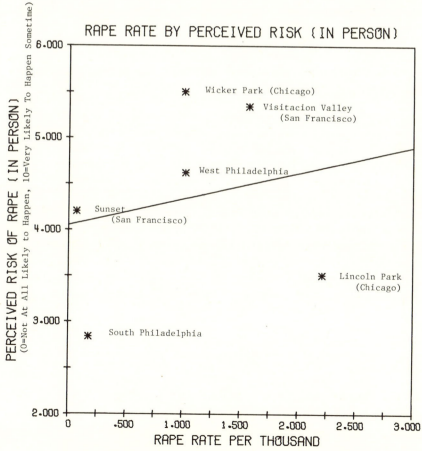

FIG. 1.—Actual rape rates (police data) by perceived risk of rape

	Unadjusted Fear	Fear Adjusted for Risk of Rape	Fear Adjusted for Vulnerability	Fear Adjusted for Risk of Rape and Vulnerability
Very Unsafe				
Somewhat Unsafe				
	(A) X			
Reasonably Safe		(C) X	(E) X	
	(B) *		(F) *	
		(D) *		(G) X
Very Safe				(H) *

FIG. 2.—Predicted fear levels for men and women. A = mean fear score for women; B = mean fear score for men; C = .117 × risk + 2.01; D = .107 × risk + 1.33; E = .383 × vulnerability + 2.01; F = .548 × vulnerability + 1.51; G = .117 × risk + .386 × vulnerability + 1.49; H = .091 × risk + .397 × vulnerability + 1.18. Points C through H are the constant terms in the regression equations—hence these points are the predicted fear scores when risk and/or vulnerability is set to zero. X = women; * = men.

This indicates that feeling vulnerable contributes more to women's fear levels than to men's, while women's perceived risk of rape affects men's and women's scores equally.

As a final step, both the vulnerability index and the rape-risk item were included in the regression equation. Men's fear scores decrease very little more than when adjusting only for risk of rape (D-H in fig. 2), but women's scores drop substantially (C-G). The correlation between vulnerability and risk for women is −.003 while for men it is +.256. Thus, the effect of rape risk and vulnerability on women's fear are independent and additive, while for men some of the effects overlap. Therefore, the perceived risk of rape and vulnerability are both substantial components of women's fear, while perceived risk plays a bigger role in the fear men report (perhaps reflecting also men's fear for others).

Self-protective Behavior

Many researchers report that women exceed men in the use of precautionary strategies.[13] Our respondents' answers to the general

13. Michael Hindelang and Bruce L. Davis, "Forcible Rape in the U.S.: A Statistical Profile," in Chappell, Geis, and Geis; Michael Hindelang, Michael Gottfredson, and James Garafalo, *Victims of Personal Crime: An Empirical Foundation for a Theory of Personal Victimization* (Cambridge, Mass.: Ballinger Publishing Co., 1978); Frederick DuBow, Edward McCabe, and Gail Kaplan, "Reactions to Crime: A Critical Review of the Literature," Reactions to Crime Project, mimeographed (Evanston, Ill.: Northwestern University, Center for Urban Affairs, 1978); Riger, Gordon, and LeBailly.

question about what they do to avoid dangerous situations in cities followed this general pattern. More women than men gave responses which indicated that their strategies were not to go out alone; not to come home alone; and to avoid dangerous areas, strangers, and other situations that could lead to danger. To specify more precisely which precautionary behaviors women engage in more than men, we used a *t*-test with a .05 significance level to sort the behaviors into three groups: (1) those which women use more frequently, (2) those which men use more frequently, and (3) those behaviors for which there was not a significant sex difference in usage (see table 3). The precautionary behaviors that women use more than men do not involve significant monetary expenditures (e.g., they go out in groups rather than individually, they stay out of dangerous parts of town, they change seats in a movie or on a bus). Most of the strategies with no significant sex differences involve major financial costs (e.g., installing a burglar alarm, moving for fear of safety, owning a dog for protection) and are behaviors intended to protect a household or a family rather than an individual. The only behavior that men use more than women is taking self-defense classes. Thirty-one percent of males but only 17 percent of females in our study had taken self-defense training. Our data, therefore, support the idea that there are sex differences in the use of precautionary behaviors, although we do not know if observations of behavior would confirm these self-reports. Although what women do more frequently may not be costly in terms of money, their strategies are undoubtedly costly in terms of personal freedom.

Avoiding Dangerous Situations

In addition to describing more worry than men in all of the situations that we asked about, women also reported being in each specific situation less often (with the sole exception of being home alone after dark, which both sexes report doing with equal frequency). In every instance, how often our respondents reported doing something was significantly and negatively related to their worry levels (see table 4). That is, those telling us they "never" did the activity in question consistently had the highest level of worry associated with that activity. The proportions of those who "never" do the activity in question vary greatly, from 8.7 percent who say they never are home alone after dark to 98 percent who say they never ride in cars with strangers. The lowest worry levels are associated with the most common situations. People feel safer nearer home, and these situations—being at home alone and walking on neighborhood streets alone at night—might be considered unavoidable.

Worry levels for going alone to laundromats, movies, downtown, and bars are higher than worry levels for unavoidable situations, and the

Table 3

Correlation between Fear and Use of Strategies by Sex

	% Who Never Do Activity*		% Who Always Do Activity†		Correlation of Fear with How Often Done	
	M	F	M	F	M	F
Strategies which women use more frequently than men ($p \leq .05$):						
How often do you restrict your going out to only during the daytime?	72	25	9	26	.3106	.5250
How often do you avoid doing things you have to do because of fear of being harmed?	78	32	6	15	-.0279	.3050
When you go out, how often do you drive rather than walk because of fear of being harmed?	56	18	13	40	.1335	.2925
How often do you not do things you want to do but do not have to do because of fear?	75	30	6	15	.1682	.2813
When you are looking for a parking place at night, how often do you think about safety?	15	5	33	71	.1512	.2350
How often do you ask for identification from salesmen or repairmen?	18	11	33	50	.0282	.2342
How often do you go out with a friend or two as protection?	50	10	4	51	-.0371	.2031
How often do you check the back seat of your car for intruders before getting in?	38	12	31	59	.0048	.1826
How often do you check to see who is at your door before opening it?	10	2	60	87	.2184	.1789
How often do you try to wear shoes that are easy to run in, in case of danger?	61	19	13	36	.1500	.1779
How often do you lock the outside door when home alone during the day?	12	3	63	79	-.0769	.1567
When on the street, how often do you avoid looking people in the eye whom you don't know?	31	18	22	29	.1334	.1531

*People who respond "never" or "no" to questions about precautionary behavior.
†People who respond "always" or "yes" to questions about precautionary behavior.

Table 3 (Continued)

	% Who Never Do Activity*		% Who Always Do Activity†		Correlation of Fear with How Often Done	
	M	F	M	F	M	F
How often do you try to avoid going downtown when making plans to go out at night?	37	21	19	24	.2715	.1489
When you are out alone, how often do you try not to dress in a provocative manner?	63	18	10	58	−.0017	.1402
How often do you lock the doors when home alone at night?	87	.3	85	95	.0215	.1340
When in a car how often do you lock the doors?	10	1	64	79	−.0665	.1288
How often do you cross the street when you see someone who seems strange or dangerous?	11	6	25	52	−.0247	.1261
How often do you stay out of parts of town you think are dangerous?	9	9	38	55	.2774	.1109
When walking on the street, how often do you make a point of being alert and watchful?	3	2	66	81	.1972	.1101
How often do you deliberately leave on lights or a radio when no one will be home?	14	5	57	65	.1504	.1037
When out alone, how often do you take something along for protection like a dog or whistle?	73	50	6	23	.1961	.0656
How often do you carry keys in your hand when going to your car?	20	4	44	82	.2260	.0596
Did you install or make sure there were special locks or bars on the doors?	43	28	57	72	.1081	.0452
Did you get an unlisted phone number?	60	43	40	57	.1985	.0399
When at a movie or on a bus, how often do you change seats if someone strange is nearby?	26	18	13	28	.0125	.0375
How often do you ask a neighbor to watch your house when no one will be home for several days?	16	5	60	75	−.1094	.0323
How often do you get your house keys out before reaching your door?	15	4	50	81	.2216	.0265

Table 3 (Continued)

	% Who Never Do Activity*		% Who Always Do Activity†		Correlation of Fear with How Often Done	
	M	F	M	F	M	F
When at a movie or on a bus, how often do you choose a seat after checking who is nearby?	23	16	33	42	−.2360	.0165
How often do you avoid using alleys or streets that are not well lit?	10	5	42	81	.1709	.0020
Before taking a job, have you thought of the safety of that neighborhood?	67	48	33	52	−.0255	.0007
Do you use initials instead of first name on your mailbox?	57	30	43	70	−.0342	−.0398
Strategies which men use more frequently than women (p<.05):						
Did you ever take a self-defense class?	69	83	31	17	−.1216	−.0929
Strategies with no significant sex difference (p>.05):						
Have you ever thought of moving to a place with a door-man because of fear for your safety?	94	82	6	12	.2149	.1500
How often do you lock the car when it is parked?	2	1	86	94	.1477	.1237
Did you install or make sure there were special locks or bars on windows?	63	60	37	40	.0679	.0896
Do you have a dog for protection?	76	68	23	31	−.0298	.0515
Have you ever moved because of fear for your safety?	83	80	17	20	−.0633	.0460
Did you install or make sure there were bright lights outside your house?	59	48	41	52	−.0747	.0246
Did you ask about the safety of your neighborhood before moving in?	85	87	14	13	.0825	−.0349
Did you install or make sure there was a burglar alarm?	93	93	7	7	−.0198	−.0434
When out alone, how often do you take a gun for protection?	91	91	0	3	−.0543	−.0641
Do you own a gun for protection?	75	80	25	20	.2053	−.0661

Table 4

Worry and Frequency of Activities

Activities	Women's Worry about Activity (0–10 Scale)	Percentages of Sample Who Respond "Never" When Asked How Frequently They Engage in Activities		Significance of Mean Sex Difference of Frequency of Activity	% Variance in Women's Worry Explained by How Often Respondent Does It
		Women	Men		
Home alone after dark...	3.3	8.7	9.0	N.S.	3
Walk in neighborhood alone after dark......	5.2	25.3	2.9	≤.01	18
Go to laundromats alone after dark..........	5.7	68.2	61.8	≤.01	20
Go to movies alone after dark...............	6.1	74.9	32.4	≤.01	30
Go downtown alone after dark...............	6.4	47.0	7.5	≤.01	20
Go to bars/clubs alone after dark............	6.5	68.4	5.4	≤.01	33
Use public transit alone after dark...........	6.6	46.3	29.4	≤.01	16
Walk by groups of boys alone after dark......	6.9	33.6	11.8	≤.01	10
Walk by bars/hangouts alone after dark.......	7.2	46.5	10.3	≤.01	18
Walk by parks/lots alone after dark...........	7.8	52.8	13.2	≤.01	16
Give rides to strangers alone after dark.......	8.8	96.7	82.1	≤.01	31
Ride with male strangers alone after dark......	9.2	98.0	91.2	≤.01	25

proportions of respondents who say they never do these things increase dramatically. Each of these actions reflects both more danger and more choice. The fear levels associated with using public transportation and with walking past groups of boys, bars, and empty lots are higher, but the proportions of the sample who never do these activities drop substantially. Once again, these behaviors have less choice associated with them. The last two items, giving rides to or accepting rides from strangers, are associated with both the highest fear levels and the highest percentages of respondents who "never" do them. In addition, they may be associated with both the greatest danger and the greatest choice.

Correlation between Fear and Precautionary Behaviors

If women express more fear of crime than men do, if women avoid certain activities more often than men do, and if women engage in more self-protective behavior than men do, what is the correlation between women's fear of crime and the extent to which they engage in self-protection? Table 3 lists the correlations between the stated use of protective behaviors and fear of crime. Seven of the self-protective behaviors correlate .20 or higher with women's fear of crime. In other words, the women who report the highest levels of fear of crime report using these self-protective measures the most. Six of the behaviors that correlate most highly with fear of crime for women are quite restrictive ones in terms of mobility: going out only in the daytime, not doing certain things for fear of crime, driving instead of walking, choosing parking places with safety in mind, and going out with a friend or two as protection. As we move down our list in terms of behavioral correlates of women's fear of crime, we notice that for some behaviors the correlation between fear and the behavior is higher for men than for women.

Inspection of the columns that indicate the percentage of respondents who reported they always or never engaged in the behavior in question sheds light on this apparent contradiction. For many of the self-protective actions, such a large percentage of women always engage in the behavior that there is little variation in its use by women. This results in low discriminating power and low correlations. For example, getting keys out before reaching the door is a behavior that correlates more highly with fear for men than for women. Closer inspection reveals that 81 percent of the women, compared with 50 percent of the men, reported always using this form of self-protection. Similarly, 81 percent of the women, compared with 42 percent of the men, told us they always avoid using badly lit alleys and streets. On the other side, the correlations between behavior and fear for men are sometimes low because the majority of men never take those precautions. For example, 78 percent of the men, compared with 32 percent of the women, reported they never avoid doing things they need to for fear of crime. From the overall pattern in table 3, we conclude that the use of self-protective behaviors is correlated more highly with fear of crime for women than for men, particularly in situations in which women vary in their use of the protective measure.

Summary and Discussion

Our findings strongly support previous research results indicating that urban fear of crime is pervasive but that women express more fear than men, whether it is measured in terms of perceptions of neighborhood safety or worry about physical safety in day-to-day activities. Our data also indicate significant differences in fear measures according to women's neighborhoods. Intuitively we would expect fear to be related to the likelihood of victimization, but residents of neighborhoods with the highest rates of personal violence did not express the highest levels of fear. Moreover, women, though victimized less often than men by most crimes, report greater fear of crime than men do.[14] Therefore, crime rates alone do not seem to explain differences in fear. However, our analyses did show that women's responses may be explained substantially by taking into account both the perceived risk of rape and feelings of vulnerability to physical attack.

Our findings also agree with previous research suggesting that behavioral correlates of this fear for women include engaging in significantly more precautionary behaviors than do men. Many of these safety measures restrict freedom of action. Although the possibility exists that women's higher level of fear produces precautionary behavior, which in turn leads to low rates of victimization, such a causal relationship has not been empirically demonstrated. In an extensive analysis of sources and conditions surrounding victimization, Hindelang, Gottfredson, and Garafalo suggest that life-style, not degree of precaution, is the critical variable in preventing victimization, since "lifestyles are related to the probability of being in places (streets, parks, and other public places) at times (especially night-time) when victimizations are known to occur."[15] Our data suggest that women may have developed life-styles that include restrictions on their freedom and behavior and that may keep them safe by limiting their chances of becoming victims.

In a review of developments in fear of crime from 1965 through

14. Stephanie Riger and Margaret Gordon, "Structure of Rape Prevention Beliefs," *Personality and Social Psychology Bulletin* 5 (1979): 186–90, and "Public Opinion and Public Policy: The Case of Rape Prevention" (paper presented at the American Psychological Association convention, Toronto, August 1978).

15. Hindelang et al., p. 255.

1975, Stinchcombe et al. found that the trend is clearly upward, "most . . . caused by a marked increase in the fear of women."[16] We may expect, therefore, that restrictions on women's daily lives are increasing, an expectation supported by the large proportions of our women respondents who simply never engage in many ordinary activities, such as walking alone in their neighborhoods at night. The irony, of course, is that these restrictions do not guarantee their safety and may, in the final analysis, result only in increased fear.

The impact of crime and fear of crime on men's lives is not as easily documented, but our data show that men are also affected. Although much less restricted than women, they also avoid certain activities and take certain precautions. Most interestingly, men's estimates of the risk of a woman being raped in their neighborhood are associated with their own feelings of safety. Possibly rape is a "bellwether" crime against which both men and women judge the general criminal environment[17] in their neighborhoods, or possibly the decrease we detect is caused by men's concern for their wives' and daughters' safety. Whatever the causal link, the existence of rape in society diminishes, at the very least, the quality of life for both men and women in our cities.

Our findings that women's perceived risk of rape and feelings of vulnerability contribute importantly to their greater fear suggest that social policies designed to reduce fear should focus on these two factors. In a study of the impact of self-defense training on women, Cohn, Kidder, and Harvey[18] point out that after the training course women reported feeling stronger, braver, more active, more in control, bigger, and safer. Therefore, policymakers might begin by promoting self-defense classes for women and other measures that enhance women's perceptions of their own strength.

A variety of rape prevention measures have been proposed. Unfortunately, too many ignore the cultural or systemic factors which support or even promote rape, such as the glorification of violence against women in some advertising.[19] In the case of rape, this has meant that women's victimization implicitly has been attributed to traits or behaviors of the rape victim (e.g., seductiveness)[20] or to psychological disorders of the rapist; consequently, preventive strategies involving changes in the social system have been overlooked.[21] When substantial energies of our

16. Stinchcombe et al., p. 48.

17. John E. Conklin, *Impact of Crime* (New York: Macmillan Publishing Co., 1975).

18. Louise Kidder, personal communication; see also Ellen Cohn, Louise H. Kidder, and Joan Harvey, "Crime Prevention: The Psychology of Two Different Reactions," *Victimology* 3 (1978): 285–96.

19. Brownmiller.

20. Lynda L. Holmstrom and Ann Burgess, *The Victim of Rape: Institutional Reactions* (New York: John Wiley & Sons, 1978).

21. Nathan Caplan and Stephen D. Nelson, "On Being Useful," *American Psychologist* 28 (March 1973): 199–211.

society's institutions are focused on eliminating rape, both men and women living in our cities will have less to fear. Failure to act against rape results in the impoverishment of our lives and of the life of our nation.

Departments of Journalism, Urban Affairs, and Sociology
Northwestern University (Gordon)

Department of Psychology
Lake Forest College (Riger)

Departments of Sociology and Urban Affairs
Northwestern University (LeBailly)

Department of Criminal Justice
University of Minnesota (Heath)

The Chicago Woman:
A Study of Patterns of Mobility and Transportation

Helena Znaniecki Lopata

A vast literature discusses the American tendency to divide the world into two spheres: that of the public world and that of the home and its private space.[1] However, the home, its occupants, and its possessions were not expected to be geographically stable. Americans have had to be able and willing to shift their households and to move objects, including themselves, in and out of the home.[2] Women, in particular, were expected to go away from their parental home and to permit their family

This paper is based on one given at the Conference on Women's Travel Issues, organized by the U.S. Department of Transportation, September 19, 1978.

1. Barbara Sicherman documents this division in her review essay on "American History" (*Signs: Journal of Women in Culture and Society* 1, no. 2 [Winter 1975]: 461–86), as does Foster Rhea Dulles in *A History of Recreation: America Learns to Play* (New York: Appleton-Century-Crofts, 1965). Betty Friedan's *The Feminine Mystique* (New York: W. W. Norton & Co., 1963) and Rose Coser's "Stay Home, Little Sheba: On Placement, Displacement and Social Change" (*Social Problems* 22, no 4 [April 1975]: 470–79) analyze the ideology which convinced American women to identify their world as focused upon the home and the resources needed to maintain it and the family, while my own *Occupation: Housewife* (New York: Oxford University Press, 1971) describes the resultant role definitions of urban and suburban homemakers.

2. The effects of immigration to America, free and forced, are treated in such classics as W. I. Thomas and Florian Znaniecki's *The Polish Peasant in Europe and America* (New York: Alfred A. Knopf, 1918–20), or Oscar Handlin's *The Uprooted* (Boston: Atlantic Monthly Press, 1951). Movement within this country is described in popular terms by Vance Packard in *A Nation of Strangers* (New York: David McKay Co., 1972). The transfer of business personnel has received attention since William H. Whyte, Jr.'s *The Organization Man* (New York: Simon & Schuster, 1956), and its effect on the wife and family has been described by Robert Weiss in *Loneliness: The Experience of Emotional and Social Isolation* (Cambridge, Mass.: M.I.T. Press, 1973); Robert Seidenberg in *Corporate Wives: Corporate Casualties* (Garden City, N.Y.: Anchor Press, 1975); Maryanne Vandervelde in *The Changing Life of the Corporate Wife* (New York: Mecox Publishing Co., 1979); and Rosabeth Moss Kanter in *Men and Women of the Corporation* (New York: Basic Books, 1977).

of procreation to follow the dictates of their husband's job or various life reconstructions.[3] Clearly, such mobility is inseparable from the transportation resources of a society. This paper examines some of the ways in which American urban women define and use those resources. Most of the data come from studies done in the metropolitan Chicago area between 1965 and 1976.[4] They are applicable to other urban centers only with the modifications that the historical and structural divergences among American cities demand.[5]

In terms of human and even American history, Chicago is a relatively new city. The population until recently consisted of first- or second-generation immigrants coming mainly from European countries. Its black segment migrated from the American south northward

3. See Peter Rossi, *Why Families Move* (New York: Free Press, 1955), for an early analysis of these patterns; my *Occupation: Housewife* for the meaning of the home and mobility to the traditional woman; and Linda Nelson and Mary Winter, "Life Disruption, Independence, Satisfaction, and the Consideration of Moving," *Gerontologist* 15, no. 2 (April 1975): 160–69, for the mobility effects of life-course events.

4. The first study commented on in this paper, culminating in *Occupation: Housewife,* involved several sets of interviews with 571 women conducted over a span of nine years, with funding from Roosevelt University, *Chicago Tribune,* and the Midwest Council for Social Research on Aging. A second project, focusing on role changes in widowhood, involved a modified area probability sample of 301 women aged fifty and over and was funded by the Administration on Aging and Roosevelt University (grant AA-4-67-030-01-A1) (see Helena Znaniecki Lopata, *Widowhood in an American City* [Cambridge, Mass.: Schenkman Publishing Co., 1973]). The research on the support systems of widows was facilitated by a contract with the Social Security Administration (SSA-71-3411) and used a sample of 1,169 current or former beneficiaries of social security. A multiframed sample with different ratios was used to insure the presence of enough young and remarried widows. When weighed by the ratio of selection, the sample represents 82,085 Chicago former or current widows (the study is discussed in Helena Znaniecki Lopata, *Women as Widows: Support Systems* [New York: Elsevier-North Holland Publishing Co., 1979]). The study of changing commitments of women to work and family roles was funded by the Social Security Administration (SSA-72-S-7703). The four-stage area mobility sample consists of 1,877 women aged twenty-five to fifty-four. Its purpose is to determine if behavioral changes in the attachment of women to the labor force are simply a response to economic need or are the outward manifestations of real changes in self-images, expectations, demands on societal institutions and plans for future role involvements (see Helena Znaniecki Lopata and Kathleen Fordham Norr, "Changing Commitments of American Women to Work and Family Roles and Their Future Consequences for Social Security: Final Report" [1979]). Thanks go to Kathleen Norr, Deb Burdeno, Cheryl Miller, and Suzanne Meyering for work with the women and work study and data analysis. In the meantime, the Mayor's Office for Senior Citizens commissioned Kirchner Associates Research firm to conduct "The Chicago Needs Assessment Survey," final report (Chicago: Mayor's Office for Senior Citizens, 1973).

5. The great range of transportation and mobility resources, and of resident definitions of needs and resource availability, in different American cities became apparent when the Gerontological Society brought several of us urban researchers for a symposium on "The City: A Viable Environment for the Elderly," under the influence of Alice Brothy as chair and Thomas O. Byers as organizer and editor (see *Gerontologist,* vol. 15, no. 1, pt. 1 [February 1975]).

primarily since World War I, often using the Illinois Central Railroad as the migration route. Transportation within Chicago itself follows mainly radial routes of trains and highways. In spite of the assumption that people work in the city and live outside, current patterns of industrial and other employer movement have resulted in arteries being filled primarily with driver-only automobiles in both directions during work-rhythm related hours. The rail-subway-elevated-bus system within the city is reputedly very good, although the elderly report congestion during work-influenced hours to an extent that makes travel difficult at those times. At the same time, Chicago's *Local Community Factbook*, describing the seventy-six "natural neighborhoods" of the city and some of its suburbs, shows that a large proportion, varying by area, of workers do not commute to the center of the city and that, the further away from the center they live, the smaller the percentage so employed.[6]

American urban, young, and single women are geographically relatively mobile within the complex of the home, school, and work roles until the birth of the first child. Most of the Chicago area women whom I have studied follow this pattern. They did not express feelings of restrictions in movement until the birth of their first child. Chicago's climate makes it particularly difficult to travel with small children during many months of the year. Full-time homemakers and mothers report feeling "tied down" for several years. Even shopping for the home becomes a problem. Carrying, watching, and controlling children while trying to shop is difficult. So is carrying objects and children home. Mass transportation facilities, such as buses, are not designed for women needing to move children or goods. The problems become complicated and changed by a household move to outlying areas of the city or to suburbs. "Good for the children" becomes the reason given most often for outward mobility. However, such areas often lack public transportation, so that a second car becomes a necessity. The combination of mortgage, transportation costs, and the drop in income after the wife quits working pushes many Chicago area families into a curtailed social life space, restricting them to informal interaction in the immediate neighborhood.[7]

Another source of constriction for women may be their husband's occupational demands. According to Mortimer, Hall, and Hill, a great deal of research supports the general American contention that wives are expected, and in actuality do, refrain from working or interrupt

6. Evelyn Kitagawa and Karl E. Taeuber, eds., *Local Community Factbook: Chicago Metropolitan Area*, 1960 (Chicago: Chicago Community Inventory, 1963); see also "The Chicago Needs Assessment Survey" and Helena Znaniecki Lopata, "The Support Systems of Elderly Urbanites: Chicago of the 1970s," *Gerontologist* 15 (February 1975): 35–41.

7. I specifically asked the *Occupation: Housewife* suburban respondents their reasons for movement to outlying areas as well as the advantages and disadvantages of suburban living and got the "for the children" as both the reason and the advantage. Isolation and transportation problems were the main disadvantages.

their employment when their husband's careers require movement to a different locale.[8] However, a sample of 1,877 women aged twenty-five to fifty-four living in a metropolitan Chicago area indicates that it is mainly concern over the children that stops women from seeking or retaining employment outside of the home once they become mothers.[9] Eighty percent of these women feel that a mother should stop working after the birth of a child; 39 percent think that the youngest children should be at least six years of age or over when she returns. On the other hand, 33 percent believe that the youngest can be one year or less, 34 percent that he or she can be between two and five years of age. Women who feel that their husbands do not want them to be employed outside of the home are also less likely to take a job, but the presence of young children in the home is a major deterrent.

The same sample suggests that when women do seek employment outside of the home, transportation or travel difficulties may be contributing a share to the constraints society and the women themselves impose on their occupational choice and on their working careers. We asked, "At the present time, would you take a job you really wanted, but which required that you . . . move to another town" or " . . . occasionally travel out of town" (see table 1). The image of the "modern women"

Table 1

Constraints Placed on Potential Jobs by Chicago
Area Adult Women

Job-related Duties	Would Take Job (%)
At the present time, would you take a job you really wanted, but which required that you:	
Work outside your own neighborhood	72
Move to another town	15
Supervise men	60
Take on a lot of responsibility	67
Occasionally work after hours to get the job done	78
Sometimes bring work home	70
Occasionally travel out of town	46
Entertain occasionally during evenings or weekends	59

SOURCE.—Helena Znaniecki Lopata and Kathleen Fordham Norr, "Changing Commitments of American Women to Work and Family Roles and Their Future Consequences for Social Security: Final Report" (1979).

8. Jeylan Mortimer, Richard Hall, and Reuben Hill point out in "Husband's Occupational Attributes as Constraints on Wives' Employment" (*Sociology of Work and Occupation* 5, no. 3 [August 1978]: 258–313) that the husband's work patterns can prevent the wife's engagement in an occupation in the first place: "Frequent travel, necessary for advancement in some careers, places the entire burden of family responsibilities upon the wife" (p. 292). See also Caroline Bird, *The Two Paycheck Marriage* (New York: Rawson, Wade Publishers, 1979).

9. See Lopata and Norr.

reflected in the mass media does not lead us to anticipate that only 15 percent of the metropolitan Chicago women aged twenty-five to fifty-four would be willing to take a really desirable job if it meant moving to another town, and that over half would not take a job involving travel out of town. Thus traditional limitations on women's employment appear to be more influential than are role demands of occupations high on prestige, authority, pay, hierarchal position in the organization, and other scales. Women who will not even consider a job involving transfers or travel are very apt to restrict themselves to inferior occupations.

The same conclusion can be drawn from table 2. The concern is again with the transportation or location characteristics a woman considers important in looking for, accepting, or rejecting a job. It is unlikely that a woman who considers a location close to where she lives to be a very important aspect of a job, as 45 percent of the respondents do, will end up in an occupation or a career line which offers the highest economic or intrinsic work rewards. The same can be said of the 51 percent of the women who consider a "location in a desirable area" to be very important, especially since they are living in metropolitan Chicago. Over two-thirds of the respondents find the convenience of working hours to be an important feature of a job; they undoubtedly include traveling time in their considerations.[10] The women's reluctance to take a job requiring movement to another town is reflected by the fact that only 6

Table 2

Importance Assigned to Various Aspects of a Job by Chicago Area Adult Women (%)
(N = 1,877)

	Importance			
Job Aspects	Very Important	Somewhat Important	Somewhat Unimportant	Very Unimportant
A location close to where you live	45	40	11	4
A location in a desirable area	51	38	8	3
Convenient work hours	69	23	7	2
Good pay	69	26	4	1
Pleasant surroundings	60	34	4	1
Challenging work	72	23	4	1

SOURCE.—Helena Znaniecki Lopata and Kathleen Fordham Norr; "Changing Commitment of American Women to Work and Family Roles and Their Future Consequences for Social Security: Final Report" (1979).

10. Julia Ericksen demonstrates in "An Analysis of the Journal to Work for Women" (*Social Problems* 24, no. 4 [April 1977]: 428–35) that mothers of small children travel shorter time distances to work than do men or women without concerns for the care of children. She also states that "as Lansing and Henricks have shown, women have less access to automobiles than men" (p. 434, referring to John Lansing and Gary Henricks, *Automobile Ownership and Residential Density* [Ann Arbor: Institute for Social Research, University of Michigan, 1967]).

percent answered affirmatively the question, posed much earlier in the interview, "Did you ever move to accept a job?" The dependency of women on the career opportunities or other decision-making events of others is implied by the yes answers of 26 percent of the metropolitan adult women who gave up a job because their families moved.

The officials of the city of Chicago are aware of the fact that many of its older residents, among whom women are statistically predominant, have even more intense problems with the use of its resources. They lack knowledge about what is available, they are timid about entering unfamiliar territory, they suffer financial and health restrictions and fear. Older women generally do not operate automobiles, having grown up while they were scarce and having lived their adulthood when cars were considered the province of men. The Chicago Mayor's Office for Senior Citizens commissioned studies of elderly urbanites of direct relevance to this paper. Though, unfortunately, not all are analyzed by sexual identity, they relate to the distance in miles to the relative, other than a child, whom the respondent could call to help with problems about money, illness, or loneliness (table 3). Although most older Americans have at least one child living within easy contact distance, as Shanas documented recently, other relatives who could be turned to for help with problems tend to be dispersed, especially in the case of the elderly born in Eastern Europe who are the latecomers to Chicago.[11] Further-

Table 3

Chicago Area Older Women's Distance in Miles to a Relative, Other than Child, Whom He or She Could Call to Help with Money, Illness, or Loneliness Problems, by Place of Birth

Distance (Miles)	Native Born U.S. (%)	Eastern European Born (%)	Other Foreign Born (%)	Total (%)	N
Lives with relative	6	1	4	5	47
1 or Less	10	11	8	10	97
2–10	15	10	12	14	141
11–20	4	6	5	5	46
21–30	4	1	1	3	33
31–40	10	4	10	10	95
41–50	45	61	54	48	479
Other	1	2	0	1	6
Don't know	5	5	5	5	47
Total					
%	75	11	14	100	...
N	743	106	141	...	991

SOURCE.—Chicago Mayor's Office for Senior Citizens, "Chicago Needs Assessment Survey," final report (Chicago: Mayor's Office for Senior Citizens, 1973); tabulations prepared by Clarence L. Fewer.
NOTE.—χ^2 (16) = 27.8, P = .05.

11. Ethel Shanas, "Social Myth as Hypothesis: The Case of the Family Relations of Old People," *Gerontologist* 19, no. 1 (February 1979): 3–9.

more, the elderly who came to the city from other countries tend to go out to public places less often than do people with longer urban backgrounds. The exception are those born in Russia, who are apt to go to movies, plays, concerts, and club meetings, or church affairs. Half or more of the Chicago residents do not travel enough to engage in activities which could or necessarily do bring them into contact with others outside of the home. Where the data are broken down by sex, as well as age, there is little difference among the different categories of people, except that the younger men and the oldest women report more frequent visitors than do their counterparts. It is somewhat startling to find that 34 percent of the women aged seventy-five and more and 30 percent of the same-aged men did no visiting the week prior to the interview. Over a fourth of most of the people aged sixty or over of both sexes had not more than one visit, or only once went out to visit a friend, neighbor, or relative during that week.[12]

Perhaps even more sharply than the elderly, widows reveal limitations on mobility, which transportation systems tend to exacerbate. Widows are women who are most likely to have been spatially somewhat restricted throughout life and/or to have been stripped of mobility resources by the death of the husband. These women also face both isolation and constrictions because of increased age and disengagement from some roles through residential changes, the death of friends, retirement, and poverty.

Many of these women in Chicago are simply "urban villagers" as Gans called similar people in Boston, born outside of the city or brought up by "foreign" city parents.[13] Most of such women do not even have a map of the city in their heads and travel only a limited number of avenues to maintain themselves and their homes. However, they are apt to have moved households several times in their lives. The immigrant women are apt to have first moved into one of Chicago's ethnic communities; many remain among members of their ethnic groups now that their community has moved out. Others are located in the Chicago Housing Authority buildings or in retirement hotels, if they can afford them.

Most of these women lack the personal resources for extensive service and social support systems, as tables 4 and 5 show. The fact that women are restricted in their use of an automobile is apparent in that so few provide transportation to other human beings and none help with car care. In addition, 87 percent receive no help from others in taking care of a car, a probable indication of the tendency to dispose of the automobile once the husband dies. Although 39 percent receive help with shopping, only 13 percent help others with such an activity which

12. "Chicago Needs Assessment Survey." The interviewers were instructed to count all visits with such people living outside of the housing unit, including those with people at meetings at clubs and in churches.

13. Herbert Gans, *The Urban Villagers* (New York: Free Press, 1962).

Table 4

Chicago Area Widows Not Receiving or Giving
Selected Service Supports (%) (N = 82,085)

Service Supports	Do Not Give or Receive Supports
In flow:	
Transportation	45
House repairing	57
Housekeeping	77
Shopping	61
Yard work	69
Car care	87
Sick care	44
Decisions	59
Legal aid	81
Out flow:	
Transportation	82
House repairing	98
Housekeeping	88
Shopping	87
Yard work	96
Child care	80
Car care	100
Sick care	64
Decisions	85
Legal aid	99

SOURCE.—Helena Znaniecki Lopata, *Women as Widows: Support Systems* (New York: Elsevier-North Holland Publishing Co., 1979).

Table 5

Chicago Area Widows Who Do Not Engage in
Selected Social Activities (%) (N = 82,085)

Social Activity	Do Not Engage in the Activity
Other activity	96
Play sports, cards, games	58
Go to public places	51
Entertain	40
Travel out of town	40
Eat lunch with someone	37
Go to church	24
Visit	21
Celebrate holidays	8

SOURCE.—Helena Znaniecki Lopata, *Women as Widows: Support Systems* (New York: Elsevier-North Holland Publishing Co., 1979).

would take them out of the home. In general, they are not strongly involved in service exchanges. Even more surprising, so many women do not engage in the typical urban social exchanges that take them out of the home or bring others into it. Over half claim not to go to public places such as movie houses, or to play sports, cards, or games. Almost 20 percent more claim never to entertain than state that they never go visiting. A strong educational and age difference exists among women who do not engage in service and social support exchanges. The more educated and middle-class women not only involve themselves in more activities but utilize a wider network of people from whom, to whom, and with whom they exchange supports.

Summary

Most transportation resources of modern urban America have been developed on the assumptions that men need them for work and that family activity involves a husband/father familiar with the main resources. American society as a whole has not been innovative in helping women reach resources other than shopping, has not provided child-care assistance even when mothers function as consumers and definitely not to ease employment or social contact. Resources for social life and even for development of children's skills and abilities are often so located that the chauffeuring restricts the time available to a woman for many years. Suburban communities assume that their residents have cars and can care for them, requiring resettling after marriage dissolution. Transportation inadequacies or difficulties are especially evident in the lives of older women, and more for older widows.

Center for the Comparative Study of Social Roles
Loyola University

What Would a Non-Sexist City Be Like? Speculations on Housing, Urban Design, and Human Work

Dolores Hayden

"A woman's place is in the home" has been one of the most important principles of architectural design and urban planning in the United States for the last century. An implicit rather than explicit principle for the conservative and male-dominated design professions, it will not be found stated in large type in textbooks on land use. It has generated much less debate than the other organizing principles of the contemporary American city in an era of monopoly capitalism, which include the ravaging pressure of private land development, the fetishistic dependence on millions of private automobiles, and the wasteful use of energy.[1] However, women have rejected this dogma and entered the paid

This paper comprised part of the text of a talk for the conference "Planning and Designing a Non-Sexist Society," University of California, Los Angeles, April 21, 1979. I would like to thank Catharine Stimpson, Peter Marris, S. M. Miller, Kevin Lynch, Jeremy Brecher, and David Thompson for extensive written comments on drafts of this paper.

1. There is an extensive Marxist literature on the importance of spatial design to the economic development of the capitalist city, including Henri Lefebre, *La Production de l'espace* (Paris: Editions Anthropos, 1974); Manuel Castells, *The Urban Question* (Cambridge, Mass.: M.I.T. Press, 1977); David Harvey, *Social Justice and the City* (London: Edward Arnold, 1974); and David Gordon, "Capitalist Development and the History of American Cities," in *Marxism and the Metropolis,* ed. William K. Tabb and Larry Sawyers (New York: Oxford University Press, 1978). None of this work deals adequately with the situation of women as workers and homemakers, nor with the unique spatial inequalities they experience. Nevertheless, it is important to combine the economic and historical analysis of these scholars with the empirical research of non-Marxist feminist urban critics and sociologists who have examined women's experience of conventional housing, such as Gerda Wekerle,

labor force in larger and larger numbers. Dwellings, neighborhoods, and cities designed for homebound women constrain women physically, socially, and economically. Acute frustration occurs when women defy these constraints to spend all or part of the work day in the paid labor force. I contend that the only remedy for this situation is to develop a new paradigm of the home, the neighborhood, and the city; to begin to describe the physical, social, and economic design of a human settlement that would support, rather than restrict, the activities of employed women and their families. It is essential to recognize such needs in order to begin both the rehabilitation of the existing housing stock and the construction of new housing to meet the needs of a new and growing majority of Americans—working women and their families.

When speaking of the American city in the last quarter of the twentieth century, a false distinction between "city" and "suburb" must be avoided. The urban region, organized to separate homes and workplaces, must be seen as a whole. In such urban regions, more than half of the population resides in the sprawling suburban areas, or "bedroom communities." The greatest part of the built environment in the United States consists of "suburban sprawl": single-family homes grouped in class-segregated areas, crisscrossed by freeways and served by shopping malls and commercial strip developments. Over 50 million small homes are on the ground. About two-thirds of American families "own" their homes on long mortgages; this includes over 77 percent of all AFL-CIO members.[2] White, male skilled workers are far more likely to be homeowners than members of minority groups and women, long denied equal credit or equal access to housing. Workers commute to jobs either in the center or elsewhere in the suburban ring. In metropolitan areas studied in 1975 and 1976, the journey to work, by public transit or private car, averaged about nine miles each way. Over 100 million privately owned cars filled two- and three-car garages (which would be con-

"A Woman's Place Is in the City" (paper for the Lincoln Institute of Land Policy, Cambridge, Mass., 1978); and Suzanne Keller, "Women in a Planned Community" (paper for the Lincoln Institute of Land Policy, Cambridge, Mass., 1978). Only then can one begin to provide a socialist-feminist critique of the spatial design of the American city. It is also essential to develop research on housing similar to Sheila B. Kamerman, "Work and Family in Industrialized Societies," *Signs: Journal of Women in Culture and Society* 4, no. 4 (Summer 1979): 632–50, which reviews patterns of women's employment, maternity provisions, and child-care policies in Hungary, East Germany, West Germany, France, Sweden, and the United States. A comparable study of housing and related services for employed women could be the basis for more elaborate proposals for change. Many attempts to refine socialist and feminist economic theory concerning housework are discussed in an excellent article by Ellen Malos, "Housework and the Politics of Women's Liberation," *Socialist Review* 37 (January–February 1978): 41–47. A most significant theoretical piece is Movimento di Lotta Femminile, "Programmatic Manifesto for the Struggle of Housewives in the Neighborhood," *Socialist Revolution* 9 (May–June 1972): 85–90.

2. *Survey of AFL-CIO Members Housing 1975* (Washington, D.C.: AFL-CIO, 1975), p. 16. I am indebted to Allan Heskin for this reference.

sidered magnificent housing by themselves in many developing countries). The United States, with 13 percent of the world's population, uses 41 percent of the world's passenger cars in support of the housing and transportation patterns described.[3]

The roots of this American settlement form lie in the environmental and economic policies of the past. In the late nineteenth century, millions of immigrant families lived in the crowded, filthy slums of American industrial cities and despaired of achieving reasonable living conditions. However, many militant strikes and demonstrations between the 1890s and 1920s made some employers reconsider plant locations and housing issues in their search for industrial order.[4] "Good homes make contented workers" was the slogan of the Industrial Housing Associates in 1919. These consultants and many others helped major corporations plan better housing for white male skilled workers and their families, in order to eliminate industrial conflict. "Happy workers invariably mean bigger profits, while unhappy workers are never a good investment," they chirruped.[5] Men were to receive "family wages," and become home "owners" responsible for regular mortgage payments, while their wives became home "managers" taking care of spouse and children. The male worker would return from his day in the factory or office to a private domestic environment, secluded from the tense world of work in an industrial city characterized by environmental pollution, social degradation, and personal alienation. He would enter a serene dwelling whose physical and emotional maintenance would be the duty of his wife. Thus the private suburban house was the stage set for the effective sexual division of labor. It was the commodity par excellence, a spur for male paid labor and a container for female unpaid labor. It made gender appear a more important self-definition than class, and consumption more involving than production. In a brilliant discussion of the "patriarch as wage slave," Stuart Ewen has shown how capitalism and antifeminism fused in campaigns for homeownership and mass consumption: the patriarch whose home was his "castle" was to work year in and year out to provide the wages to support this private environment.[6]

3. *Transit Fact Book,* 1977–78 ed. (Washington, D.C.: American Public Transit Association, 1978), p. 29; *Motor Vehicle Facts and Figures* (Detroit, Mich.: Motor Vehicle Manufacturers Association, 1977), pp. 29, 31, 53.

4. Gordon, pp. 48–50, discusses suburban relocation of plants and housing.

5. Industrial Housing Associates, "Good Homes Make Contented Workers," 1919, Edith Elmer Wood Papers, Avery Library, Columbia University. Also see Barbara Ehrenreich and Deirdre English, "The Manufacture of Housework," *Socialist Revolution* 5 (1975): 16. They quote an unidentified corporate official (ca. 1920): "Get them to invest their savings in homes and own them. Then they won't leave and they won't strike. It ties them down so they have a stake in our prosperity."

6. Stuart Ewen, *Captains of Consciousness: Advertising and the Social Roots of the Consumer Culture* (New York: McGraw-Hill Book Co., 1976).

Although this strategy was first boosted by corporations interested in a docile labor force, it soon appealed to corporations who wished to move from World War I defense industries into peacetime production of domestic appliances for millions of families. The development of the advertising industry, documented by Ewen, supported this ideal of mass consumption and promoted the private suburban dwelling, which maximized appliance purchases.[7] The occupants of the isolated household were suggestible. They bought the house itself, a car, stove, refrigerator, vacuum cleaner, washer, carpets. Christine Frederick, explaining it in 1929 as *Selling Mrs. Consumer,* promoted homeownership and easier consumer credit and advised marketing managers on how, to manipulate American women.[8] By 1931 the Hoover Commission on Home Ownership and Home Building established the private, single-family home as a national goal, but a decade and a half of depression and war postponed its achievement. Architects designed houses for Mr. and Mrs. Bliss in a competition sponsored by General Electric in 1935; winners accommodated dozens of electrical appliances in their designs with no critique of the energy costs involved.[9] In the late 1940s the single-family home was boosted by FHA and VA mortgages and the construction of isolated, overprivatized, energy-consuming dwellings became commonplace. "I'll Buy That Dream" made the postwar hit parade.[10]

Mrs. Consumer moved the economy to new heights in the fifties. Women who stayed at home experienced what Betty Friedan called the "feminine mystique" and Peter Filene renamed the "domestic mystique."[11] While the family occupied its private physical space, the mass media and social science experts invaded its psychological space more effectively than ever before.[12] With the increase in spatial privacy came pressure for conformity in consumption. Consumption was expensive.

7. Richard Walker, "Suburbanization in Passage," unpublished draft paper (Berkeley: University of California, Berkeley, Department of Geography, 1977).

8. Christine Frederick, *Selling Mrs. Consumer* (New York: Business Bourse, 1929).

9. Carol Barkin, "Home, Mom, and Pie-in-the-Sky" (M. Arch. thesis, University of California, Los Angeles, 1979), pp. 120–24, gives the details of this competition; Ruth Schwartz Cowan, in an unpublished lecture at M.I.T. in 1977, explained GE's choice of an energy-consuming design for its refrigerator in the 1920s, because this would increase demand for its generating equipment by municipalities.

10. Peter Filene, *Him/Her/Self: Sex Roles in Modern America* (New York: Harcourt Brace Jovanovich, 1974), p. 189.

11. Betty Friedan, *The Feminine Mystique* (1963; New York: W. W. Norton & Co., 1974), p. 307, somewhat hysterically calls the home a "comfortable concentration camp"; Filene, p. 194, suggests that men are victimized by ideal homes too, thus "domestic" mystique.

12. Eli Zaretsky, *Capitalism, the Family, and Personal Life* (New York: Harper & Row, 1976), develops Friedman's earlier argument in a more systematic way. This phenomenon is misunderstood by Christopher Lasch, *Haven in a Heartless World* (New York: Alfred A. Knopf, 1977), who seems to favor a return to the sanctity of the patriarchal home.

More and more married women joined the paid labor force, as the suggestible housewife needed to be both a frantic consumer and a paid worker to keep up with the family's bills. Just as the mass of white male workers had achieved the "dream houses" in suburbia where fantasies of patriarchal authority and consumption could be acted out, their spouses entered the world of paid employment. By 1975, the two-worker family accounted for 39 percent of American households. Another 13 percent were single-parent families, usually headed by women. Seven out of ten employed women were in the work force because of financial need. Over 50 percent of all children between one and seventeen had employed mothers.[13]

How does a conventional home serve the employed woman and her family? Badly. Whether it is in a suburban, exurban, or inner-city neighborhood, whether it is a split-level ranch house, a modern masterpiece of concrete and glass, or an old brick tenement, the house or apartment is almost invariably organized around the same set of spaces: kitchen, dining room, living room, bedrooms, garage or parking area. These spaces require someone to undertake private cooking, cleaning, child care, and usually private transportation if adults and children are to exist within it. Because of residential zoning practices, the typical dwelling will usually be physically removed from any shared community space—no commercial or communal day-care facilities, or laundry facilities, for example, are likely to be part of the dwelling's spatial domain. In many cases these facilities would be illegal if placed across property lines. They could also be illegal if located on residentially zoned sites. In some cases sharing such a private dwelling with other individuals (either relatives or those unrelated by blood) is also against the law.[14]

Within the private spaces of the dwelling, material culture works against the needs of the employed woman as much as zoning does, because the home is a box to be filled with commodities. Appliances are usually single-purpose, and often inefficient, energy-consuming machines, lined up in a room where the domestic work is done in isolation from the rest of the family. Rugs and carpets which need vacuuming, curtains which need laundering, and miscellaneous goods which need maintenance fill up the domestic spaces, often decorated in "colonial," "Mediterranean," "French Provincial," or other eclectic styles purveyed by discount and department stores to cheer up that bare box of an

13. Rosalyn Baxandall, Linda Gordon, and Susan Reverby, eds., *America's Working Women: A Documentary History, 1600 to the Present* (New York: Vintage Books, 1976). For more detail, see Louise Kapp Howe, *Pink Collar Workers: Inside the World of Woman's Work* (New York: Avon Books, 1977).

14. Recent zoning fights on the commune issue have occurred in Santa Monica, Calif.; Wendy Schuman, "The Return of Togetherness," *New York Times* (March 20, 1977), reports frequent illegal down zoning by two-family groups in one-family residences in the New York area.

isolated house. Employed mothers usually are expected to, and almost invariably do, spend more time in private housework and child care than employed men; often they are expected to, and usually do, spend more time on commuting per mile traveled than men, because of their reliance on public transportation. One study found that 70 percent of adults without access to cars are female.[15] Their residential neighborhoods are not likely to provide much support for their work activities. A "good" neighborhood is usually defined in terms of conventional shopping, schools, and perhaps public transit, rather than additional social services for the working parent, such as day care or evening clinics.

While two-worker families with both parents energetically cooperating can overcome some of the problems of existing housing patterns, households in crisis, such as subjects of wife and child battering, for example, are particularly vulnerable to its inadequacies. According to Colleen McGrath, every thirty seconds a woman is being battered somewhere in the United States. Most of these batterings occur in kitchens and bedrooms. The relationship between household isolation and battering, or between unpaid domestic labor and battering, can only be guessed, at this time, but there is no doubt that America's houses and households are literally shaking with domestic violence.[16] In addition, millions of angry and upset women are treated with tranquilizers in the private home—one drug company advertises to doctors: "You can't change her environment but you can change her mood."[17]

The woman who does leave the isolated, single-family house or apartment finds very few real housing alternatives available to her.[18] The typical divorced or battered woman currently seeks housing, employment, and child care simultaneously. She finds that matching her complex family requirements with the various available offerings by landlords, employers, and social services is impossible. One environment that unites housing, services, and jobs could resolve many difficulties, but the existing system of government services, intended to stabilize households and neighborhoods by ensuring the minimum conditions for a decent home life to all Americans, almost always assumes that the traditional household with a male worker and an unpaid homemaker is the goal to be achieved or simulated. In the face of massive demographic changes, programs such as public housing, AFDC, and food stamps still

15. Study by D. Foley cited in Wekerle (see n. 1 above).

16. Colleen McGrath, "The Crisis of Domestic Order," *Socialist Review* 9 (January–February 1979): 12, 23.

17. Research by Malcolm MacEwen, cited in *Associate Collegiate Schools of Architecture Newsletter* (March 1973), p. 6.

18. See, for example, Carol A. Brown, "Spatial Inequalities and Divorced Mothers" (paper delivered at the annual meeting of the American Sociological Association, San Francisco, 1978); Susan Anderson-Khleif, research report for HUD on single-parent families and their housing, summarized in "Housing for Single Parents," *Research Report, MIT-Harvard Joint Center for Urban Studies* (April 1979), pp. 3–4.

attempt to support an ideal family living in an isolated house or apartment, with a full-time homemaker cooking meals and minding children many hours of the day.

By recognizing the need for a different kind of environment, far more efficient use can be made of funds now used for subsidies to individual households. Even for women with greater financial resources the need for better housing and services is obvious. Currently, more affluent women's problems as workers have been considered "private" problems—the lack of good day care, their lack of time. The aids to overcome an environment without child care, public transportation, or food service have been "private," commercially profitable solutions: maids and baby-sitters by the hour; franchise day care or extended television viewing; fast food service; easier credit for purchasing an automobile, a washer, or a microwave oven. Not only do these commercial solutions obscure the failure of American housing policies, they also generate bad conditions for other working women. Commercial day-care and fast-food franchises are the source of low-paying nonunion jobs without security. In this respect they resemble the use of private household workers by bourgeois women, who may never ask how their private maid or child-care worker arranges care for her own children. They also resemble the insidious effects of the use of television in the home as a substitute for developmental child care in the neighborhood. The logistical problems which all employed women face are not private problems, and they do not succumb to market solutions.

The problem is paradoxical: women cannot improve their status in the home unless their overall economic position in society is altered; women cannot improve their status in the paid labor force unless their domestic responsibilities are altered. Therefore, a program to achieve economic and environmental justice for women requires, by definition, a solution which overcomes the traditional divisions between the household and the market economy, the private dwelling and the workplace. One must transform the economic situation of the traditional homemaker whose skilled labor has been unpaid, but economically and socially necessary to society; one must also transform the domestic situation of the employed woman. If architects and urban designers were to recognize all employed women and their families as a constituency for new approaches to planning and design and were to reject all previous assumptions about "woman's place" in the home, what could we do? Is it possible to build non-sexist neighborhoods and design non-sexist cities? What would they be like?

Some countries have begun to develop new approaches to the needs of employed women. The Cuban Family Code of 1974 requires men to share housework and child care within the private home. The degree of its enforcement is uncertain, but in principle it aims at men's sharing what was formerly "women's work," which is essential to equality. The Family Code, however, does not remove work from the house, and relies upon private negotiation between husband and wife for its day-to-day enforcement. Men feign incompetence, especially in the area of cooking, with tactics familiar to any reader of Patricia Mainardi's essay, "The Politics of Housework," and the sexual stereotyping of paid jobs for women outside the home, in day-care centers for example, has not been successfully challenged.[19]

Another experimental approach involves the development of special housing facilities for employed women and their families. The builder Otto Fick first introduced such a program in Copenhagen in 1903. In later years it was encouraged in Sweden by Alva Myrdal and by the architects Sven Ivar Lind and Sven Markelius. Called "service houses" or "collective houses," such projects (figs. 1 and 2) provide child care and cooked food along with housing for employed women and their families.[20] Like a few similar projects in the USSR in the 1920s, they aim at offering services, either on a commercial basis or subsidized by the state, to replace formerly private "women's work" performed in the household. The Scandinavian solution does not sufficiently challenge male exclusion from domestic work, nor does it deal with households' changing needs over the life cycle, but it recognizes that it is important for environmental design to change.

Some additional projects in Europe extend the scope of the service house to include the provision of services for the larger community or

FIG. 1.—Sven Ivar Lind, Marieberg collective house, Stockholm, Sweden, 1944, plan of entrance (*entré*), restaurant (*restaurang*), and day nursery (*daghem*). (1) entrance hall; (2) doorman's office; (3) restaurant delivery room; (4) real estate office; (5) connecting walkway to Swedberg house; (6) restaurant anteroom; (7) main dining room; (8) small dining room; (9) restaurant kitchen; (10) to day nursery's baby carriage room; (11) day nursery's baby carriage room; (12) office for day nursery's directress; (13) to Wennerberg house's cycle garage.

19. Patricia Mainardi, "The Politics of Housework," in *Sisterhood Is Powerful*, ed. Robin Morgan (New York: Vintage Books, 1970). My discussion of the Cuban Family Code is based on a visit to Cuba in 1978; a general review is Carollee Bengelsdorf and Alice Hageman, "Emerging from Underdevelopment: Women and Work in Cuba," in *Capitalist Patriarchy and the Case for Socialist Feminism*, ed. Z. Eisenstein (New York: Monthly Review Press, 1979). Also see Geoffrey E. Fox, "Honor, Shame and Women's Liberation in Cuba: Views of Working-Class Emigré Men," in *Female and Male in Latin America*, ed. A. Pescatello (Pittsburgh: University of Pittsburgh Press, 1973).

20. Erwin Muhlestein, "Kollektives Wohnen gestern und heute," *Architese* 14 (1975): 3–23.

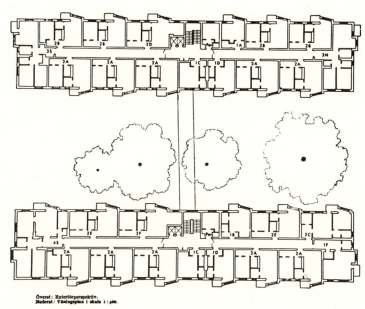

Överst: Exteriörperspektiv.
Nederst: Våningsplan i skala 1 : 400.

FIG. 2.—Plan of residential floors. Type 2A contains two rooms, bath, and kitchenette. Types 1C and 1D are efficiency units with bath and kitchenette. Type 4S includes four rooms with bath and full kitchen.

society. In the Steilshoop Project, in Hamburg, Germany, in the early 1970s, a group of parents and single people designed public housing with supporting services (fig. 3).[21] The project included a number of former mental patients as residents and therefore served as a halfway house for them, in addition to providing support services for the public-housing tenants who organized it. It suggests the extent to which current American residential stereotypes can be broken down—the sick, the aged, the unmarried can be integrated into new types of households and housing complexes, rather than segregated in separate projects.

Another recent project was created in London by Nina West Homes, a development group established in 1972, which has built or renovated over sixty-three units of housing on six sites for single parents. Children's play areas or day-care centers are integrated with the dwellings; in their Fiona House project the housing is designed to facilitate shared baby-sitting, and the day-care center is open to the neighborhood residents for a fee (fig. 4). Thus the single parents can find jobs as day-care workers and help the neighborhood's working parents as well.[22] What is most exciting here is the hint that home and work can be

21. This project relies on the "support structures" concept of John Habraken to provide flexible interior partitions and fixed mechanical core and structure.

22. "Bridge over Troubled Water," *Architects' Journal* (September 27, 1972), pp. 680–84; personal interview with Nina West, 1978.

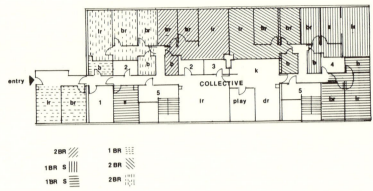

FIG. 3.—"Urbanes Wohnen" (urban living) Steilshoop, north of Hamburg, Germany, public housing for 206 tenants, designed by the tenant association in collaboration with Rolf Spille, 1970–73. Instead of seventy-two conventional units they built twenty multifamily units and two studios. Twenty-six mental patients were included in the project, of whom twenty-four recovered. Partial floor plan. Units include private bedrooms (br), living rooms (lr), and some studies (s). They share a collective living room, kitchen, dining room, and playroom. Each private apartment can be closed off from the collective space and each is different. (1) storage room; (2) closets; (3) wine cellar; (4) *buanderie;* (5) fire stair.

reunited on one site for some of the residents, and home and child-care services are reunited on one site for all of them.

In the United States, we have an even longer history of agitation for housing to reflect women's needs. In the late nineteenth century and early twentieth century there were dozens of projects by feminists, domestic scientists, and architects attempting to develop community services for private homes. By the late 1920s, few such experiments were still functioning.[23] In general, feminists of that era failed to recognize the problem of exploiting other women workers when providing services for those who could afford them. They also often failed to see men as responsible parents and workers in their attempts to socialize "women's" work. But feminist leaders had a very strong sense of the possibilities of neighborly cooperation among families and of the economic importance of "women's" work.

In addition, the United States has a long tradition of experimental utopian socialist communities building model towns, as well as the

23. Dolores Hayden, *A "Grand Domestic Revolution": Feminism, Socialism and the American Home, 1870–1930* (Cambridge, Mass.: M.I.T. Press, 1980); "Two Utopian Feminists and Their Campaigns for Kitchenless Houses," *Signs: Journal of Women in Culture and Society* 4, no. 2 (Winter 1979): 274–90; "Melusina Fay Peirce and Cooperative Housekeeping," *International Journal of Urban and Regional Research* 2 (1978): 404–20; "Challenging the American Domestic Ideal," and "Catharine Beecher and the Politics of Housework," in *Women in American Architecture,* ed. S. Torre (New York: Whitney Library of Design, 1977), pp. 22–39, 40–49; "Charlotte Perkins Gilman: Domestic Evolution or Domestic Revolution," *Radical History Review,* vol. 21 (Winter 1979–80), in press.

example of many communes and collectives established in the 1960s and 1970s which attempted to broaden conventional definitions of household and family.[24] While some communal groups, especially religious ones, have often demanded acceptance of a traditional sexual division of labor, others have attempted to make nurturing activities a responsibility of both women and men. It is important to draw on the examples of successful projects of all kinds, in seeking an image of a non-sexist settle-

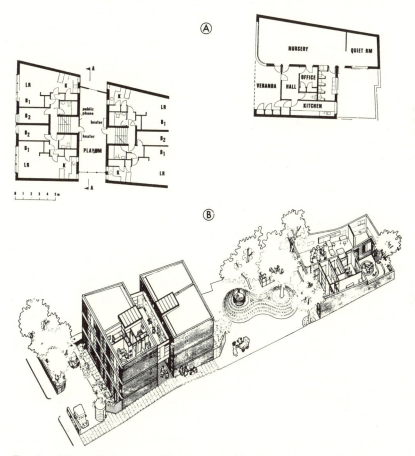

FIG. 4.—*A*, Fiona House, second-floor plan, main building, showing corridor used as playroom, with kitchen windows opening into it; first-floor plan, rear building, showing nursery school. *B*, Axonometric drawing, Fiona House, Nina West Homes, London 1972, designed by Sylvester Bone. Twelve two-bedroom units for divorced or separated mothers with additional outdoor play space, and neighborhood nursery school facility. Flats can be linked by intercom system to provide an audio substitute for baby-sitting.

24. Dolores Hayden, *Seven American Utopias: The Architecture of Communitarian Socialism, 1790–1975* (Cambridge, Mass.: M.I.T. Press, 1976), discusses historical examples and includes a discussion of communes of the 1960s and 1970s, "Edge City, Heart City, Drop City: Communal Building Today," pp. 320–47.

ment. Most employed women are not interested in taking themselves and their families to live in communal families, nor are they interested in having state bureaucracies run family life. They desire, not an end to private life altogether, but community services to support the private household. They also desire solutions which reinforce their economic independence and maximize their personal choices about child rearing and sociability.

What, then, would be the outline of a program for change in the United States? The task of reorganizing both home and work can only be accomplished by organizations of homemakers, women and men dedicated to making changes in the ways that Americans deal with private life and public responsibilities. They must be small, participatory organizations with members who can work together effectively. I propose calling such groups HOMES (Homemakers Organization for a More Egalitarian Society). Existing feminist groups, especially those providing shelters for battered wives and children, may wish to form HOMES to take over existing housing projects and develop services for residents as an extension of those offered by feminist counselors in the shelter. Existing organizations supporting cooperative ownership of housing may wish to form HOMES to extend their housing efforts in a feminist direction. A program broad enough to transform housework, housing, and residential neighborhoods must: (1) involve both men and women in the unpaid labor associated with housekeeping and child care on an equal basis; (2) involve both men and women in the paid labor force on an equal basis; (3) eliminate residential segregation by class, race, and age; (4) eliminate all federal, state, and local programs and laws which offer implicit or explicit reinforcement of the unpaid role of the female homemaker; (5) minimize unpaid domestic labor and wasteful energy consumption; (6) maximize real choices for households concerning recreation and sociability. While many partial reforms can support these goals, an incremental strategy cannot achieve them. I believe that the establishment of experimental residential centers, which in their architectural design and economic organization transcend traditional definitions of home, neighborhood, city, and workplace, will be necessary to make changes on this scale. These centers could be created through renovation of existing neighborhoods or through new construction.

Suppose forty households in a U.S. metropolitan area formed a HOMES group and that those households, in their composition, represented the social structure of the American population as a whole. Those forty households would include: seven single parents and their fourteen children (15 percent); sixteen two-worker couples and their twenty-four children (40 percent); thirteen one-worker couples and their twenty-six children (35 percent); and four single residents, some of them "displaced homemakers" (10 percent). The residents would include sixty-nine adults and sixty-four children. There would need to be forty private dwelling units, ranging in size from efficiency to three bedrooms, all with private fenced outdoor space. In addition to the private housing, the group would provide the following collective spaces and activities: (1) a day-care center with landscaped outdoor space, providing day care for forty children and after-school activities for sixty-four children; (2) a laundromat providing laundry service; (3) a kitchen providing lunches for the day-care center, take-out evening meals, and "meals-on-wheels" for elderly people in the neighborhood; (4) a grocery depot, connected to a local food cooperative; (5) a garage with two vans providing dial-a-ride service and meals-on-wheels; (6) a garden (or allotments) where some food can be grown; (7) a home help office providing helpers for the elderly, the sick, and employed parents whose children are sick. The use of all of these collective services should be voluntary; they would exist in addition to private dwelling units and private gardens.

To provide all of the above services, thirty-seven workers would be necessary: twenty day-care workers; three food-service workers; one grocery-depot worker; five home helpers; two drivers of service vehicles; two laundry workers; one maintenance worker; one gardener; two administrative staff. Some of these may be part-time workers, some full-time. Day care, food services, and elderly services could be organized as producers' cooperatives, and other workers could be employed by the housing cooperative as discussed below.

Because HOMES is not intended as an experiment in isolated community buildings but as an experiment in meeting employed women's needs in an urban area, its services should be available to the neighborhood in which the experiment is located. This will increase demand for the services and insure that the jobs are real ones. In addition, although residents of HOMES should have priority for the jobs, there will be many who choose outside work. So some local residents may take jobs within the experiment.

In creating and filling these jobs it will be important to avoid traditional sex stereotyping that would result from hiring only men as drivers, for example, or only women as food-service workers. Every effort should be made to break down separate categories of paid work for women and men, just as efforts should be made to recruit men who accept an equal share of domestic responsibilities as residents. A version of the Cuban Family Code should become part of the organization's platform.

Similarly, HOMES must not create a two-class society with residents outside the project making more money than residents in HOMES jobs that utilize some of their existing domestic skills. The HOMES jobs should be paid according to egalitarian rather than sex-stereotyped attitudes about skills and hours. These jobs must be all classified as skilled work rather than as unskilled or semiskilled at present, and offer full social security and health benefits, including adequate maternity leave, whether workers are part-time or full-time.

Many federal Housing and Urban Development programs support

the construction of nonprofit, low- and moderate-cost housing, including section 106b, section 202, and section 8. In addition, HUD section 213 funds are available to provide mortgage insurance for the conversion of existing housing of five or more units to housing cooperatives. HEW programs also fund special facilities such as day-care centers or meals-on-wheels for the elderly. In addition, HUD and HEW offer funds for demonstration projects which meet community needs in new ways.[25] Many trade unions, churches, and tenant cooperative organizations are active as nonprofit housing developers. A limited-equity housing cooperative offers the best basis for economic organization and control of both physical design and social policy by the residents.

Many knowledgeable nonprofit developers could aid community groups wishing to organize such projects, as could architects experienced in the design of housing cooperatives. What has not been attempted is the reintegration of work activities and collective services into housing cooperatives on a large enough scale to make a real difference to employed women. Feminists in trade unions where a majority of members are women may wish to consider building cooperative housing with services for their members. Other trade unions may wish to consider investing in such projects. Feminists in the co-op movement must make strong, clear demands to get such services from existing housing cooperatives, rather than simply go along with plans for conventional housing organized on a cooperative economic basis. Feminists outside the cooperative movement will find that cooperative organizational forms offer many possibilities for supporting their housing activities and other services to women. In addition, the recently established national Consumer Cooperative Bank has funds to support projects of all kinds which can be tied to cooperative housing.

In many areas, the rehabilitation of existing housing may be more desirable than new construction. The suburban housing stock in the United States must be dealt with effectively. A little bit of it is of architectural quality sufficient to deserve preservation; most of it can be aesthetically improved by the physical evidence of more intense social activity. To replace empty front lawns without sidewalks, neighbors can create blocks where single units are converted to multiple units; interior land is pooled to create a parklike setting at the center of the block; front and side lawns are fenced to make private outdoor spaces; pedestrian paths and sidewalks are created to link all units with the central open space; and some private porches, garages, tool sheds, utility rooms, and family rooms are converted to community facilities such as children's play areas, dial-a-ride garages, and laundries.

Figure 5*A* shows a typical bleak suburban block of thirteen houses,

25. I am indebted to Geraldine Kennedy and Sally Kratz, whose unpublished papers, "Toward Financing Cooperative Housing," and "Social Assistance Programs Whose Funds Could Be Redirected to Collective Services," were prepared for my UCLA graduate seminar in spring 1979.

constructed by speculators at different times, where about four acres are divided into plots of one-fourth to one-half acre each. Thirteen driveways are used by twenty-six cars; ten garden sheds, ten swings, thirteen lawn mowers, thirteen outdoor dining tables, begin to suggest the wasteful duplication of existing amenities. Yet despite the available land there are no transitions between public streets and these private homes. Space is either strictly private or strictly public. Figure 6*A* shows a typical one-family house of 1,400 square feet on this block. With three bedrooms

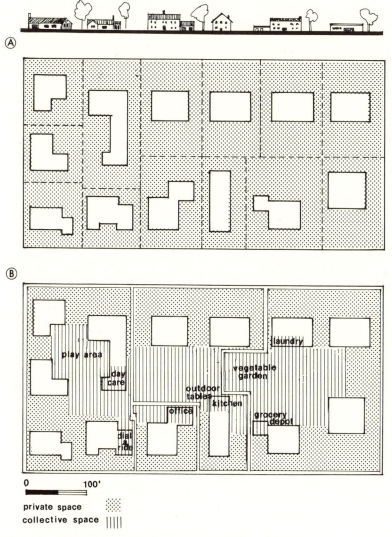

Fig. 5.—*A*, Suburban neighborhood, block plan. *B*, Proposed HOMES revitalization, same suburban block with new common space and facilities.

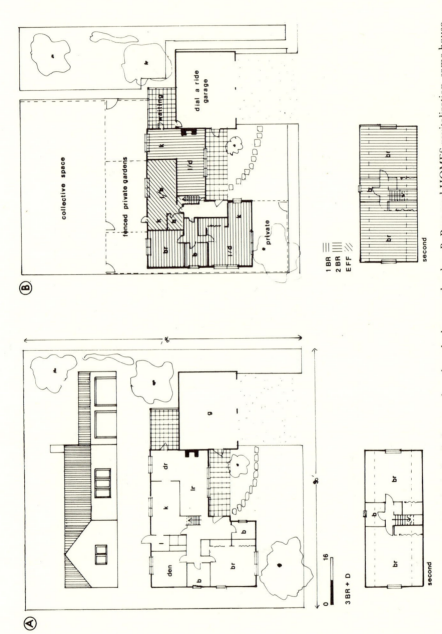

FIG. 6.—A, Suburban single-family house, plan, three bedrooms plus den. B, Proposed HOMES revitalization, same house converted to three units (two bedroom, one bedroom, and efficiency), plus dial-a-ride garage and collective outdoor space.

and den, two-and-a-half baths, laundry room, two porches, and a two-car garage, it was constructed in the 1950s at the height of the "feminine mystique."

To convert this whole block and the housing on it to more efficient and sociable uses, one has to define a zone of greater activity at the heart of the block, taking a total of one and one half to two acres for collective use (fig. 5B). Essentially, this means turning the block inside out. The Radburn plan, developed by Henry Wright and Clarence Stein in the late 1920s, delineated this principle very clearly as correct land use in "the motor age," with cars segregated from residents' green spaces, especially spaces for children. In Radburn, New Jersey, and in the Baldwin Hills district of Los Angeles, California, Wright and Stein achieved remarkably luxurious results (at a density of about seven units to the acre) by this method, since their multiple-unit housing always bordered a lush parkland without any automobile traffic. The Baldwin Hills project demonstrates this success most dramatically, but a revitalized suburban block with lots as small as one-fourth acre can be reorganized to yield something of this same effect.[26] In this case, social amenities are added to aesthetic ones as the interior park is designed to accommodate community day care, a garden for growing vegetables, some picnic tables, a playground where swings and slides are grouped, a grocery depot connected to a larger neighborhood food cooperative, and a dial-a-ride garage.

Large single-family houses can be remodeled quite easily to become duplexes and triplexes, despite the "open plans" of the 1950s and 1960s popularized by many developers. The house in figure 6A becomes, in figure 6B, a triplex, with a two-bedroom unit (linked to a community garage); a one-bedroom unit; and an efficiency unit (for a single person or elderly person). All three units are shown with private enclosed gardens. The three units share a front porch and entry hall. There is still enough land to give about two-fifths of the original lot to the community. Particularly striking is the way in which existing spaces such as back porches or garages lend themselves to conversion to social areas or community services. Three former private garages out of thirteen might be given over to collective uses—one as a central office for the whole block, one as a grocery depot, and one as a dial-a-ride garage. Is it possible to have only twenty cars (in ten garages) and two vans for twenty-six units in a rehabilitated block? Assuming that some residents switch from outside employment to working within the block, and that for all residents, neighborhood shopping trips are cut in half by the presence of day care, groceries, laundry, and cooked food on the block, as well as aided by the presence of some new collective transportation, this might be done.

26. See also the successful experience of Zurich, described in Hans Wirz, "Back Yard Rehab: Urban Microcosm Rediscovered," *Urban Innovation Abroad* 3 (July 1979): 2–3.

What about neighbors who are not interested in such a scheme? Depending on the configuration of lots, it is possible to begin such a plan with as few as three or four houses. In Berkeley, California, where neighbors on Derby Street joined their backyards and created a cooperative day-care center, one absentee landlord refused to join—his entire property is fenced in and the community space flows around it without difficulty. Of course, present zoning laws must be changed, or variances obtained, for the conversion of single-family houses into duplexes and triplexes and the introduction of any sort of commercial activities into a residential block. However, a community group that is able to organize or acquire at least five units could become a HUD housing cooperative, with a nonprofit corporation owning all land and with producers' cooperatives running the small community services. With a coherent plan for an entire block, variances could be obtained much more easily than on a lot-by-lot basis. One can also imagine organizations which run halfway houses—for ex–mental patients, or runaway teenagers, or battered women—integrating their activities into such a block plan, with an entire building for their activities. Such groups often find it difficult to achieve the supportive neighborhood context such a block organization would offer.

I believe that attacking the conventional division between public and private space should become a socialist and feminist priority in the 1980s. Women must transform the sexual division of domestic labor, the privatized economic basis of domestic work, and the spatial separation of homes and workplaces in the built environment if they are to be equal members of society. The experiments I propose are an attempt to unite the best features of past and present reforms in our own society and others, with some of the existing social services available in the United States today. I would like to see several demonstration HOMES begun, some involving new construction following the program I have laid out, others involving the rehabilitation of suburban blocks. If the first few experimental projects are successful, homemakers across the United States will want to obtain day-care, food, and laundry services at a reasonable price, as well as better wages, more flexible working conditions, and more suitable housing. When all homemakers recognize that they are struggling against both gender stereotypes and wage discrimination, when they see that social, economic, and environmental changes are necessary to overcome these conditions, they will no longer tolerate housing and cities, designed around the principles of another era, that proclaim that "a woman's place is in the home."

School of Architecture and Urban Planning
University of California, Los Angeles

Review Essay

Women in the Urban Environment

Gerda R. Wekerle

Within the last five years, the issues of women in urban settings have come to the fore, receiving long overdue attention. Academics and policymakers, both of whom have been loathe to admit that there even was a perspective on urban problems unique to women, are not only concerning themselves with these problems but also are realizing that the solutions will benefit both women as a special group and the society as a whole.

Today, interest in women and the urban environment is at an all-time high.[1] Since the first review of the field, *Women, Planning and Change,* appeared in 1974 and the last review essay in *Signs* in 1976,[2] there has been an explosion of research and writing about women and urban environments by scholars in half a dozen disciplines and by government agencies in several countries. From the situation five years ago, when it seemed impossible to find sufficient material to launch a one-term course or compile an edited book, the current work is astounding.

I would like to thank Brent Rutherford and William Michelson for their detailed comments on a draft of this essay. Without the encouragement and support of Slade Lander, Dolores Hayden, and Catharine Stimpson, this essay would not have been written.

1. This review does not cover the growing body of research on women and urbanization which is summarized in an annotated bibliography, Hasia R. Diner, *Women and Urban Society—a Guide to Information Guide Series* (Detroit: Gale Research Co., 1979).

2. Karen Hapgood and Judith Getzels, eds., *Women, Planning and Change* (Chicago: American Society of Planning Officials, 1974); Dolores Hayden and Gwendolyn Wright, "Architecture and Urban Planning," *Signs: Journal of Women in Culture and Society* 1 (Spring 1976): 923–33.

There have been several review essays and books, a number of books in progress, special issues of urban and women's journals, many articles, and some annotated bibliographies. In addition, the number of organizations and networks of women in the planning and design professions has grown by leaps and bounds (see Appendix). This review essay attempts to provide a guide to the scattered literature in this rapidly growing field—outlining the basic themes, some of the gaps, and directions for future work.

There is no central focus to the work on women and the urban environment: it is as broad and as eclectic as the fields of urban studies and planning. Research is being done in several disciplines—urban and architectural history, urban geography, urban sociology, economics, political science, planning, architecture, and appropriate technology. Much of this work is pioneering—the first of its kind in the field—posing an initial definition of the problem, developing a perspective, presenting a case study, or collecting facts to document the existence of a problem. There are few comparative studies, longitudinal studies, or studies which are able to build on a body of previous work. Much of the work is done independently, by people working in isolation from one another—inevitable in a "field" which is so large and where the numbers of scholars is so small.

Integration of the rapidly growing body of work on women in the urban environment and the development of theories and paradigms to explain women's urban experience are still far in the future. Three dominant paradigms (either used separately or in combination) guide the current work reviewed in this essay: (1) there is an emphasis on the dichotomy between private and public spheres under industrial capitalism, the importance of the private world of the family, and the necessity of integrating the private/personal and public/political (this is often the focus of research by historians, architects, and sociologists); (2) the environment and behavior paradigm emphasizes the "fit" between women's activities and the environments of home, neighborhood, and city and how users of environments might participate more fully in their planning and design (empirical research has usually come from sociologists, environmental psychologists, planners, and architects); (3) the environmental equity model focuses primarily on women's right to equal access to public goods and services such as transportation, housing, and social services (this includes work by geographers, sociologists, and urban activists and guides government studies and programs designed to document discrimination and redress grievances).

The Private-Public Dichotomy

A dominant paradigm in the women's studies literature is the segregation of male and female roles and how this is inextricably linked with women's isolation within the private sphere of the family and men's dominance in the public world of work and politics. Scholars such as Oakley, Zaretsky, and Boulding have developed a historical analysis of the roots of the privatization of family life within capitalist society and the shrinkage of women's realm to the home.[3]

Boulding argues that the seclusion of women in the home was a direct result of the growth of urbanism.[4] In the process of urbanization women's work was removed from the communal work spaces of the village and relegated to the private space of the individual home. The loss was significant since communications networks and political skills had developed in these communal spaces and were prevented from emerging when women's work became isolated in the home.[5]

The focus of much current work is on the relations of reproduction. Detailed empirical studies of women's unpaid household work and childcare within the home show the severe time constraints under which many women are forced to operate.[6] Women in the paid labor force are characterized as multiple job holders with limited opportunities for participation in the wider public world. The major conclusion of much of this work is that changing the gender-based division of labor in the home is the key to breaking down the female-dominated domestic sphere and a male-dominated public sphere.[7] But there is wide agreement that this will only come about indirectly through changes in the wider social world—changes in the hours of work, the availability and acceptability of part-time work, and an increasing network of support services and alternatives to the isolated nuclear family.

Housework and the Single-Family Home

A new contribution to the debate about the segregation of the private and public spheres comes from architectural historians and urbanists

3. Ann Oakley, *Woman's Work: The Housewife, Past and Present* (New York: Vintage Books, 1974); Eli Zaretsky, *Capitalism, the Family and Personal Life* (New York: Harper Colophon, 1976); Elise Boulding, *The Underside of History: A View of Women through Time* (Boulder, Colo.: Westview Press, 1976).

4. Elise Boulding, *Women in the Twentieth Century World* (New York: Sage Books, 1977), p. 41.

5. The decline of women's communal work and increasing isolation in apartments is described by Donna Gabaccia, "Housing and Household Work: Sicily and New York, 1890–1910" (paper presented at a conference on Italian Immigrants in North America, Ontario Institute of Studies in Education, Toronto, November 1977).

6. Alexander Szalai, *The Use of Time* (The Hague: Mouton, 1972); Sara F. Berk, "The Household as Workplace: Wives, Husbands and Children," in *New Space for Women,* ed. Gerda R. Wekerle, Rebecca Peterson, and David Morley (Boulder, Colo.: Westview Press, 1980); Oakley.

7. Jessie Bernard, *The Future of Motherhood* (New York: Penguin, 1975); Nona Glazer and Helen Youngelson Waehrer, eds., "Introduction," in *Women in a Man-made World,* 2d ed. (Chicago: Rand McNally College Publishing, 1977); Rosemary Ruether, "Toward New

who focus on its spatial expression in the physical design and planning of the home, neighborhood, and city. Other researchers had treated these environments as a given—a context within which women operate, but not a factor which might independently affect women's opportunities.

Scholars are beginning to uncover some of the historical roots of the associations in our culture among the single-family house, the nuclear family, women's roles, and industrial capitalism. Hayden and Wright[8] review the recent historical literature on changes in housing form, domestic technology, and women's attitudes to their domestic roles. Wright examines the relationship between the social reform movement, the rise of home economics, and the role of women as household consumers.[9] She shows that the use of home appliances and the increasing privatization of services within the home was encouraged to create a new market for the output of industry and effectively eliminated neighborhood-based services to the home. Hayden discusses how women became increasingly trapped in the role of caretaker of the home with the emergence of the new field of domestic economy and the emphasis on efficient and professionalized home management.[10] Wright provides plans of "model" domestic environments from the "efficient" labor-saving home of the early twentieth century to the functional homes of the World War II era.[11]

Feminist architects argue that architects and builders have constructed homes which unnecessarily isolate women in the home and even increase household work through poor design.[12] Rock, Torre, and Wright point out that homes are usually not designed to accommodate the sharing of household tasks; they suggest design changes which would provide private space outside the kitchen for women and encourage a greater sharing of domestic work. Architects Birkby and Weisman

Solutions—Working Women and the Male Workday," *Christianity and Crisis* 37 (February 1977): 3–8.

8. Dolores Hayden, *A Grand Domestic Revolution: American Visions of Household Liberation* (Cambridge, Mass.: M.I.T. Press, 1980); Gwendolyn Wright, *Moralism and the Model Home: Domestic Architecture and Cultural Conflict in Chicago 1873–1913* (Chicago: University of Chicago Press, 1980).

9. Gwendolyn Wright, "Sweet and Clean: The Domestic Landscape in the Progressive Era," *Landscape* 10 (October 1975): 38–43.

10. Dolores Hayden, "Catharine Beecher and the Politics of Housework," in *Women in American Architecture: A Historic and Contemporary Perspective,* ed. Susana Torre (New York: Watson Guptill Publications, 1977).

11. Gwendolyn Wright, "The Model Domestic Environment: Icon or Option?" in Torre.

12. Maureen Taylor, "The Official View of the Female User," *Architectural Design* 45 (August 1975): 471–72; Cynthia Rock, Susana Torre, and Gwendolyn Wright, "The Appropriation of the House, Changes in Design and Concepts of Domesticity," in Wekerle et al.; Susana Torre, Cynthia Rock, and Gwendolyn Wright, "Rethinking Closets, Kitchens, and Other Forgotten Spaces," *Ms* 6 (December 1977): 54–55; Hayden and Wright (n. 8 above).

have collected drawings of women's "fantasy environments," many of which are based on women's familiarity with household objects and show the great gap between existing housing design and what women feel they need.[13]

While feminist architects have focused new attention on how the North American obsession with the single-family house works to keep women in the home, it is still not clear whether home design is an independent factor affecting the amount of housework that is done and who does it. From Michelson's research we know that high-rise apartment dwellers spend less time on housework than do residents of single-family homes.[14] However, these differences may be due to life-style or other characteristics of residents and are not necessarily attributable to the design. Careful empirical evaluations of alternative housing designs to assess their effects on household labor and the sharing of household tasks are still needed.

The Industrialization of Housework

Proposals to industrialize housework have long been popular and involve shifting some of the tasks which tie women to the home into the public sector of paid labor. Economists from Engels to Galbraith have argued that the privatization of services within the home is antithetical to women's emancipation.[15] Galbraith points out that the increase in women's labor force participation has increased the market for external services such as child care, dry-cleaning services, and especially fast food, and replaced wife-operated individual services in the home. He predicts further growth in such services and suggests that this is a solution to women's confinement within the domestic sphere.

But this is a limited solution, since the high cost of services in the marketplace excludes many of the women who are most pressed for time and need relief. Besides, industrializing some household tasks does not necessarily promote any fundamental changes in women's prime responsibility for the domestic sphere. It maintains (and even expands) the consumer role of the nuclear family and does not challenge either existing sex roles within the family or the sanctity of the single-family house. To free women from their responsibilities as primary caretakers of the home, it is necessary to restructure the whole network of services to the home and family now provided by schools, stores, public utilities, and

13. Noel Phyllis Birkby and Leslie Kanes Weisman, "A Woman Built Environment—Constructive Fantasies," *Quest* 2 (Summer 1975): 7–18, "Women's Fantasy Environments—Notes on a Project in Process," *Heresies* 2 (May 1977): 116–17.

14. William Michelson, *Environmental Choice, Human Behavior and Residential Satisfaction* (New York: Oxford University Press, 1977).

15. Frederick Engels, *The Origins of the Family, Private Property, and the State* (Chicago: Charles H. Kerr & Co., 1902); John Kenneth Galbraith, *Economics and the Public Purpose* (Boston: Houghton Mifflin Co., 1973).

service people which operate on a 9:00–5:00 basis and assume a full-time housewife in the home. There has been little discussion on how such basic changes might be made. Nona Glazer and her colleagues have proposed an ingenious solution which addresses some of the major issues.[16] They suggest the establishment of federally funded neighborhood service houses called Neighbors in Community Helping Environments (NICHE) to provide some of the services now carried out by a full-time person in the home: supervising children's play and homework, visiting sick children, providing access to repair and delivery people, preparing hot meals for families to take home with them. A similar service has been institutionalized in Sweden, where a position called "Samaritan" is supplied and paid for by the municipality. The Samaritan provides extra support to the sick and the homebound— minding sick children when parents are at work; visiting homebound elderly once a week, cleaning for them, and leaving them hot food. What is significant about the Samaritan role and the NICHE proposal is the recognition that the community holds some responsibility to support people in their daily functioning (not just for emergencies) whose multiple roles prove too much of a burden. Proposals merely to industrialize housework, on the other hand, throw all the costs on the individual nuclear family.

The Collectivization of Housework

A third response to women's isolated work within the home are proposals for the collectivization of housework. These represent a challenge both to the private home and to the nuclear family, since they attempt to eliminate some of the distinctions between the private and public realms by transforming the private world of housework into a new "communal" sector. Groundbreaking research has been done by architect and historian Dolores Hayden, who has unearthed a feminist tradition of home design and community planning which has gone unrecognized in the design professions. Hayden's research on nineteenth and early twentieth century communitarian experiments shows that domestic architecture and community planning were deliberately used to free women from isolated domestic drudgery.[17] Hayden concludes that one of the major achievements of these movements was to end the

16. Nona Glazer, Linda Majka, Joan Acker, and Christine Bose, "The Homemaker, the Family, and Employment: Some Interrelationships," mimeographed (prepared for American Women in a Full Employment Economy. A compendium for the Use of the Joint Economic Committee of Congress, 1976).

17. Hayden, *A Grand Domestic Revolution,* "Redesigning the Domestic Workplace," *Chrysalis* 1 (1977): 19–29, "Challenging the American Domestic Ideal," in Torre, "Melusina Fay Peirce and Cooperative Housekeeping," *International Journal of Urban and Regional Research* 2 (October 1978): 404–20, and "Two Utopian Feminists and Their Campaigns for Kitchenless Houses," *Signs: Journal of Women in Culture and Society* 4, no. 2 (Winter 1978): 274–90.

isolation of the housewife by organizing household tasks such as cooking, cleaning, and child care collectively and defining housework as a concern of the total community. Further, case studies of collective housekeeping experiments in American communities in the nineteenth century provide models for alternatives in contemporary housing design and community planning which are sorely needed.

There is a growing interest in collective housing and housekeeping arrangements as more women work outside the home and the number of single parents and single-person households increases. Besides turning to historical models, North Americans have long been intrigued by Scandinavian housing projects which provide a wide range of collective services to support family life. Göran Lindberg analyzes the initial growth, decline, and new interest in Swedish service houses which provide such collective facilities as a common central kitchen, communal dining hall, child care, and assistance for minor illnesses.[18] Ellen Perry Berkeley describes two services houses she visited as being especially attractive to single parents because of available day-care and collective-food services.[19] In some Danish housing projects, expanded services to replace the household labor of women are routinely provided, and the projects designed as collectives have been sold out while others have stood empty.[20]

Swedish service houses and Danish housing projects with services for families were developed to emancipate women from household tasks and to provide a support system for family life. However, there is little information on how these arrangements actually work for women— whether they decrease women's home responsibilities and encourage participation in the paid labor force and wider public sphere.[21] What is needed is some cross-national research which examines the inter-relationships between housing design, community social services, housework, and role sharing within the home and involves an inter-disciplinary group of scholars—including historians, architects, sociologists, and urban planners. Particularly since proposals for new forms of housing and neighborhood designs, such as that developed by Hayden in this volume, are seen by feminists as increasingly necessary to emancipate women from isolation in the home, there is need to examine more closely existing options in other countries.

18. Göran Lindberg, "Arguments for Studying Collective Houses" (paper presented at the World Congress of Sociology, Uppsala, 1978).

19. Ellen Perry Berkeley, "The Swedish Servicehus," *Architecture Plus* 1 (May 1973): 56–59.

20. Alfred J. Kahn and Sheila B. Kamerman, *Not for the Poor Alone: European Social Services* (Philadelphia: Temple University Press, 1975); Allen Konya and Karl Agehenk, "Danish Community Housing," *Architects Journal* 161 (April 21, 1975): 717–32.

21. When queried, architect Kirsten Knudsen, who has worked on Danish community housing projects and is active in an organization of Danish women architects, responded that they know very little about the effects of different designs and services on women.

Women in Public Space

Scholars using the private-public paradigm have focused primarily on the private sphere and the circumstances that keep women there. Little attention has been directed to the nature of the public environment—especially the public places and facilities of the city and how they inhibit or encourage women's participation in the urban public realm. Elise Boulding's macrohistory, *The Underside of History,*[22] documents women's changing relationship to the private and public spheres and the diminution of women's public roles with the industrial revolution and urbanization. This is an exception. On the whole, discussions of public behavior tend to ignore women as separate actors. For example, Richard Sennett's book, *The Fall of Public Man,*[23] is aptly titled—women's public role is hardly discussed. Sennett argues that "public" came to mean a life passed outside the family and that the growth of public spaces for men occurred at the same time as the home was newly defined as a refuge from the world. Women were identified with the family—the "weaker" sex, not strong enough to associate with strangers in the coffee houses, cafés, restaurants, clubs, and pedestrian parks which emerged in the eighteenth century. In the nineteenth century the public sphere was defined as an immoral domain where women were at risk, and their mere presence in public spaces provoked anger and violence.

This situation continues today. In "The City: Off-Limits to Women,"[24] two French urbanists argue that, for women, the city consists of an endless series of "keep-out" signs. Women are still not accepted in many urban public spaces: lounging in cafés, eating alone in restaurants, strolling in woods or public parks. Little research has been done on women's actual usage of public space and facilities, how women are given the message that they are "out of place," the kinds of changes that would make women feel both entitled to use and socially accepted in using the urban public environment.[25]

In most major North American cities, a new urban phenomenon is the emergence of a network of women's spaces—women's buildings,

22. See n. 4 above.

23. Richard Sennett, *The Fall of Public Man: On the Social Psychology of Capitalism* (New York: Vintage Books, 1974).

24. Claude Enjeu and Joana Savé, "The City: Off-Limits to Women," *Liberation* 8 (July–August 1974): 9–15. In "Skyscraper Seduction—Skyscraper Rape," *Heresies* 2 (May 1977): 108–15, Dolores Hayden analyzes the development of a high-rise city which benefits the male corporate structure while workers and other residents pay most of the costs.

25. Women's restricted territory is often a rational response to the fear of sexual assault. An analysis of how this limits women's mobility is provided by Rebecca Dreis, "Innovations in Transportation for Women" (master's research paper, Department of Sociology, University of California, Santa Barbara, Spring 1978). Dreis points out that warnings about the dangers to women in public places are frequent in the rape-prevention literature, and these reinforce the image that the urban environment is a dangerous place for women.

coffee shops, bookstores, bars, and restaurants—which represent an attempt by the women's community to provide an alternative but protected public environment for women. While many women's facilities originated in small groups meeting in members' homes, a major step forward in the seventies has been to make these activities public. This is exemplified by the Los Angeles Woman's Building which has grown from a small group of feminist artists meeting together to a public center for women's culture serving the whole metropolitan area.[26] Just as coffee shops and pubs were important as gathering places and sources of information to men in the eighteenth century, today women's spaces and services are vital in providing opportunities for the geographically scattered women's community to meet, socialize, exchange new ideas, and to move out of the restricted space of the home.[27]

Little scholarly attention has been directed to the study of women's spaces and services. There is little concrete data on who uses these services or whether women's services are more effective in meeting women's needs than public services. Since many women's services have been organized along feminist principles of nonhierarchical decision making and collective responsibility, they provide potential models for the reorganization and humanization of the workplace and deserve detailed study.[28] Finally, there is the question of whether it is necessary (or desirable) to create segregated female environments or whether women might not be better served by applying pressures to make the urban public environment more accessible to all women. Elise Boulding argues for men and women sharing public space on the grounds that women will have a broader training and a wider range of role models than if the spaces of women were more restricted.[29]

Another issue is the extraordinarily high cost to women of trying to build and maintain a parallel urban service structure based on volunteer labor and little money at the same time as they are required to pay for public services which do not adequately meet their needs. As social service budgets are slashed, the survival of many women's services which have become standard in American cities, such as women's health clinics, is threatened. A key question for the eighties is the kind of strategies that women should use to prevent the dismantling of services that have been the successes of the women's movement in the last two decades. Greater

26. Sheila Levrant de Bretteville, "The Los Angeles Woman's Building: A Public Center for Women's Culture," in Wekerle, Peterson, and Morley (n. 6 above).

27. Bonnie Loyd, "Community in California," *California Geographer* 17 (1977): 73–81; Bonnie Loyd and Lester Rowntree, "Radical Feminists and Gay Men in San Francisco: Social Space in Dispersed Communities," in *An Invitation to Geography,* ed. David A. Lanegran and Risa Palm, 2d ed. (New York: McGraw-Hill Book Co., 1978).

28. An extended discussion of women's innovations in the urban environment is found in "Introduction," in Wekerle, Peterson, and Morley.

29. Boulding, *Women in the Twentieth Century World,* p. 26.

attention to organizational analysis and intervention strategies as these apply to women's institutions is needed.

The Fit between the Urban Environment and Women's Changing Roles

The second paradigm guiding research on women and the urban environment is derived from the multidisciplinary field of environment and behavior.[30] Women have only recently been the subjects of these studies, and the range of women and environments studies is still limited.[31] The most surprising results of the research to date are the findings which show that women's experience of the urban environment is substantially different from men's and that the structure of current land uses and planning practices create serious disadvantages for urban women.

Women and Suburbia

The women and environment studies have focused primarily on two related areas: housing and community planning. Most of the work has examined one specific environment—suburban low-density communities, environments which create particularly high costs for women due to the reliance on the single-family house, the segregation of land uses, and the absence of collective services. Fava's paper reviews the literature on suburbia and demonstrates how the suburban environment confines women in ways it does not confine men.[32] Fava also examines the costs of suburban residence to older women, teenagers, blacks, and minority women. She discusses two trends—the growing heterogeneity of suburban residents and the decentralization of jobs and their potential impact on women's lives.[33]

Several recent empirical studies have focused specifically on the

30. J. Douglas Porteous, *Environment and Behavior* (New York: Addison-Wesley Publishing Co., 1977); David Popenoe, *The Suburban Environment: Sweden and the United States* (Chicago: University of Chicago Press, 1977); William Michelson, *Man and His Urban Environment* (New York: Addison-Wesley Publishing Co., 1970).

31. See Rebecca Peterson, Gerda Wekerle, and David Morley, "Women and Environments: An Overview of an Emerging Field," *Environment and Behavior* 10 (December 1978): 511–34, for a more detailed discussion of how this perspective can be applied to women.

32. Sylvia F. Fava, "Women's Place in the New Suburbia," in Wekerle, Peterson, and Morley.

33. Janet L. Abu-Lughod's "Designing a City for All," in Hapgood and Getzels (n. 2 above), further explores the trend to exurban living where women and children are confined in bedroom suburbs while men keep city apartments and are rarely home.

costs and benefits to women of living in low-density environments.[34] What is new about this work is that, for the first time, data have been collected on men and women living in the same household, thus allowing for some comparisons of reactions to living space and neighborhood rather than assuming that the experience of one family member represents that of the whole family.

The results have been surprising. Studies by Michelson in Toronto and Saegert and Winkel in the New York City area show that men gain most from living in suburban neighborhoods; women have the most to lose. Michelson finds that after a move to suburbia women feel more alone and more isolated. In contrast, when families move to a downtown apartment a woman gains most: her travel time declines and the family makes greater use of the public and cultural facilities of the city. Saegert and Winkel's study shows similar results in another city.

Popenoe's book, *The Suburban Environment: Sweden and the United States,* presents some alternatives to women's experience of isolation and frustration in the typical North American suburb. In comparing the lives of women, children, and the elderly in a typical American and Swedish suburb, he finds that the Swedish suburb encourages women to hold jobs. Women's roles outside the home are supported by community planning and the provision of a wide range of social services. He con-

34. William Michelson, "The Place of Time in the Longitudinal Evaluation of Spatial Structures by Women" (Toronto: University of Toronto, Center for Urban and Community Studies, 1973), and *Environmental Choice* (n. 14 above); Susan Saegert and Gary Winkel, "The Home: A Critical Problem for Changing Sex Roles," in Wekerle, Peterson, and Morley. For a review of the literature on men's relationship to domestic space, see Jerome Tagnoli, "Men's Relationship with Domestic Space" (paper presented at the Environmental Design Research Association, Tucson, 1978). Other studies of women in suburbia which reinforce the view that women suffer real deprivation in this environment include Donald N. Rothblatt, Daniel J. Garr, and Jo Sprague, eds., *The Suburban Environment and Women* (New York: Praeger Publishers, 1979); Suzanne Keller, "Women in a Planned Community," Land Policy Roundtable Basic Concept Series, no. 10 (Cambridge, Mass.: Lincoln Institute of Land Policy, 1978); Gerda R. Wekerle and Novia Carter, "Urban Sprawl: The Price Women Pay," *Branching Out—Canadian Magazine for Women* 5 (August 1978): 13–14; Karla Werner, "Swedish Women in Single Family Housing," in Wekerle et al. There has been considerable research on women in Australian and New Zealand suburbs. This includes the fictional account, Wendy Sarkissian, "Planning as If Women Mattered: The Story of Brown Hills," *Makara* 3 (Fall 1978): 9–12; research and planning reports, Wendy Sarkissian, "Planning as Though Women Mattered," *Council and Community* 1 (July 1977): 12–14; Marilyn Reynolds and Bonny Stephanie, "Woman's World: Houses and Suburbs" (Auckland: Society for Research on Women in New Zealand, 1976); and Antoinette Logan, "Decentralists Forget Jobs for the Girls," *Royal Australian Planning Institute Journal* 14 (July/October 1976): 55–59; also, C. Donaldson Spagnoletti, *Women and Planning,* Library Bibliography, no. 20 (Adelaide: South Australian Housing Trust, 1974), provides a comprehensive listing. The suburban environment taken to its extreme is described in two articles examining women's isolation and deprivation in resource towns: Claire Williams, "Working Class Women in an Australian Mining Town," *Hecate* 2 (January 1976): 7–20, and "Northern British Columbia Women's Task Force Report on Single Industry Resource Towns," mimeographed (Vancouver: Women's Research Center, 1977).

cludes that American suburbs must be urbanized—built to higher densities providing a wider range of housing and services and better access to public transit if they are to adequately meet the needs of women, children, and the elderly.

Of the large body of literature on women in suburbia, the overwhelming impression is that women have been the passive victims of post–World War II suburban development, forced to subordinate their own interests to those of husbands and children. This interpretation is too simplistic, for women, as well as men, share the American dream of homeownership and have willingly chosen suburban locations.[35] These studies make apparent the narrow range of environmental alternatives available to most people and the forced choice between access to jobs or safety in the city and an environment suitable for child rearing but lacking in stimulation for adults in the suburbs. A wider range of options is needed, and particularly community designs which acknowledge women's labor force participation and support it.

Women in the City

We know far less about women living in the city that we do about suburban women. A report by economists Gerard and McCormick on "The Impact of Women on the Economy of New York City" shows that the city attracts career women because of a concentration of jobs in which women are highly paid and appropriate services like apartments and public transportation.[36] But women have also been hardest hit by the suburbanization of jobs, and the total number of women employed in New York City has declined in the seventies. In part, this is due to the increase in the numbers of poor and minority women living in the city. (More than 35 percent of the families living in New York City are single women or women heads of families, and approximately half of the families headed by women receive payments through the aid to dependent children program.) New York City is often viewed as a bellwether for other cities, and the increasing concentration in inner-city neighborhoods of powerless and poor women with a need for a high level of social services, in an impoverished city whose economy is dominated by large multinational corporations, is cause for concern. Frances Fox Piven argues that the fundamental oppression of center-city women is their extreme poverty and a need for very basic services: decent housing; clean, safe, streets; parks; schools; shopping facilities; and local jobs.[37]

35. Saegert and Winkel and Keller emphasize the value conflicts faced by women in making housing choices.

36. Karen Gerard and Mary McCormick, *The Impact of Women on the Economy of New York City* (New York: Chase Manhattan Bank, 1978).

37. Frances Fox Piven, "Planning for Women in the Central City," in Hapgood and Getzels.

Carol Brown examines the environmental supports needed by mother-led families to live independent lives.[38] She finds that neighborhoods labeled "disorganized" and declining by planners often provide precisely the kinds of services that divorced mothers need: jobs, welfare services, child care, shopping, apartment houses, and public transportation. In contrast to the family-oriented suburbs, there is also a greater acceptance of single-parent families and their life-styles. Stamp describes a similar community in Toronto where divorced mothers create supportive neighborhood networks around their own and their children's needs. Milne's study of the housing needs of single parents in Australia also supports the view that older city neighborhoods often provide the most supportive environments for these families.[39]

In contrast to the many books which chronicle men's subcultures and daily lives in urban neighborhoods,[40] there are few detailed case studies of women living in urban settings which might provide planners and designers with information for creating more responsive environments for women. Lyn Lofland analyzes this gap in the urban literature and concludes that predominately male ethnographers have invariably chosen to study the public life of ethnic and working-class communities, where women's roles were private and highly circumscribed.[41] Further, she suggests that researchers have been able to obtain funding for studies of deviants and urban troublemakers, and since women rarely fell into either category they were excluded. Now that women are becoming urban troublemakers, leading tenant strikes and squatters takeovers, especially in the United Kingdom, their struggles and contributions to urban social movements have been chronicled in several recent books.[42]

The exception to the great gap in behavioral studies of women's urban experience is the large body of work on the elderly, many of whom are women. Geographers have studied the experience of old people living in different urban neighborhoods.[43] There are many

38. Carol A. Brown, "Spatial Inequality and Divorced Mothers" (paper presented at the American Sociological Association, San Francisco, 1978).

39. Judy Stamp, "Toward Supportive Neighborhoods: Women's Role in Changing the Segregated City," in Wekerle et al.; Phillipa Milne, "Housing Single Parent Families: A Problem on the Increase" (Adelaide: South Australia Housing Trust, July 1976).

40. E.g., William F. Whyte, *Street Corner Society* (Chicago: University of Chicago Press, 1943); Eliot Liebow, *Tally's Corner* (Boston: Little, Brown & Co., 1967).

41. Lyn Lofland, "The 'Thereness' of Women: A Selective Review of Urban Sociology," in *Another Voice: Feminist Perspectives on Social Life and Social Science,* ed. Marcia Millman and Rosabeth Moss Kanter (New York: Anchor Press, 1975).

42. Marjorie Mayo, ed., *Women in the Community* (London: Routledge & Kegan Paul, 1977); Cynthia Cockburn, *The Local State: Management of Cities and People* (London: Pluto Press, 1977).

43. E.g., Joey Edward Helms, "Old Women in America: The Need for Social Justice," *Antipode* 6 (July 1974): 26–33.

studies of the housing needs of the elderly,[44] and case studies include mobile homes and retirement communities.[45] Particular attention has been paid to translating behavioral data into design and planning proposals.

Gaps and Future Directions for Women and Environment Studies

There are substantial gaps in the kinds of environments and the types of women that have been studied. We know little about the single parents who choose to stay in suburbs after a divorce and how they cope with an environment organized around the two-parent nuclear family; there are few data on women in ethnic neighborhoods and their more segregated urban worlds. The studies by Michelson and Saegert and Winkel suggest that dual-career families often prefer inner-city neighborhoods and apartment living,[46] and economist Eli Ginzberg argues that this will contribute to the revitalization of the inner city, but this assumption remains to be tested.[47]

The environment and behavior studies, like those using the private-public paradigm, have tended to focus on the private world of women—their housing and immediate neighborhood. Considerably less empirical research has been done on women using the public environment. Except for several studies of environmental hazards,[48] little attention has been directed to the environment of the workplace. Yet the layout and design of many contemporary workplaces reflect status hierarchies and affect communication among workers. Similarly, there is virtually no research on women's use of public environments such as airports, civic buildings, public malls, and shopping centers even though anecdotal stories emphasize their unsuitability, especially for women with small children.

By focusing primarily on the experiences of individual users, behavioral studies have also not gone far enough in stressing the implications of their findings for present and future land-use patterns. Current trends in zoning, questions about the desirability of centralizing or de-

44. E.g., M. P. Lawton, *Planning and Managing Housing for the Elderly* (New York: John Wiley & Sons, 1975).

45. Sheila K. Johnson, *Idle Haven: Community Building among the Working Class Retired* (Berkeley: University of California Press, 1971); Arlie Hochschild, *The Unexpected Community* (Englewood Cliffs, N.J.: Prentice-Hall, Inc., 1973).

46. See n. 34 above.

47. Eli Ginzberg, "Who Can Save the City?" *Across the Board—the Conference Board Magazine* 15 (April 1978): 24–26. Gerda R. Wekerle, "A Woman's Place Is in the City," Land Policy Roundtable Basic Concept Series, no. 102 (Cambridge, Mass.: Lincoln Institute of Land Policy, 1979), summarizes the arguments for making the city a more attractive place for women.

48. Jeanne Stellman, *Women's Work, Women's Health* (New York: Pantheon Books, 1978); Andrea Hricko, with Melanie Brent, *Working for Your Life: A Women's Guide to Health Hazards* (Berkeley: University of California Press, 1976).

centralizing public services, support for either suburban single-family housing or inner-city revitalization all have potentially significant impacts on women's lives in the urban environment.

Hapgood and Getzels describe zoning as the most influential tool which planners employ to control the use of land.[49] Yet, there are virtually no data on the effects of zoning on women's day-to-day lives. Zoning requires the segregation of home and work. It excludes home occupations from residential neighborhoods, thereby making it more difficult for women and men to combine work and family roles.[50] Zoning limits the location of child-care facilities and often forces families to travel far out of their neighborhood.[51] Zoning ordinances which define "family" in very restrictive terms make it illegal for single parents and older women to share housing in a single-family neighborhood. Cooperative living arrangements and group homes such as battered-women's shelters are often relegated to transitional neighborhoods—areas of higher crime, poorer schools, and fewer amenities. Zoning ordinances which require the construction of single-family homes on large lots and exclude moderate and low-cost multifamily units discriminate against women, who comprise a large proportion of the low-income population. Judicial challenges to this "exclusionary zoning" have been supported by low-income groups and minorities, and it is important that women add their voice.[52]

Zoning can also be used positively to permit mixed uses, encourage a range of housing types and public services. Although a long-term trend has been the centralization of services such as hospitals, schools, health centers, and shopping, there are also new pressures from neighborhood control advocates and the appropriate technology movement for a greater decentralization of urban services to the neighborhood level.[53] There is need for information on the costs and benefits to women of the centralization and decentralization of urban services and the kinds of changes that would be most appropriate.

49. See n. 2 above.

50. A review of zoning bylaws which limit home occupations is available in William Toner, "Planning for Home Occupations," report no. 316, American Society of Planning Officials, Planning Advisory Service Report, April 1976.

51. A recent study in Toronto showed that parents and children traveled an average of twenty-six blocks to day care (Laura Climenko Johnson, *Who Cares? A Report of the Project Child Care Survey of Parents and Their Child Care Arrangements* [Toronto: Social Planning Council of Metro Toronto, 1977]); and research in Los Angeles found that over 90 percent of parents want care close to their home (Karen Hill-Scott, "Child Care in the Black Community" [Los Angeles: School of Architecture and Urban Planning, University of California, October 1978]).

52. Jerome G. Rose and Robert E. Rothman eds., *After Mount Laurel: The New Suburban Zoning* (Rutgers, N.J.: Center for Policy Research, 1977).

53. E.g., Milton Kotler, *Neighborhood Government: The Local Foundations of Political Life* (Indianapolis: Bobbs-Merrill Co., 1969); David Morris and Karl Hess, *Neighborhood Power: The New Localism* (Boston: Beacon Press, 1975); Richard Register, "Integral Urban Neighborhood," *Seriatim—Journal of Ecotopia* 3 (Winter 1978): 37–41.

The environment and behavior studies have begun to provide solid evidence of the costs to women of living in urban environments which do not readily accommodate women's participation in the labor force or changing family patterns. But this research is still missing any link with a wider feminist analysis of women's position in a class society or an analysis of how power and decision making in the city relate to the kinds of environments that are planned and created. This perspective is more evident in the work using the environmental equity paradigm, which is discussed next.

Women and Environmental Equity

The third major paradigm guiding research and action on women's position in the urban environment addresses the issue of environmental equity and, specifically, women's equal access to housing, transportation, and public services. An approach to urban analysis used by Marxist geographers and urban sociologists has been the examination of the hidden mechanisms of resource allocation in the city—how housing policies and the location of housing and access to transportation and public services affect the real income and life chances of various groups in the urban population.[54] Studies of the impact of spatial allocation decisions on the poor and racial minorities show that accessibility and proximity affect the ability to use urban services,[55] but until recently women have not been defined as a group that might be unfairly disadvantaged by public decisions or might require special consideration in the location of public goods and services.

Transportation

The study of women and transportation is very new. The conference organized by the U.S. Department of Transportation in September 1978, "Women's Travel Issues: Research Needs and Priorities," focused national attention on the topic and brought together researchers doing some of the first empirical studies in the field.[56] They found that women's transportation patterns differ from men's on several dimensions: the journey-to-work trip, the use of public transit, and the

54. David Harvey, *Social Justice and the City* (Baltimore: Johns Hopkins University Press, 1973); Manuel Castells, *The Urban Question* (London: Edward Arnold, 1977); and C. G. Pickvance, ed., *Urban Sociology* (London: Tavistock Publications, 1977).

55. Robert L. Lineberry, *Equality and Public Policy: The Distribution of Municipal Public Services* (Beverly Hills, Calif.: Sage Publications, 1977); John C. Falcocchio and Edmund J. Cantilli, *Transportation and the Disadvantaged* (Lexington, Mass.: Lexington Books, 1974).

56. A conference report will be available early in 1980 from the U.S. Department of Transportation.

kinds of trips made. Madden and White's review essay covers the empirical research on women's work trips and evaluates the adequacy of existing transportation models as these apply to women's trip behavior.[57] They point out that the basic models assume traditional family patterns where each household has a single worker and housing location decisions are designed to minimize the husband's journey to work. Few models incorporate the more complex travel patterns of dual-career families.

Transportation studies conducted over the past two decades consistently show that women have shorter journeys to work than men.[58] Women try to reduce the distance between home and work and the time spent in commuting; the shortest journey-to-work trips are found among married women.[59] As a result, women tend to confine themselves to a much smaller work-preference area than men do, and this either diminishes women's chances of competing in the job market or limits them to lower-paying local jobs.[60]

Overall, the general tendency to decentralize jobs to suburban locations has resulted in an increase in the average length of work trips for all workers, but women have been more disadvantaged than men by this trend.[61] For women, a move to the suburbs has often resulted in either a forced job change or unemployment.[62]

In part, the effects of the suburbanization of jobs and housing weigh more heavily on women than on men because women have less access to private automobiles and are more dependent on public transportation for mobility.[63] Women, and especially elderly women and women heads of families, are disproportionately represented among the poorest groups living in metropolitan areas. Unable to afford a car, they use public transportation for all activities.[64]

57. Janice Fanning Madden and Michele J. White, "Women's Work Trips: An Empirical and Theoretical Overview" (paper presented at conference on Women's Travel Issues, U.S. Department of Transportation, Washington, D.C., September 1978).

58. Ibid.; Julia A. Ericksen, "An Analysis of the Journey to Work for Women," *Social Problems* 24 (April 1977): 428–35.

59. Ericksen.

60. Ibid; Phyllis Kaniss and Barbara Robins, "The Transportation Needs of Women," in Hapgood and Getzels (n. 2 above); Mary Cichocki, "Women's Travel Patterns in a Suburban Development," in Wekerle et al. (n. 6 above).

61. Ericksen; Falcocchio and Cantilli.

62. Keller (n. 34 above) and Popenoe (n. 30 above) report a higher incidence of unemployment among women after a move to the suburbs due to an absence of local jobs. In a study of the Paris region, J. Coutras and J. Fagnani, "Femmes et transports en milieu urbain," *International Journal of Urban and Regional Research* 2 (October 1978): 432–39, report that 40 percent of women moving from central city to outer areas change employment to reduce travel time contrasted with 22 percent of males. At the same time, Ericksen notes that the decentralization of jobs affects women living in the center city who are now reported to have longer than average trips to work.

63. Kaniss and Robins.

64. This is reflected in the study by Donald L. Foley, "Differentials in Personal Access to Household Motor Vehicles: Five County San Francisco Bay Area, 1971," Working Paper

Transportation studies have not been sensitive to the fact that even within the same household men and women often have differential access to family resources including time, money, and use of the family car. Thus, even in affluent families, women may suffer serious spatial disadvantages when compared with their husbands. This is reflected in the finding that when there is only one automobile it is frequently the husband who uses it on a regular basis.[65] The evidence from studies conducted in a larger number of North American cities shows that the proportion of female workers using public transit is consistently twice and three times that of male workers using it.[66] Women workers' heavier dependence on public transportation affects their ability to take paid work and the extent of the job search area in which they can look for work. It increases the hours spent in work-related activities and cuts into time for family and leisure activities. Paradoxically, women's increased labor force participation creates a greater demand for public transportation at a time when there are cutbacks in both the quality and availability of services.

Transportation systems are designed primarily to carry workers to and from their jobs during peak commuting hours. Planning does not take into account the fact that the journey to work for women workers is often more time consuming, more costly, and more complicated than men's. Women frequently use public transportation for shopping and household errands, and women workers combine these trips with the journey to work to save precious time.[67] Yet fare structures and the location of transit lines do not accommodate this trip pattern. In addition, mothers are generally responsible for taking children to child-care facilities and picking them up. These trips are not reflected in transportation models even though they require an extra trip twice a day, sometimes in a direction away from work, and involve additional time and

---

no. 197 (Berkeley: University of California, Institute of Urban and Regional Development, 1972), which shows that 72 percent of all persons sixteen and older with no access to a car were women and that 42.5 percent of all women older than sixteen lack access to cars, contrasted with 19 percent of males.

65. This is documented by Kaniss and Robins and Coutras and Fagnani. In addition, Cichocki finds that women are most often accompanied or are passengers during trips while men enjoy more independent movement.

66. In Philadelphia, 30 percent of women workers use public transit compared with 15 percent of male workers; in Los Angeles 10 percent of working females and 3 percent of working males use public transit; in Boston, 28 percent of women workers use transit compared with 15 percent of males. These and other statistics are found in Kaniss and Robins.

67. Louise Skinner and Karen Borlaug, "Shopping Trips: Who Makes Them and When?" and Susan Hanson and Perry Hanson, "Impact of Women's Employment on Household Travel Patterns" (papers presented at the conference on Women's Travel Issues, U.S. Department of Transportation, Washington, D.C., September 1978); Cichocki; and Irene Bruegel and Adah Kay, "Women and Planning, *"Architectural Design* 45 (August 1975): 499–500, present some British data.

money. There has been virtually no research on the spatial distribution of child-care facilities—how this affects aggregate travel patterns, parents' travel time, and choice of work location. One of the first studies on this topic, conducted in the Paris region,[68] concludes that women are subjected to daily harassment in trying to coordinate work hours and commuting schedules with the hours of these facilities.

Although the differences between women's and men's travel patterns have been noted in many transportation studies, only the recent studies provide adequate explanations for these differences. Geographers Palm and Pred were among the first to emphasize the critical connection between women's domestic roles, their travel patterns, and access to jobs, leisure activities and social services;[69] while Fava, Ericksen, and Madden and White point out that women's home responsibilities severely restrict the time they can spend in commuting and increases the "accessibility costs" of getting to jobs and urban services.

The research on women's travel patterns makes an important contribution not only to the transportation field, but also to theories of spatial inequality and resource allocation within the city. By linking women's mobility and access to urban resources directly to the segregation of roles within the home, this research ties into the work on the private sphere of the home and the sexual division of labor. The prevailing theories of spatial inequality rely on poverty, residential segregation, and urban power structures to explain differences among groups,[70] but this research on women crosses class and racial boundaries and requires a revision of existing theories.

One response to women's need for greater mobility in the city has been the formation of a small number of transit services created by women for women. Started in 1976, the Yukon Women's Minibus Society in Whitehorse remains the only known example of a transit system started by a women's organization which now serves the whole community.[71] It carries 750–900 passengers daily in five minibuses, employs fifteen women, and continues to expand. Rebecca Dreis's research on women's transit services in Madison and Milwaukee, Wisconsin, shows how a concern with rape prevention has developed into a local transportation service for women at night.[72] She stresses the difficulty of main-

68. Regina Fodor, "Day-Care Policy in France and Its Consequences for Women: A Study of the Metropolitan Paris Area," *International Journal of Urban and Regional Research* 2 (October 1978): 463–81.

69. Risa Palm and Allan Pred, "A Time-Geographic Perspective on Problems of Inequality for Women," Working Paper no. 236 (Berkeley: University of California, Institute of Urban and Regional Development, 1974).

70. Harvey and Castells (n. 54 above).

71. Wekerle and Carter (n. 34 above); "Yukon Minibus Update," *Women and Environments International Newsletter* 3 (Spring 1979): 5.

72. Dreis (n. 25 above); see also Marianne Goss, "Women's Transit Authority," *Women—a Journal of Liberation* 6, no. 1:30–31.

taining what amounts to a parallel transportation system with volunteers and little money.

Access to transportation plays a critical role in providing access to many essential services in the North American city, and public transportation must be made serviceable to a wider population, particularly now when automobile ownership is becoming increasingly prohibitive to more segments of the population. To date, women's groups (unlike the elderly) have not developed a lobby around transportation issues. Unless they do, they will be left out of the process of setting priorities for the allocation of resources during a period of increasing scarcity.

Housing

Hearings and fact-gathering surveys conducted in the mid-seventies established that women experience severe discrimination in housing. The housing market is still largely oriented toward the traditional nuclear family and has not responded to the huge increases in the number of households headed by women, one third of whom have incomes below the poverty level.[73] Due to their low income, families headed by women are more likely to live in central cities, to rent rather than own a house, and to reside in public housing.[74] Regardless of race or income level, female heads of households spend a larger portion of their income than the national average for adequate housing. Poor women have one chance in five of living in inadequate housing; this figure rises to better than one chance in four for minorities and large families.[75]

Discrimination in the housing market has aggravated the problems of women. Women of all ages, family types, income groups, and races have been subjected to blatant and systematic discrimination by lenders, landlords, insurance agencies, and public housing officials. Married women seeking to purchase a house (or contribute to its purchase) have been most discriminated against in the mortgage market; single women and women heads of families have experienced the most discrimination in rental housing.[76]

The hearings on women and housing in five American cities orga-

73. U.S. Department of Housing and Urban Development, Office of Policy Development and Research, "How Well Are We Housed? 2-Female-Headed Households" (Washington, D.C.: Superintendent of Documents, November 1978).

74. Beverly L. Johnson, "Women Who Head Families, 1970–77: Their Numbers Rose, Income Lagged," *Monthly Labor Review* 101 (February 1978): 32–37.

75. U.S. Department of Housing and Urban Development, Office of the Assistant Secretary for Neighborhoods, Voluntary Associations and Consumer Protection, "The Women's Policy and Programs Staff—Questions and Answers," mimeographed (Washington, D.C.: WPP staff, 1979).

76. Elizabeth A. Roistacher and Janet S. Young, "Two-Earner Families in the Housing Market: 1969–1976" (paper presented at St. Michael's College Symposium, "Women and Society: Past, Present, Future," Winooski Park, Vt., March 24, 1979).

nized by the National Council of Negro Women in 1975 documented these inequities. This study and another by the U.S. Commission on Civil Rights showed that, until recently, working-women's income was automatically discounted, that is, counted as less than 100 percent—and often only 50 percent—in determining a family's mortgage eligibility.[77] (Now prohibited by law in the United States, this is still standard practice in countries such as Canada, the United Kingdom, and Australia.) Discounting prevented many families from buying homes, and minority families were worst hit since fewer can rely solely on the husband's income for mortgage eligibility.[78] Lenders gave preference in mortgage lending to married couples and males; women living outside husband-wife households found themselves at a serious disadvantage in seeking a mortgage and were required to present a stronger credit and income status than single men.[79]

Several unchallenged and unsubstantiated myths justified these practices: that married women's participation in the labor force is temporary; that single women are a less reliable credit risk than single men because they are less attached to work; that men generally repair and maintain a house and single women do not have the skills to do so.[80] A consultant's report commissioned by HUD showed that many of these stereotypes were unfounded and concluded that there is no statistical justification for different treatment of women borrowers and coborrowers.[81]

Women have experienced the greatest discrimination in the rental market. Because of their lower incomes, difficulty in obtaining mortgages, and need for housing close to collective services, single women, widowed, separated, and divorced women represent a large share of the market for apartment units. The National Council of Negro Women found that the least wanted tenants are women, especially elderly females and single women with children. Low vacancy rates in

77. National Council of Negro Women, *Women and Housing—a Report on Sex Discrimination in Five American Cities* (Washington, D.C.: Department of Housing and Urban Development, Office of the Assistant Secretary for Fair Housing and Equal Opportunity, June 1975); U.S. Commission on Civil Rights, *Twenty Years after Brown: Equal Opportunity in Housing* (Washington, D.C.: Commission on Civil Rights, December 1975).

78. U.S. Commission on Civil Rights, p. 42; Roistacher and Young show that wives' earnings in white two-earner families account for 25.5 percent of family earnings but 32.4 percent in black two-earner families.

79. National Council of Negro Women; Barbara Grant, "Sex and Marital Status Discrimination in Residential Mortgage Lending" (master's thesis, Columbia University, 1975).

80. National Council of Negro Women.

81. Ketron, Inc., "Women in the Mortgage Market" (Washington, D.C.: Department of Housing and Urban Development, Office of Policy Development and Research, March 1976).

many cities allow landlords to be selective and keep out families with children; single women are often stereotyped as irresponsible parents. Women on low or fixed incomes are left with the dregs of the housing market: substandard buildings, basement apartments, rooms where they share facilities, and public housing. This is the same whether the country is the United States, Canada, the United Kingdom, or Australia,[82] and the long-term costs to women and children are only now being documented.

In the United States, the response to the widespread discrimination against women in the housing market has been the passage of legislation at both the state and federal levels.[83] At the federal level several statutes prohibit sex discrimination in housing: the Equal Credit Opportunity Act of 1975 which affects lending practices, the Housing and Community Development Act of 1974, and the 1974 amendment to the Fair Housing Act of 1968. The United States experience serves as a model for other countries which lag behind in enacting legislation.

Most observers are agreed that the U.S. laws have not been enforced and have been largely ineffective. Gelb and Palley document the passage of the Equal Credit Opportunity Act, the coalitions formed by women's organizations to gain its passage, and its limitations.[84] They note that responsibility for enforcement was spread through a dozen federal agencies, that little money was allocated for enforcement, and that procedures are only now being established for monitoring lenders. In 1976 alone, over 2,000 women complained to the Federal Trade Commission, which is only one of the enforcement agencies.[85] There is little systematic information on how well the laws are being enforced. Currently HUD is funding a "Women and Mortgage Credit Project" which involves a national media campaign to inform women of their legal rights, educate lenders about what constitute discriminatory practices, and compile data on compliance with the law.[86] Congress has started to prod federal bank agencies to establish practices to turn up violations of the law.[87] But for

82. National Council of Negro Women; Peggy Gurstein and Nancy Hood, "Housing Needs of One Parent Families" (Vancouver: YWCA, November 1975); Sue Laurence, "The Single Woman and the Nuclear Family in the State Housing Sector," mimeographed (London: University College, School of Environmental Studies, 1978); Milne (n. 39 above).

83. Roistacher and Young review the state legislation.

84. Joyce Gelb and Marian Lief Palley, "Women and Interest Group Politics: A Case Study of the Equal Credit Opportunity Act," *American Politics Quarterly* 5 (July 1977): 331–52.

85. June Kronholz, "Women Complain That New Equal Credit Law Is Applied Unevenly, Enforced Haphazardly," *Wall Street Journal* (January 21, 1977), p. 32.

86. Project director is JoAnn McGeorge in the Office of the Assistant Secretary for Policy Development and Research, Department of Housing and Urban Development, Washington, D.C.

87. Linda E. Demkovich, "Enforcing the Laws against Discriminatory Credit Practices," *National Journal* 10 (October 14, 1978): 1646–47.

the most part, enforcement relies on individual women bringing suit—a costly and time-consuming process—and the area of worst discrimination, the rental housing market, has hardly been touched.

The Housing Needs of Single Parents

Recent British studies focus on the plight of single mothers in the state housing sector and utilize a Marxist perspective to examine how state housing policy exercises social control and reinforces the traditional patriarchal family. Sue Laurence points out that council housing gives preference to the intact working-class family and automatically views single mothers as less respectable and uncreditworthy.[88] Single parents have a lesser chance of being rehoused in permanent local authority housing, and when they are they tend to be placed on the most depressed and remote estates.

Several articles examine the growth of the British movement for battered women and the establishment of women's refuges as a response to women's homelessness. Hilary Rose presents an account of the history of Women's Aid in Britain: how violence against women became defined as a social problem, the political struggles involved, and the emergence of a women's network and new forms of collective organization. Sutton covers the same ground, but also adds information on the struggles with local housing authorities who allocated the worst housing to encourage women to return to their husbands.[89] Articles by Galper and Washburne and Cools, describing two shelters for women in North American cities, show that the problems are much the same, but they do not link their experiences to a broader class analysis as the British studies do.[90]

One response to the acute need for housing for single mothers has been the organization of small communal housing projects for single parents and their children. In England, Nina West Homes (described by Hayden in this volume) provides flats for single mothers which combine opportunities for some communal sharing, child care, and resident management. Gurstein and Hood describe several housing projects in

88. Laurence; Elizabeth Wilson, *Women and the Welfare State* (London: Tavistock Publications, 1977).

89. Jalna Hanmer, "Community Action, Women's Aid and the Women's Liberation Movement," and Angela Weir, "Battered Women: Some Perspectives and Problems," in *Women in the Community,* ed. Marjorie Mayo (London: Routledge & Kegan Paul, 1977); Hilary Rose, "In Practice Supported, In Theory Denied: An Account of an Invisible Urban Movement," *International Journal of Urban and Regional Research* 2 (October 1978): 521–37; Helen Sachs, "Women's Self-Help," *Architectural Design* 45 (August 1975): 493–96; Jo Sutton, "The Growth of the British Movement for Battered Women," *Victimology* 2 (1977–78): 576–84.

90. Miriam Galper and Carolyn Kott Washburne, "A Women's Self-Help Program in Action," *Social Policy* 6 (March/April 1976): 46–52; Anne Cools, "Emergency Shelter: The Development of an Innovative Women's Environment," in Wekerle et al. (n. 6 above).

British Columbia for single parents, including a twenty-nine-unit town-house complex in Victoria which provides low rental housing, child care, and after school and summer programs for residents and single parents in the surrounding community. New projects and proposals which deal specifically with the housing needs of single parents include a proposed housing complex designed by women public housing tenants in Ottawa, Canada,[91] a completed rehabilitation project by women ex-offenders in Harlem, and several repair services and self-help housing projects.[92]

The various studies of the housing needs of single parents tend to emphasize that housing for this group involves more than shelter and must include a network of social services such as crisis services, counseling, child care, educational, and recreational facilities.[93] These requirements give some indication of why housing subsidies alone, without a package of attached services, will not make single parents independent. They also show how the problems of homeless women differ substantially from those of homeless men. A policy question raised by Milne and Gurstein and Hood centers around the desirability of providing segregated housing for single parents or whether their needs might be better met by living in the general community and receiving rent subsidies. On the one hand, concentration raises the fear of stigma and neighbor prejudice; on the other hand, single mothers need contact and opportunities for communal sharing, and the popularity of the few existing projects is shown by their long waiting lists.

Women and Community Activism

Women's concern with the home has led them to become increasingly more active in community issues and self-help movements to improve living conditions related to housing, child care, food cooperatives, and neighborhood planning. Birch describes the key role played by women and organized women's groups in the reform movement which obtained the passage of the first public housing legislation in the United States; Lawson, Barton, and Joselit document women's leadership in tenant organizing and rent strikes in New York City from the nineteenth century to the present.[94] They conclude that women have been most active in tenant organizing at the individual building level, but when organizations become larger and real political power is involved, men

91. Mary Soper, "Housing for Single Parents: A Women's Design," in Wekerle et al.

92. Gerda R. Wekerle, "Women House Themselves," *Heresies,* vol. 11 (1980), forthcoming.

93. Gurstein and Hood (n. 82 above); Milne (n. 39 above); Ann McAffee, "High Density Family Housing," *Urban Forum* 4 (November–December 1978): 6–15.

94. Eugenie L. Birch, "Women-made America: The Case of Early Public Housing Policy," *AIP Journal* 44 (April 1978): 130–44; Ronald Lawson, Stephen Barton, and Jenna Joselit, "From Kitchen to Storefront: Women in the Tenant Movement," in Wekerle et al.

often take over leadership roles. Several authors have documented the vanguard role that working women have played in British housing and community struggles,[95] and interviews with community organizers in two U.S. cities show that housing and neighborhood organizing are top priorities for women in American working-class communities.[96] From these few examples, it seems that women in working-class communities define planning and housing issues as concerns which affect them directly, while the organized women's movement has yet to define urban planning as a "women's issue."

Conclusions

The new research on women in the urban environment is very radical in its implications. As in other fields where women have been neglected, this new work has the potential of requiring fundamental revisions in many of the accepted theories and empirical findings in urban studies. Much of the current work implies the necessity for fundamental changes in some of the most basic elements of the modern city—its zoning patterns, neighborhood planning, transportation system and housing industry, and social service structure.

While this review essay summarizes a rich and extremely varied body of work, I would emphasize that it represents only the smallest beginnings of scholarship and policy analysis related to women's needs in the urban environment. It is not so much an area of study as a loose network of a small number of individuals spread thinly across three continents. As an indication of the lack of legitimacy given to the study of women's environmental needs, there is not one planning school in North America which offers a course on this topic as part of its permanent curriculum. As yet, there is no cumulative body of work. Many of the articles consist of anecdotal accounts or descriptive case studies documenting the emergence of women's urban institutions which may eventually form the basis for the development of a more comprehensive theory. The social surveys—for instance, those on women's housing experiences or transportation patterns—are important because they provide empirical evidence of women's disadvantage and can readily be used by women's organizations and urban policymakers to plead the case for new programs or legislation. However, the development of theoretical frameworks which integrate these new data either into existing urban

95. Sachs; also see articles by Elizabeth Wilson, Ann Gallagher, Jan O'Malley, and Cynthia Cockburn in Marjorie Mayo (n. 42 above).

96. Juanita Weaver, "It's Always the Women: An Interview with Community Organizer Marie Nahikian," *Quest—a Feminist Quarterly* 4 (Fall 1978): 42–57; Maureen Fahey, "Block by Block—Women in Community Organizing." *Women—a Journal of Liberation* 6, no. 1:14–19.

or feminist theory or achieve a synthesis of the two is still lacking. Much of the current work remains at the level of fact gathering—documenting the extent of problems or the nature of solutions. An analysis of the economic, institutional, and political context in which urban decision-making takes place and women's potential role within that structure is still missing. Some of these gaps will be filled as more work is completed and the topic gains greater visibility and credibility. But in the long run, the development of scholarship on women in the urban environment will also require greater collaboration among interdisciplinary groups of scholars and policymakers, since the study of the city, by its very nature, cuts across disciplinary lines and leads to social action.

Appendix

The review essays are Lyn Lofland, "The 'Thereness' of Women: A Selective Review of Urban Sociology," in *Another Voice: Feminist Perspectives on Social Life and Social Science,* ed. Marcia Millman and Rosabeth Moss Kanter (New York: Anchor Press, 1975); Rebecca Peterson, Gerda Wekerle, and David Morley, "Women and Environments: An Overview of an Emerging Field," *Environment and Behavior* 10 (December 1978): 511–34; David Morley, Rebecca Peterson, and Gerda Wekerle, "A Different Place: An Introduction to the Study of Women and Their Environments," in *Women: Public and Private Spaces,* special issue of *Centerpoint,* ed. F. Kaplan, R. Lamont, and S. Saegert (New York: City University Graduate Center, Fall 1979); Gerda R. Wekerle, "A Woman's Place Is in the City," Land Policy Roundtable Basic Concepts Series, no. 102 (Cambridge, Mass.: Lincoln Institute of Land Policy, 1979). Books include Susana Torre, ed., *Women and American Architecture: A Historic and Contemporary Perspective* (New York: Watson Guptill Publications, 1977); Marjorie Mayo, ed., *Women and the Community* (London: Routledge & Kegan Paul, 1977); David Popenoe, *The Suburban Environment: Sweden and the United States* (Chicago: University of Chicago Press, 1977). Several books in progress are Gerda R. Wekerle, Rebecca Peterson, and David Morley, eds., *New Space for Women* (Boulder, Colo.: Westview Press, 1980); Dolores Hayden, *A Grand Domestic Revolution: American Visions of Household Liberation* (Cambridge, Mass.: M.I.T. Press, 1980); Gwendolyn Wright, *Moralism and the Model Home: Domestic Architecture and Cultural Conflict in Chicago 1873–1913* (Chicago: University of Chicago Press, 1980). Special issues of journals and magazines include an issue on "Women and the Environment," *Branching Out: Canadian Magazine for Women,* vol. 3 (August 1978); an issue on "Women in Their Community," *Quest—a Feminist Quarterly,* vol. 4 (Fall 1978); "Women and the City," *International Journal of Urban and Regional Research,* vol. 2 (October 1978); "Women in Geographic Curricula," *Journal of Geography,* vol. 77 (September/October 1978); "Women and Architecture," *Heresies,* vol. 11 (October 1979). The first overview of women in appropriate technology which also includes a resource list of names is Judy Smith, *Something Old, Something New, Something Borrowed, Something Due: Women and Appropriate Technology* (Butte, Mont.: National Center for Appropriate Technology, August 1978). Annotated bibliographies include C. Donaldson Spagnoletti, *Women and Planning,* Library Bibliography, no. 20 (Adelaide: South Australia Housing Trust, 1974); and Bonnie Loyd, *Women and Geography: An Annotated Bibliography and Guide to Sources of Information,* C.P.L. Exchange Bibliography, no. 1159 (Monticello, Ill.: Council of Planning Librarians, 1976). Sample course outlines on women in geography are available in *Journal of Geography,* vol. 77 (September/October 1978), and a women and environments course is described in Gerda R. Wekerle, Rebecca Peterson, and David Morley, "Trial Balloon: The Story of a Course," *Branching Out* 5 (August 1978): 26–29. The Women's School of Planning and Architecture is described by Leslie Kanes Weisman, "The Women's School of Planning and Architecture," in *Not by Degrees: Essays on Feminist Education,* ed. Charlotte Bunch (Houston: Daughters, Inc., 1980); and Mary Vogel, "Women's School of Planning and Architecture: Reflections of 1978," *Women and Environments International Newsletter,* vol. 3 (Spring 1979). The *Women and Environments International Newsletter* links researchers and professionals in several countries. (It is available from the Faculty of Environmental Studies, York University, 4700 Keele Street, Downsview, Ontario M3J 2R2, Canada, for $5.00 a year.) Organizations of women environmental professionals include Sisters for a Humane Environment (SHE) in Seattle; the Organization of Women Architects (OWA) in San Francisco; the Organization of Women in Landscape Architecture (OWL); the Union International des Femmes Architects which held its fifth International Congress in Seattle, October 1979; and the newly organized Division on Planning for Women of the American Planning Association. Torre's book includes a complete listing of these and related organizations.

Faculty of Environmental Studies
York University

Women, Housing Access, and Mortgage Credit

Emily Card

The topic "men, housing access, and mortgage credit" is so encompassing and well covered that it would be difficult to add anything of interest to the scholar in a journal essay on the subject. Not surprisingly, the reverse is true for women, housing access, and mortgage credit. In a recent study commissioned by the Department of Housing and Urban Development (HUD), a literature search revealed that the number of serious sources that dealt directly and exclusively with women, housing access, and mortgage credit could be reviewed in less than twenty pages.[1]

The history of the exclusion of this subject as one of scholarly focus parallels that of women's exclusion in statistical terms from the housing market. Homeownership is an important aspect of life for the majority of Americans. While in some urban areas apartment dwelling is the norm, in most American cities homeownership is critical to full participation in the life of the city. Homeowners are taxpayers. They are perceived as powerful, stable, and solid citizens. The quality of life for homeowners in many cities is higher. They cannot be excluded if they have children. In short, owning a home is another means for women to take control of their own lives. Seventy-five percent of all housing units

---

1. Emily Card, "Women and Mortgage Credit: An Annotated Bibliography," mimeographed (prepared for the U.S. Department of Housing and Urban Development, Office of Policy Development and Research, May 1979). Regina Steele contributed to the research for this study and research note.

in the country are owner occupied.[2] Yet, despite the symbolic and economic importance of "a home of one's own," until very recently women have been excluded by custom, law, and economics from direct participation in homeownership. Women's participation has almost always been ancillary to that of their husbands or parents.

Two points about women and the traditional practices of homeownership should be made. First, homeownership and home purchasing are not identical. One can own a home without having had the original means to purchase it. Second, as a practical matter, purchasing a home today involves being able to obtain a mortgage.

As recently as five years ago, homeownership by a woman was usually concomitant with marriage. Although, over the past 100 years, all of the adopted provisions have reduced or abolished the common-law disabilities of marriage, traditional attitudes about married women's roles have continued to influence the property dealings of both married and single women. There were three socially acceptable models for homeownership by women: Separated and divorced women usually retained the family home and stayed there to raise children; widows lived their lives out in their married locations; and single "spinsters" might inherit a home from their parents. In none of these cases did homeownership ordinarily involve a purchase, the exception being primarily the case in which a widow used her insurance funds to purchase a home outright.

There were few positive role models for the woman homeowner. Sociopsychological barriers operated to discourage women who were not trained to think in terms of incurring debt. Mortgages, although backed by equity in times of market fluctuation, appeared to be awesome responsibilities and were not readily obtainable. There were also concerns on the part of both women and lenders about women's ability to engage in home repairs; the notion that men also had to hire repairpersons did not fit culturally accepted imagery. In addition, being alone in a home appeared to be lonelier, and women, for some very sound reasons, have had to concern themselves with physical safety.

The perception of discrimination against women in housing is a recent development. Since women were permitted joint ownership with their husbands, sex discrimination in housing was not as easy to observe as racial segregation in geographically distinct areas. Civil rights legislation in the 1960s reflected this oversight. The 1968 Fair Housing Act prohibited discrimination in the sale, rental, and financing of housing on account of race, color, religion, and national origin, but discrimination because of sex was not prohibited.[3]

2. U.S. Commission on Civil Rights, *Social Indicators of Equality for Minorities and Women* (Washington, D.C.: Government Printing Office, 1978), p. 69.

3. Fair Housing Act, 1968, Public Law—90-284, 42 U.S.C. 3605.

Rather than outlawing sexual discrimination in the 1968 Fair Housing Act, the federal government was the backbone of the system supporting discrimination against women. The federal government, through its lending regulatory agencies, ensures the safety and soundness of the U.S. banking system. Sound business practice excluded or severely limited women in the mortgage market because their incomes were thought to be unstable. Regulatory guidelines encouraged lenders to follow sound business practices, which suited their prejudices perfectly: The idea of women as homeowners was looked upon in horror by lenders and their industry spokespeople.

The spectre of pregnancy dominated the lending world's view; the fear of having to evict a lonely widow for mortgage default ran a close second. To lenders, all women under the age of fifty were candidates for marriage and motherhood. It was considered self-evident that as soon as a woman married, or shortly thereafter, she would drop out of the work force and thereby render herself incapable of sustaining a mortgage payment. If she were married and continued in the perverse habit of working, only after all other avenues had been exhausted would a lender consider counting a wife's income toward a mortgage.[4]

These practices were consolidated under a system of "income discounting" for married women. Single women had to present a substantially stronger paper picture to qualify for a mortgage. Although the exact parameters varied, the "lender's rule of thumb" was commonly accepted by lenders, although virtually unknown to women. These rules provided a formula whereby a mortgage was prorated or "discounted" in proportion to a woman's age and potential childbearing status. An additional characteristic of these rules of thumb was that occupation was counted.[5]

The federal government supported these prejudices not only through the regulation of lending institutions but also through the practices of its own agencies. In a bulletin issued in February 1973, the Veterans Administration (VA) affirmed that it did not count a wife's income for a veteran's home loan unless the veteran himself could not qualify. The bulletin went on to enumerate the circumstances in which her income would be counted: These included "her age, the nature and length of her employment, and the composition of the family." The "composition of the family" was a euphemism for "number of children,"

---

4. U.S. Congress, Senate, "Remarks of Senator Brock Introducing S. 1605," *Congressional Record*, 93d Cong., 1st sess., 1973, 119:S7540–43. Senator Brock was the main Senate sponsor of the Equal Credit Opportunity Act (ECOA). As a research fellow in his office, I was responsible for the staff work on the ECOA and the Title VIII amendment.

5. U.S. Commission on Civil Rights, *Mortgage Money: Who Gets It? A Case Study in Mortgage Lending Discrimination in Hartford, Connecticut,* Clearinghouse Publication no. 48 (Washington, D.C.: Commission on Civil Rights, June 1974), pp. 33 ff.

on the assumption that if a woman had had her 2.5 standard children she was a preferable candidate for the loan.[6]

The parade of horrors did not stop here. If a couple really wanted a home and the wife were suspiciously young, then the VA, and other lenders and lender guarantor as well, might inquire as to birth-control practices, although by 1973 mounting criticism of this practice lead the VA to include the following explanation: "In certain instances, a veteran and his wife may be unable to have children and supporting medical evidence may be submitted to the lender for transmittal to the VA to establish the likelihood of the wife continuing to work. If such a medical statement is voluntarily submitted by the veteran to the lender, it cannot very well be refused upon receipt in VA."[7] This feudalistic public concern with fertility brought to light a case where a wife had been required to sign papers agreeing to an abortion if she were to become pregnant while having her income count toward a mortgage in Virginia.

The Senate passage in July 1973 of the Equal Credit Opportunity Act (ECOA) changed, almost overnight, this discriminatory situation. The act prohibited discrimination in the granting of credit on account of sex and marital status. A companion bill added prohibitions against discrimination on account of sex to the provisions of Title VIII, the Fair Housing Act. With the final passage of this legislation in 1974, the traditional exclusion of women from the housing and mortgage market was dealt a stunning blow. These laws formed the basis for homeownership on a wide scale for women for the first time in American history.[8] The scale of the potential impact can be compared with the passage of the VA and FHA legislation which expanded homeownership potential after the Second World War.

Several factors prevented the immediate recognition of women's home-buying potential. Women who learned of the equal credit legislation thought in terms of consumer rather than mortgage credit since the direct experience of discrimination was most likely in the consumer credit area. Very few women were aware of the extent of mortgage-credit discrimination. In fact, the Title VIII amendment was initially opposed by the Justice Department attorneys on the grounds that it was not "needed" and was "unworkable."

Once women recognized their home-buying potential, other factors intervened to make their purchasing homes more difficult. The 1974–75 recession and increased unemployment slowed home sales. Of more

6. U.S., Veterans Administration, "Wives' Income," Information Bulletin DVB 1B 26-73-1, mimeographed (Washington, D.C.: Department of Veterans' Benefits, February 2, 1973).

7. Ibid.

8. Equal Credit Opportunity Act, 1973, Public Law—940249, 15 U.S.C. 1667; Fair Housing Act (n. 3). The Fair Housing Act was amended in 1974.

fundamental importance from women's point of view, the passage of this legislation occurred at a point when the attention of the women's movement was turned toward ERA ratification and the disintegrating presidential administration kept equal credit education and enforcement for women a low priority. Only in 1978 did the issue of women and mortgage credit emerge as a concern of the federal government, and most of the lending regulatory agencies have just begun in 1979 to keep statistics according to sex.[9]

In 1979, five years after the passage of Title VIII and the ECOA, the outlook for women as home purchasers is mixed. Changes in expectations about marriage and childbearing in relation to work, and the increase in numbers of women with lifetime work plans, have contributed to the possibility that more women might buy homes; but the circumstances of the marketplace have made homeownership an expensive and elusive goal. The numbers of women owning mortgages, related to dimensions of age and race and examined before and after passage of the new laws in 1974, must be compared to women's income in order to see whether the legislated change met the reality of income possibilities.

In attempting to gather comparable figures across time, it has come to my attention that the Bureau of the Census did not publish much of the data needed prior to the 1970 census, and some of it is still not published. For example, in 1960, women's homeownership is obscured by several factors, including the reporting of "single" owner-occupied housing according to the categories "under 65" and "over 65" and not by sex. Similarly, if married people resided together, the home was invariably reported as belonging to the man. Further, no information was published about women's participation in the mortgage market.[10] Discussions with Bureau of the Census and HUD officials revealed that this lack of reporting was not viewed as a problem until recently.

In order to prove assertions about women's homeownership across time, other information sources will have to be developed. The research cited herein is part of a project with this information base as one goal. HUD's national Women and Mortgage Credit Project now underway (in which I am participating) may also add to the interest and information about women and homeownership.

Program for the Study of Women and Men in Society
University of Southern California

9. U.S. Department of Housing and Urban Development, "Information Kit," mimeographed (Washington, D.C.: Women and Mortgage Credit Project, Office of Policy Development and Research, March 9, 1979).

10. U.S. Bureau of the Census, *1960 Census of Housing*, vol. 5, *Residential Finance*, pt. 1, *Homeowner Properties* (Washington, D.C.: Government Printing Office, 1963).

Revisions/Reports: Notes on Research

Working Women and City Structure: Implications of the Subtle Revolution

Elizabeth A. Roistacher and Janet Spratlin Young

> The rise in the number of women who work for pay amounts to a "Subtle Revolution" looming at least as large as the Industrial Revolution that shook Europe nearly two centuries ago.[1]

Today, the "subtle revolution" of women at work, which is altering the character of the American family, also seems destined to alter the structure of our cities.[2] The traditional family in which the husband is employed outside the home while the wife serves as a full-time homemaker is becoming increasingly less common, while households with working women are becoming the norm. Three household types—the single

---

1. Ralph Smith, quoted in Alfred L. Malabre, Jr., "Women at Work," *Wall Street Journal* (August 28, 1978); Ralph Smith et al. have recently completed *The Subtle Revolution: Women at Work* (Washington, D.C.: Urban Institute, 1979) which discusses not only the labor market trends of the subtle revolution but their causes and implications and recommendations for appropriate public policy.

2. See, e.g., Beverly L. Johnson, "Changes in Marital and Family Characteristics of Workers, 1970–78," *Monthly Labor Review* 102 (April 1979): 49–52; Paul Ryscavage, "More Wives in the Labor Force Have Husbands with 'Above-Average' Incomes," *Monthly Labor Review* 102 (June 1979): 40–42; U.S. Department of Commerce, Bureau of the Census, "Divorce, Child Custody, and Child Support," *Current Population Reports*, Special Studies, ser. P-23, no. 84 (Washington, D.C.: Government Printing Office, 1979); Beverly L. Johnson, "Women Who Head Families, 1970–77: Their Numbers Rose, Income Lagged," *Monthly Labor Review* 101 (February 1978): 32–37.

woman, the two-earner family, and the household headed by a divorced woman—will shape the economy of cities by their impact not only on the labor market but also on the demand for housing, tenure choice (whether to own or rent), and particularly on choice of residential locations.

How are residential location decisions made? According to the standard economic model, individual households take as given the existing housing and employment options at various locations within their particular urban area. The housing decision simultaneously determines the household's housing consumption and its accessibility to both jobs and neighborhood amenities. Since jobs tend to be centrally located, the location decision is fundamentally a trade-off between the expense of commuting to work and the cost of space. The closer to the center, the lower the commuting costs; the farther from the center, the lower the cost of space. Given this profile of housing prices and commuting costs, income and family structure are key variables in determining the residential location of a particular household. For the postwar family with children, only one worker outside the home, and a relatively high income, this model predicts a suburban location, since transportation costs are a relatively inconsequential part of the family budget and the demand for space looms large.[3] Add to this the tax benefits from home ownership that are broadly available primarily in the single-family home market, and the high quality of the schools in the suburbs, and such a family's preference for the suburbs is even more pronounced.

Lower-income families, however, find transportation costs to be a more significant part of their budget and space to be an extravagance they cannot afford. Hence, theory predicts that these households will live closer to the center, paying more per square foot for housing than they would in the suburbs but spending less on housing and transportation combined.

The new demographics, however, suggest a change in these patterns. For the two-earner family, transportation costs are more significant, and if there are no children (or if children are delayed), the demand for space is lower and the demand for centrality increases.[4] Two-earner families are also tending to choose central locations to satisfy their demand for urban amenities, a preference which may be replacing, at least temporarily, the traditional family's desire for children. Currently, the higher prices of energy and the more widespread availability of homeownership benefits in multiple dwellings (condominiums and

3. The basic economic model of residential location choice assumes that a given increase in income results in a more than proportionate increase in the demand for space, and the decentralization of households is predicted on the basis of higher incomes rather than presence of children.

4. This is similar to the explanation of "gentrification" posited by Anthony Yezer, "Living Patterns: Why People Move into the Inner City," *Washington Post* (June 25, 1979).

cooperatives) are further promoting central city living. Singles, both male and female, have less demand for space and even greater demand for the amenities of urban living, so that the growing numbers in this population group, due to the postwar baby boom, coupled with delayed marriages, are contributing strongly to the demand for central city living.

The increasing numbers of two-earner families and affluent singles have bolstered the current high demand for luxury, multifamily units and have supported the much-touted "gentrification" of deteriorating neighborhoods in a number of cities (the return of middle-class families to the city and the concomitant rehabilitation of the central city housing stock).

The residential location decision is particularly complex for working women who are also household heads, a group that is burgeoning as a result of the rising divorce rates. Most of these women must work to support their families, and therefore they may find a city residence attractive in that it can provide easy access to a wide range of employment opportunities. Like singles, divorced women may also be attracted by the social activities available in cities. However, the disamenities of poor schools and the lack of public safety may discourage these families from locating in many cities. Whereas some two-earner households may have sufficiently high incomes to afford private schools and high-security residences, the relatively low average earnings of women preclude such options for most female-headed households. At the same time, their lower earnings induce female households to locate near the center to economize on transportation and reduce total housing outlays by conserving on space.

Not only are two-earner families more able to substitute private alternatives for deteriorating public services, but their high incomes also place them in strong positions in the housing market.[5] As housing markets respond to the changing income distribution that results from the growing number of two-earner families and affluent singles, many cities have developed very tight rental housing markets. This has adversely affected not only the existing lower-income population—a category in which female-headed households and widows are disproportionately represented—but also the single females and newly divorced women who may be new entrants to both the labor and housing markets. Single women and divorcees with no children have the option of either conserving on space by renting studio apartments or doubling up to share larger apartments. Divorced women with families are in a more difficult position because they are less able to compromise on space and are also less likely to want to share an apartment (or to find people who would be willing to share with them).

5. Elizabeth A. Roistacher and Janet Spratlin Young, "Two-Earner Families in the Housing Market," *Policy Studies Journal* (in press).

What types of families currently tend to choose central cities? Annual housing survey data indicate that husband and wife families in which the head is less than sixty-five years old are still more likely to be suburbanites (table 1). However, the tendency for centrality is increased when both husband and wife are earners and when there are no children. Female-headed families are much more likely to live centrally, in part because of their low incomes, but here, too, the absence of children increases the probability of choosing a central city location. Regardless of household type, older people are more likely to live in cities.

What impact are current demographic trends having on our cities? A recent study based on national data has found that despite the press given to the gentrification movement, there continues to be tremendous net emigration from the central cities, although Northeastern cities are now losing population less rapidly than cities in other parts of the country. What is important and somewhat surprising is that families with children are not leaving the city at a faster rate than those without children and, more important, higher-income households are not substantially more likely to leave the city than lower-income households. However, changing marital status is still an important determinant of

Table 1

SMSA* Households Residing in Central Cities for Selected Family Types (%)

Family Types	SMSA Households Residing in Central City
Husband works outside home, wife does not:	
Head less than 65:	
Children under 18 years old	33.4
No children	39.5
Head 65 or older	45.0
Husband and wife both work outside home:	
Head less than 65:	
Children under 18 years old	36.2
No children	39.3
Head 65 or older	51.5
Single female heads:	
Head less than 65:	
Children under 18 years old	58.8
No children	78.1
Head 65 or older	61.0
Divorced or separated female heads:	
Head less than 65:	
Children under 18 years old	57.2
No children	59.8
Head 65 or older	57.1
All households in SMSAs	45.1

Source.—U.S. Department of Commerce, Bureau of the Census, Annual Housing Survey, unpublished data, 1976.
*Standard Metropolitan Statistical Areas as defined by the U.S. Department of Commerce.

where a household will move. Among those movers who report changing marital status as a motivation for relocating, suburb-to-city movers are more likely to have been recently widowed, separated, or divorced, while city-to-suburb movers are more likely to have been recently married.[6]

One of the factors currently bolstering urban living is the large cohort of post–World War II children that is now reaching the age of household formation. Data indicate that a significant fraction of movers from the suburbs to the city are children leaving their parents' homes to set up their own households. Delayed marriage combined with delayed childbearing has increased the impact of the postwar baby boom on the demand for urban space. The critical question is, Where will these households choose to locate when they marry and have children? If these families move on to the suburbs and are replaced by the next (smaller) cohort of new households, the demand for urban space will weaken. If, as recent data seem to indicate, children are becoming a less important factor in suburbanization, the prospects for our central cities may be brighter. Cities have much to gain from increasing their attractiveness to families with children.

Households with working women should be a target population for any attempts to retain or attract households to the nation's cities. In particular, two-earner families, with their high incomes, are potentially significant net contributors to city revenues. While it is true that single women without children and divorced women do not have high incomes as compared with families headed by men, especially compared with two-earner families, their high rates of participation in the labor force and their high educational attainments place them in a strong economic position relative to widows and single women with children, many of whom are net users of public revenues rather than net contributors.[7] Hence, from the standpoint of the city treasury, single and divorced women are also desirable residents.

The solution of the urban crisis may require contributions from sources other than municipal governments. In some instances, the private sector may be able to help fill the gap in essential services. For example, the business community is already beginning to provide more flexible working hours, and some firms have been experimenting with providing child care.[8] It is also true that cities may be able to shift more of the burden for financing health and welfare services to higher levels of government.

6. John L. Goodman, Jr., *Urban Residential Mobility: Places, People, and Policy* SURI 23100 (Washington, D.C.: Urban Institute, 1978), and "Reasons for Moving out of and into Large Cities," *Journal of the American Planning Association*, vol. 45 (October 1979).

7. Johnson, "Women Who Head Families, 1970–77," pp. 32–37.

8. Jane Kronholz, "Women at Work: Management Practices Change to Reflect the Role of Women Employees," *Wall Street Journal* (September 13, 1979).

The increased labor force participation of women has the potential to improve significantly the economic base of our cities. However, working women, in particular those with the responsibility for families, have special needs which must be met by their working and living environments. By providing residential amenities within their boundaries, cities are in a position to capitalize on an expanding resource, the working woman.

Department of Housing and Urban Development (Roistacher)

Merrill Lynch Pierce Fenner & Smith (Young)

The History, Status, and Concerns of Women Planners

Jacqueline Leavitt

Those concerned with the changing conditions of American women in the cities might expect guidance about policy from women in the planning profession. Unfortunately, the expansion of planning in the 1950s did not lead to an entry of women into the profession, or a sensitizing of the profession to issues affecting women.[1] In that decade, the membership of the American Institute of Planners (AIP) doubled from a little less than 1,000 to over 2,000. The American Society of Planning Officials (ASPO), many of whose members were also in AIP, almost doubled, going from less than 1,500 to about 2,800. Women planners in both organizations numbered at most a little more than 100; within AIP itself women were less than 5 percent of the membership at the beginning and end of the decade.[2] In the 1970s, women have been estimated to be

1. This discussion is based on a larger body of work where the author traces the evolution of women and planning, beginning with women as "public housekeepers" who through their club activities promoted planning in its earliest period from 1890 through the 1920s. The parallel and intersecting developments of women's stereotyped role, as characterized by the "mother of civilization" concept, and of the profession, are examined through the postwar period. Planning's focus on suburban development, perhaps unwittingly, assisted in the creation of conditions that perpetuated a female stereotype, inherited by current planning. As this article shows, with the increase of women planners in the 1970s, it is possible that stereotypes can be repudiated and alternatives to them presented by women who are now inside the profession.

2. Lucien C. Faust, "An Analysis of Selected Characteristics of the Membership of the American Institute of Planners" (Master's thesis, University of North Carolina, 1959);

between 10.5 and 15.0 percent of the planning population, now number-ing between 20,000 and 25,000.[3]

The reasons for the small numbers of women in planning in the 1950s, and into the 1960s, may be attributed to several forces. Fewer women were entering any professions compared to an earlier period. A conscious effort would have to have been made for women to enter a graduate planning program.[4] Once there, a woman would find few role models. Only two women faculty members were identified in twenty-one planning programs in 1954, a time when faculties were being expanded. Moreover, when women chose work, they either sought jobs that mini-mally interfered with their traditional home and family roles or careers that were identified with "feminine" fields.

One might imagine that planning, although not a feminine field, had had earlier alliances with municipal housekeeping and could pro-vide a complementary outlet for work. However, we may speculate that issues of zoning, journey to work, land use, and infrastructure—professional issues of the 1950s—were not as identified with the feminine as tree planting, art improvement, and street cleaning, now perceived as less critical planning problems. As planning became in-creasingly integrated into government, the planner "finds himself called upon to deal with problems that are consonant with public management—fiscal operations, capital plant construction, integration of departmental activities."[5] These were implicitly perceived as mas-culine. Further, it might have been difficult for a woman to live and work in the same town where public functions of planning, such as attending night meetings or testifying at hearings, called attention to the fact that the professional woman was not there when children came home from school or her husband returned from work. Finally, in the late 1950s and early 1960s the planning profession itself was undergoing contraction.

Jacqueline Leavitt, "There's More to Affirmative Action Than Gaining Access: The Case of Female Planners," in *New Space for Women,* ed. Gerda Wekerle, Rebecca Peterson, and David Morley (Boulder, Colo.: Westview Press, 1980).

3. Robert A. Beauregard, in "The Occupation of Planning: A View from the Census" (*Journal of the American Institute of Planners* 42, no. 2 [April 1976]: 187–92), reports that the 1973 Census of Occupational Characteristics indicates that there are 9,214 planners, of whom 89.5 percent are male and 10.5 percent are female. Recent figures are drawn from the membership roll of the American Planning Association (the merged AIP and ASPO) and other updated available information gathered by the author for a study on career patterns of male and female planners.

4. There is reason to suspect, from the author's study of career patterns, that women who were engaged in volunteer civic improvement activities in the 1950s entered planning as professionals. I speculate that they waited until the 1970s when, consciously or not, they were influenced by the impact of mid-1960s programs that created jobs for planners, the women's movement, affirmative action, and their greatly reduced child-rearing re-sponsibilities.

5. William I. Goodman, "The Future of Staff Planning," *Journal of the American In-stitute of Planners* 22, no. 1 (Winter 1956): 24–29.

In just two years 1957 staffing projections were proving to be wrong. There were fewer unfilled professional planning positions reported in 1959 than in 1957, and fewer positions offered at the 1959 professional planning conference than in 1957 and 1958. In its 1959 report of planning agencies, ASPO speculated that "the general economic conditions, the slow-down in approval of 701 funds, the 1958 cutback in urban renewal appropriations, and an increase in the supply of planners—or at least in the supply of persons that agencies are willing to hire for planning positions—may all have had an effect on the number of openings. . . ."[6]

The profile of women in planning begins to change after 1970. In 1968, the first year ASPO disaggregates school enrollment by sex, only forty-six females, 7.5 percent of 610 men and women graduates, received planning degrees. Throughout the seventies the numbers of women receiving degrees steadily increased from 155 to 755. The percentage has been climbing since 1973 from 18.9 percent, 246 out of 1,302, to 1977–78 when it was 31.0 percent, 775 out of 2,500. Despite the increase, any one office may have no more than one or two women. In 1971, ASPO conducted a study on staffing that included numbers of women employees by jurisdiction—city, county, joint city-county, and metropolitan or regional—and by category—professional planners, specialized professionals, and technical staff.[7] Let us look at the city agencies, the majority of the 594 respondents. Less than two-thirds of the 334 city agencies reporting had no women employees. A little more than a third, 123, reported one or more women employees. If we only consider the categories, professional and specialized professional planners, who are at a higher position and salary than technical staff, fifty-four of the 123 reported one woman, thirty-nine, two or more. Staff sizes ranged from one to 122; at least half of the reporting agencies with only one woman had nine or less employees. Women were a majority of the staff in four cases, all in small city agencies. Subsequent ASPO reports on staffing do not disaggregate by sex, so we cannot elaborate on national trends. In 1979, a survey of Oregon female planners reports that a little more than half of the 134 respondents were either the only one or one of two women planners on the staff.[8] We doubt that nationwide women comprise more than a few professional planners other than in the larger agencies.

Two countervailing forces influence whether women planners express concerns about women's issues through their planning work. If, on

6. American Society of Planning Officials, *Expenditures and Staff of Local Planning Agencies*, report no. 122 (Chicago: ASPO, 1959), p. 6.

7. James Hannah, *Expenditures, Staff, and Salaries of Planning Agencies, 1971*, report no. 268 (Chicago: ASPO, 1971).

8. Mary T. Schoolcraft, *The Status of Women in Planning, Oregon, 1979* (Eugene: Oregon Chapter, APA, 1979).

the one hand, they are a token or minority in an agency, they may find it difficult to advance views on a traditional planning subject *and* integrate issues about women.[9] This may be true even if they are a majority, or more rarely, the director of an agency.[10] Their graduate training would not have prepared them for this except in a few scattered cases. The structure of planning, usually organized around functional and geographic areas, does not encourage analyzing clients' needs,[11] working with constituents, or integrating a feminist analysis.

On the other hand, an emerging national network is positively affecting the female practitioner whose concerns are women's issues. Accompanying the increase in the numbers of women trained in and practicing planning has been the development of action around women's issues within professional organizations. There has been an evolution from an April 1970 condemnation of the exclusion of women and women's issues at an ASPO conference; to the 1972 AIP Confer-In where women's issues were specifically discussed; to the 1973 special conference and subsequent publication of *Planning, Women, and Change;* to the 1975 establishment of quotas for women's admission into planning school, planning offices, and positions of authority; to the 1977 AIP endorsement of the Equal Rights Amendment; to the 1978 petition to the American Planning Association (APA), the merged AIP and ASPO, for a task force on women's issues; to the 1979 establishment of a technical division on planning and women within the APA.[12] To be sure, issues raised by supporters of the technical division concern individual planning careers and opportunities, but there is as much concern about the impact on planning of changing life-styles of women, and about women and housing, social services, transportation, land use, and design.

No one unifying issue in planning is perceived to affect women dramatically and uniquely. Planners working on issues of women have tended to begin with the content of their own daily work. Some researchers have started with what is typically part of planning's object— the city, suburbia, neighborhoods, new towns—and applied women's particular conditions to that analysis. Some practitioners have started with planning programs—for example, the community development block grant—and tried to identify the woman's issue in that. Others have identified problems affecting constituents—battered wives, female-headed households—and designed proposals to meet needs.

9. Rosabeth M. Kanter, *Men and Women of the Corporation* (New York: Basic Books, 1977), pp. 206–41.

10. In 1974, ASPO reported only eight female planning directors in 670 agencies.

11. Jerome L. Kaufman, "An Approach to Planning for Women," in *Planning, Women, and Change,* ed. Karen Hapgood and Judith Getzels (Chicago: American Society of Planning Officials, 1974), pp. 72–76.

12. At the 1979 APA conference in Baltimore, Maryland, the title of the division was changed from Planning for Women to Planning and Women.

The history and formation of the less-than-year-old APA technical division on planning and women indicates that practitioners are poised to explore and raise issues. The increase of women planners over the 1970s means they are now accruing experience and are in line to assume positions of authority. Within the short history of women as planning practitioners, they have probably not ever been in as fortuitous a position to improve their own conditions and those of other women. The upcoming professional issues are women's issues. They concern cities where nonnuclear families are concentrated; suburbs where the needs of traditional family units are affected by working wives; poverty, which is increasingly recognized as a woman's problem because of low earnings and discrimination; transportation, where women are primarily dependent on rapid transit. What would appear necessary to avoid would be the addressing of these and other issues only from a traditional professional stance, where contact with the public is usually limited to formal hearings. The identification of women's issues in planning raises the possibility of establishing networks with women outside planning and opening the profession's emphasis from primarily physical and administrative to human considerations.

School of Architecture and Urban Planning
Columbia University

Breaking Down the Barriers: Women in Urban Management

Ruth Ann Burns

A number of forces converge to make municipal management a significant profession: interest in the political process; concern about the quality of urban life; and the growing impact of social, economic, environmental, and administrative problems on community affairs. The responsibilities of a city manager/chief administrative officer will vary. Under council/manager government the city manager has overall responsibility for the day-to-day operations of the city. This includes appointing and dismissing department heads, developing the budget and implementing it after council approval, and recommending policy to the council.

Under a mayor/council form of government, the chief administrative officer is appointed by the mayor to relieve the elected officials of certain duties. The degree of responsibility and authority, while less than that of a city manager, differs widely depending on local needs, preferences, and political culture. For both forms of government, the national trend in municipal management is toward greater professionalization. More and more city managers and municipal administrators are recruited and hired for their technical expertise. They are responsible for shaping policy initiatives as well as for guiding elected officials.

If women are to influence community decisions, generate creative responses to urban problems, and shape public policy at the local level, more of them might consider municipal management. In 1979, the Center for the American Woman and Politics completed the first research project to focus attention on the women who do work to manage cities.[1] We surveyed three groups: women in municipal management, men in municipal management,[2] and women elected officials serving in the same community with a female or male manager in the survey. We mailed questionnaires to a nationwide sample of three targeted populations. Three-hundred seventy-three female municipal managers (48 percent response rate), 217 male municipal managers (30 percent response rate), and 288 female elected officials (46 percent response rate) answered. Approximately 10 percent of female and 10 percent of male respondents were targeted for the in-depth telephone interviews. Attendance at the national meetings of the International City Management Association and the American Society for Public Administration gave project staff additional opportunities to interact with municipal administrators.

Women do not comprise a significant portion of the total municipal management team in any state or section of the nation. They held an

1. The project was supported by a grant from the Office of Policy Development and Research, U.S. Department of Housing and Urban Development. A copy of the complete report, "Women in Municipal Management: Choice, Challenge, and Change," is available from the Center for the American Woman and Politics, Eagleton Institute of Politics, Rutgers–The State University, New Brunswick, New Jersey 08903. The study had two primary objectives: (1) to begin to identify the barriers, routes of opportunity, credentialing requirements, necessary skills, and support systems related to the recruitment, hiring, and promotion of women as municipal managers in urban governments; and (2) to explore relationships which may exist between the roles of women municipal managers and women elected officials within the same municipality; what roles, if any, women elected officials play as mentors in the recruitment, hiring, and promotion of women in municipal management in their communities; what roles, if any, women in municipal management play in the political careers of women elected officials in their communities. The full report documents: (1) who the women in municipal management are—occupational distribution, personal characteristics; (2) numbers and location of female municipal managers and the characteristics of the communities where they work—national and regional distribution, population, form of government, community character; (3) educational credentials of female and male municipal managers—formal educational background, internships, workshops; (4) recruitment and career paths of female and male managers—means of finding first and present job in public service, influence of family history in public sector employment, and/or political party activity, feelings toward relocation, future job preferences; (5) duties on the job and self-assessments—salary, supervisory responsibilities, self-assessment of administrative power and personal efficacy, hidden level of management; (6) relationships to elected officials—impact of political parties on policymaking, barriers to administrator/politician relationships, linkages between elected and appointed women, networking among women; and (7) barriers—community receptivity to professional women in government, human sexuality in the work environment, special advantages to being a woman in municipal management, support systems for female municipal managers, ranking of barriers in three career contexts: recruitment/hiring, promotion, effectiveness.

2. Municipal management positions studied: city manager/chief administrative officer, assistant city manager, finance officer, department head, public works director, assistant department head, analyst/planner, and administrative assistants.

average of 10.5 percent of the total number of local administrative positions nationally in 1978.[3] The issue of barriers necessarily arises. Why are so few women in urban managerial positions? We asked female and male managers and female elected officials to rate eleven different barriers for their impact on three critical areas of a woman municipal manager's career: recruitment/hiring, promotion, and effectiveness. The list included: exclusion from influential informal male networks (e.g., business associations, clubs, etc.); lack of training and/or educational qualifications; insufficient numbers of women in the management labor pool; family responsibilities; inability to travel and relocate; discrimination by employers; discrimination by party officials; prejudice of public and governmental employees; stereotypes about women's roles in society; difficulty in being taken seriously; and individual personality traits (e.g., too aggressive, not aggressive enough).

Female managers are the most likely to perceive barriers to women's advancement in the field; male managers are the least likely. Elected women tend to share the perceptions of their female administrative peers rather than the outlook of the male administrators. Male managers name insufficient numbers of women in the managerial labor pool, lack of training and/or educational qualifications, and individual personality traits as the top three barriers women managers face. All place the blame for women's comparative absence in municipal management on the woman herself, not on the system. In contrast, women name individual personality traits, discrimination by employers, and stereotypes about women's roles in society as their top three barriers. While the perception that individual personality traits operate to stifle women's advancement places some of the blame on women, the combination of this with the other two points to serious problems within the workplace and society in general that impede women's opportunities and upward mobility in municipal management.

Both female and male managers believe that lack of training and/or educational qualifications and the insufficient numbers of women in the management labor pool are critical stumbling blocks. In the educational credentialing section of this report we find that men do have more formal educational credentials and training than their female colleagues. Sixty percent of males have a graduate degree or have completed some advanced training, but only 33 percent of females have. Less than 1 percent of males report no college training; 25 percent of females have none. Only 11 percent of male managers have no bachelor's degree compared with 52 percent of female managers. This finding is tempered by the fact that younger females entering municipal management at the

3. Sources: *Directory of Assistants 1976–1977* (International City Management Association [ICMA]), 1140 Connecticut Avenue, N.W., Washington, D.C. 20036. The Municipal Yearbook, 1978, vol. 45 (ICMA), 1140 Connecticut Avenue, N.W., Washington, D.C. 20036.

beginning and middle levels have started to resemble their male counterparts in educational achievement. More women are entering graduate programs of public and business administration around the nation. They will provide a larger proportion of women in the pool of educationally credentialed young professionals.[4] As women continue to make breakthroughs through affirmative action, their own educational achievements, and their growing confidence on the job, these two barriers should become less and less prohibitive across time.

In contrast, the next three barriers not only highlight sharp disagreement between female and male managers, but also challenge employers and male colleagues to eliminate discrimination in the workplace and to include women in the powerful networks that affect decision making at the municipal level. Women cite discrimination by employers, difficulty in being taken seriously, and exclusion from male networks as serious obstacles to career advancement. Men consider these issues as less important in understanding women's status. The fact that male managers perceive as least important three barriers that women rate as very important explains some of the difficulty in overcoming them. The familiar refrain heard over and over during the course of this study—"Attitudes change slowly"—implies that these barriers erode incrementally and are likely to confront and trouble municipal managerial women for some time to come. Women administrators describe the frustration of watching younger, less experienced men being groomed and given assignments that lead to a city manager's post while they are left waiting in a support position. Skepticism about a woman's ability to handle the dual career demands of work and family life is also present. Discrimination by employers is best summarized by the familiar situation that while men can be average, women must be outstanding.

Difficulty in being taken seriously or the "credibility dilemma" takes many forms. Often women's phone calls or requests for information are neither returned nor answered. Their presence and suggestions at meetings are ignored. They are left out of the decision-making process. Even when they are asked for an opinion, they are frequently second-guessed by a male. Exclusion from informal male networks also exists and operates in towns across the nation, whether they are urban or rural, large or small. A network's nucleus can consist of powerful businessmen in a community or of familial patriarchs who exert considerable influence on community decision making. Sometimes a network extends from male connections in school and college to the workplace. These networks operate informally, usually outside of the 9 A.M. to 5 P.M. office day. One

4. In 1973, only 10 percent of the 12,600 MPA students were female, according to a survey conducted by the National Association of Schools of Public Affairs and Administration (NASPAA). In their 1977 survey, females represented 22 percent of the 24,836 students reported. *1978 Directory, Programs in Public Affairs and Administration* (NASPAA), 1225 Connecticut Avenue, N.W., Washington, D.C. 20036.

female manager compares the "old boys' network" to a tinker toy construction set reaching from the governor's office right down to the city hall janitor. Another female manager captures the gender differences that characterize professional networks in a sarcastic phrase, "urinal clubs."

Women rank three other barriers consistently higher than their male colleagues: individual personality traits; stereotypes about women's roles in society; and the prejudice of public and governmental employees. The "behavioral bind" that female managers experience if they are either too assertive or not assertive enough makes the issue of individual personality traits one that women cannot address completely on their own. Male reaction to the "domineering" woman manager is in part the result of stereotyping that places women in supportive and passive roles, nurturing and helping men. The problems of stereotyping and the prejudices of public and governmental employees require attitudinal readjustments that cast women in new societal roles, especially in a broad range of leadership and managerial positions.

Both female and male administrators in our telephone interviews overwhelmingly cite more disadvantages than advantages to being a woman in city management in 1979, yet they do name some advantages.

Both agree that male overprotection operates in professional settings when men treat women with kid gloves or shield them from tough situations or criticisms. This is viewed as a dubious advantage. Feminine charm is mentioned as a quality that soothes egos and smooths ruffled tempers. Yet this is a double-edged advantage that easily translates into other kinds of sexual problems in the workplace. Both female and male managers perceive women to be more empathic to the needs of their communities, better listeners, and more sensitive to the concerns of their employees. This positive attribute often raises an important question about whether women will bring new approaches to problem solving in the workplaces they enter as influential professional managers. Finally, female managers experience the temporary advantage of high visibility that comes with a sexually imbalanced professional world. They may also benefit from the long-range, cumulative forces that help women to change that imbalance: new attitudes stimulated by the women's rights movement; the legal mandates for equal employment opportunities; and the federal administrative guidelines calling for affirmative action.

Despite the barriers, female and male administrators targeted for our telephone interviews (60 women and men) remained generally optimistic about the prospects for change in employment and promotion for women in the urban management field. Approximately 75 percent of the females interviewed and 87 percent of the males perceived a difference either in the number of women hired for administrative jobs or in the power that those women have relative to the recent past. In an era when big government and multinational corporations have awed and often overwhelmed the power of the individual in society, it was refreshing to hear about the number of times change is attributed to individual effort. They believe progress can be managed. For example, a female department head in Texas says: "Change occurs here because our manager believes it is important. He is taking those steps personally to see that it happens and he is making it clear to the assistant managers who work for him that that sort of thing is expected and that everybody is given a chance." A male city manager in Ohio states: "Yes, change occurs because of me probably more than anything else. I think that it is just going to take time for us men to become aware of the fact that we are passing up a hell of a reserve of people. We don't have to look too far, the talent is there." In other cases, the women administrators initiate action. Some of our interviewees have gone on local television, helped put together commissions on the status of women, have written the town's first affirmative action ordinance, testified before personnel committees, protested personally when they found discrimination present in the city manager's office, required strict adherence to affirmative action timetables for minorities, hired paraprofessional women, pushed their secretaries into administrative and professional career paths, supported subordinates who file Equal Employment Opportunity (EEO) complaints, and served as role models themselves.

A transition period of evolving values, which challenges women and men to work out new professional relationships, has generated its own set of problems and challenges. Women get tired of making others aware of offensive and discriminatory treatment. Yet, it is critical that men understand the frustration, anger, and disillusionment that women feel as they move into a traditionally closed profession. It is equally critical that women understand the confusion and frustration of their male colleagues whose comfortable patterns of behavior are suddenly under attack. New behavior and new expectations often cause surprise, confusion, and some resistance. The voices of female managers repeat that decision making, assertiveness, and accountability make the managerial career path a lonely one. Exercising power calls on behaviors that not all women practice well. Sometimes a woman manager feels "awkward" expressing her views first and asking for the opinions of others second, taking action instead of reacting, exercising personal power rather than sharing it.

For men, the entrance of women into city hall increases the potential for relationships involving a closeness they fear could lead to sexual exchange. Threatened, anxious, or perhaps just worried that the town will talk, male managers and their wives may not welcome the presence of women in municipal management.

For women, the issue is how to relate to a male colleague whose first evaluation of her may center on her sexuality rather than on her capabilities and technical talents. Forming friendships and creating collegiality with both men and other women are perhaps new skills that will have to be learned in the process of opening up employment opportunities in management. New support systems will have to be formed for circumventing some of the barriers women face as they enter new roles. Women will have to rely on support from other women because they are excluded from informal male networks. If the numbers of women in management are sparse for a while, women throughout municipal government will have to seek each other out and build their own support system.

Some may find the evidence of progress modest and fragile. Nonetheless, it is there, manifested in the growing number of young women who are equally credentialed compared with their male colleagues, in female managers' performance on the job, and in women's ambitions. If women's numbers in municipal management continue to increase, and if their power matches their titles, city management in the 1990s will reflect a new kind of leader across the country.

Center for the American Woman and Politics,
Eagleton Institute of Politics
Rutgers University

Revisions/Reports: Notes on Research

A Rape Prevention Program in an Urban Area

Community Action Strategies to Stop Rape

Women Against Rape of Columbus, Ohio, has recently completed a three-year research-demonstration project on rape prevention in a large urban university area. The project, Community Action Strategies to Stop Rape (CASSR), is one of the first systematic research evaluation studies of rape prevention programs fielded by a grass-roots feminist organization. The project team's objective was to assess the impact of theoretically grounded feminist prevention programs that combined education, experiential learning, and community action in the target-area community.[1]

The demonstration component of the project included four community prevention programs: a series of women's rape prevention workshops that included discussions of the politics of rape and feminist prevention strategies, confrontation training, and self-defense; a Whistle Alert program; a Shelter House program; and a Women's Rape Prevention Network. The research evaluation component of the project was a quasi-experimental time-series study of the effectiveness of the four community awareness and action programs. The project team pre- and posttested program participants in the women's rape prevention workshops at the time of the workshops and did a follow-up two months later.

1. The project was funded by the National Center for the Prevention and Control of Rape of the National Institute of Mental Health, grant R18 MH29049. The project team members who developed the project are Bat-Ami Bar On, Deborah Chalfie, Sunny Graff, Karen Jensen, Sarah McKinley, Elaine McCrate, and Caroline Sparks.

Members of the Women's Rape Prevention Network received pretests when they joined the network and posttests three to six months later. All participant data were compared with data from random samples of the general community population who were questioned at yearly intervals over the three-year project period. We monitored the Whistle Alert and Shelter House programs and obtained corollary information about changes in media coverage of rape and in rape prevention programming by community organizations.

The project's primary goal was to change women program-participants' attitudes about their status as potential rape victims and increase their ability to act to alter their status. The secondary goal was to increase community concern about rape and community responsiveness to programs in which women were encouraged to act to reduce their vulnerability to rape. The CASSR project team approached rape as a social and political problem that affects all women and developed a theoretical model of rape prevention upon which to base the research and demonstration components of the project. Our approach to rape included the following points:

1. that rape is a mode of systemic violence against women;
2. that rape functions as a control mechanism in patriarchy, serving a maintenance function in it, while its occurrence is facilitated by existing patriarchal conditions;
3. that women's vulnerability to rape needs to be understood in terms of women's place in patriarchy;
4. that rape prevention efforts need to be directed toward the elimination of women's status as potential victims; and
5. that rape prevention work needs to be conducted on both individual and communal levels with women leading the change.

Within this conceptual framework, the problem of rape has two dimensions: the actual incidence of rape and the threat of rape that affects women who may never become actual victims. Rape prevention also has two dimensions: reduction of actual rapes and the reduction of the effects of the threat of rape.

The CASSR team developed a theoretical construct for rape prevention in which we operationally defined women's status as potential rape victims as women's vulnerability to rape. Rape prevention, therefore, is defined as the reduction or elimination of women's vulnerability that would require changes in the structural and cultural conditions that contribute to women's vulnerability. The three contributing conditions that CASSR posited are: (1) lack of information and understanding of rape; (2) women's subordinate relationship to men in patriarchy and the characteristics women develop as a result of sex-role socialization and dependence; and (3) women's isolation from other women and their isolation in the larger community. Since these conditions are sociopolitical, rape prevention is a process of change that will ultimately produce systemic change in women's status in society.

Given this orientation, where prevention is viewed as both an end product and a process of change, the CASSR project staff confronted the difficult problem of designing short-run interventions that relate to long-range prevention goals and of finding measures of effectiveness that distinguish between the two. The project team considered the four prevention programs offered in the target area to be first steps in developing strategies that parallel the three areas of vulnerability outlined above. We designed the programs to inform women about rape, to decrease their isolation from one another in the community, and to begin to increase women's power to change their condition of dependence upon men under patriarchy. We designed indices of impact that would show change in a direction that leads toward the elimination of women's vulnerability to rape. The short-range changes that we sought were changes in awareness about rape that were expected to impact first on women's isolation and ultimately on women's dependent status. Within our time frame, however, we hoped at best to create some of the preconditions for this kind of social change. The staff intended to work primarily with women to enable them to become catalysts for change in the rest of the community, in its agencies, and in its institutions. By taking charge of rape prevention efforts, women could begin to change the patriarchal "rules" governing rape and reduce their dependence upon men for protection.

We were concerned that strategies designed to reduce women's vulnerability not be accompanied by undesirable social change. The project team, therefore, established four criteria to be used to evaluate specific prevention strategies. Strategies ought to (1) build women's strength, (2) extend women's mobility, (3) promote women's independence, and (4) guarantee women's freedom.

Once the project team had posited three contributing conditions of women's vulnerability to rape, we identified specific components under each of the three conditions. These components were an initial subset of conditions that the project team thought had important consequences for women's ability to develop rape prevention strategies. Once defined, they gave the project team a set of content areas around which to develop program materials and specific strategies.[2] This framework allowed us to identify the ways in which each of the four prevention programs fit into an overall schema for changing women's vulnerability to rape even if a given program addressed only a small area of change. For example, we presented self-defense as a change in socializing practices that keep women physically dependent upon men for protection.

---

2. A complete discussion and illustration of the components of vulnerability is beyond the scope of this brief report but does appear in the project's final report.

Framing the tactic in this way permits women to see the value of self-defense not only as a practical individual prevention tactic but as a means for creating alternatives to women's traditional dependent status.

The project team designed its outcome measures to assess changes along each of the components of vulnerability that the programs addressed. Data analysis of the first two years of the project indicates that the rape prevention workshops had a striking effect on participants in several areas that the project had identified as important for prevention. Participants' knowledge of rape was more accurate at the end of the workshops, and their attitudes and beliefs about rape and rape prevention were strongly profeminist by the end of the workshops. Support for social change prevention tactics increased, as did awareness of women's oppression. Participants reported increased practice of confrontation and self-defense skills, decreased fear, and increased confidence in their ability to defend themselves if attacked—effects that were sustained over the two-month follow-up period. The project considered these changes a sign of increased readiness to act both individually and in support of organized action on the part of women. The general community showed a heightened awareness of the problem of rape, awareness of crime prevention programs, and belief in the utility of various prevention tactics. Knowledge of the two neighborhood programs, Whistle Alert and Shelter Houses, doubled over a year's period, although Whistle Alert was the more popular program. In contrast to the workshop participants, the general public maintained support for a number of popular myths about rape and showed stronger support for restrictive prevention tactics than social change tactics. We are currently analyzing the Women's Rape Prevention Network data and the third-year survey data. Results of all three years of project data will be available after June 1, 1980.

Columbus, Ohio

REVISIONS/REPORTS:
NOTES ON RESEARCH

Spatial and Temporal Dimensions of Child Care

William Michelson

We have considerable research and political interest in the factors that enable women to enter the labor force and remain there. We ask about equal opportunity and pay and about the services, like child care, that support people's ability to handle an increasing number of demanding daily responsibilities. Our discussions of such questions have included time and space dimensions. We recognize, for example, that part-time work can facilitate the conduct of other activities that full-time work might crowd into a daily timetable.[1] We know, too, that fusing traditional and new roles may add up to an overly large set of time demands for one person, which can be relieved by the transfer of some responsibilities to another person (or persons) in the same family.[2] Similarly, discussions of

This research note is a report on a study project being undertaken by the author in collaboration with Linda Hagarty, Susan Hodgson, and Suzanne Ziegler funded under the National Welfare Grants Programme of Health and Welfare Canada, whose support is gratefully acknowledged. The study ought to be finished in 1981. I am grateful to Willem van Vliet for helpful research assistance; to Hagarty, Hodgson, and Martha Friendly for constructive comments on an earlier draft of this paper; to Sue Ray, who typed the manuscripts; and to the editors of *Signs* for constructive editorial advice.

1. T. W. Moore, "Effects on the Children," in *Working Mothers and Their Children*, ed. S. Judkin and A. Holme (London: Michael Joseph, Ltd., 1963).

2. See, e.g., K. Walker, "Household Work Time: Its Implication for Family Decisions," *Journal of Home Economics* 65, no. 7 (1973): 7–11; T. W. Weisner and R. Gallimore, "My Brother's Keeper: Child and Sibling Caretaking," *Current Anthropology* 18, no. 2 (1977): 169–80; A. Oakley, *The Sociology of Housework* (New York: Random House, 1974); S. S. Angrist, J. R. Lave, and R. Mickelsen, "How Working Mothers Manage: Socio-

day care include some spatial dimensions, arguing for centers near the home or job to cut down on needless travel (and time consumption) by parent and child alike.[3]

Nonetheless, we have failed to deal with time and space as systematic phenomena which form a context in the local urban environment relevant to the everyday lives people lead. Time and space do form a context together. It takes time to traverse space. While the relationship is not linear (due to differential means of travel and site-specific impediments to movement), the location of facilities (vis-à-vis each other and users) and the density of residence affect the use of time. Conversely, the nature of individuals' time schedules limits the extent that they are free to make various lengths of trips. The day is a zero-sum game.[4] It has only twenty-four hours and is extremely unlikely to change overnight. Hence, daily activities have both absolute and relative time limits. None can exceed twenty-four hours a day, and those pursued have to compete with each other for a finite amount of time. Any new or expanded activities, because they take time away from others, represent a reorganization of the performance of or access to the activity. Consistent with this, spatial dimensions of activities limit what an individual can do in a day. There is an absolute limit on the territory that can fit into the daily timetable (amount of accessible territory a function of available transportation).

Research has already substantiated many of the points related to these truisms. The employed mother, for example, has been shown in time-use studies in many different nations[5] to sleep less than any other segment of the population. Studies fail to confirm that employed mothers do everything they previously did in addition to their outside jobs (the so-called double load); but they still do *much* of it, without, on the average, significant increases in help from other family members.[6] Typically, housework is done more selectively and at different times.[7] Furthermore, even in affluent nations, the average employed mother is second in line for ownership and use of a family car, often a time-saver.[8]

Economic Differences in Work, Child Care, and Household Tasks," *Social Science Quarterly* 56, no. 4 (1976): 631–37; S. F. Berk and C. W. Berheide, "Going Backstage: Gaining Access to Observe Household Work," *Sociology of Work and Occupations* 4, no. 1 (1977): 27–48.

3. L. C. Johnson, *Who Cares?* (Toronto: Social Planning Council of Metropolitan Toronto, 1977); J. Maudit and A. M. Raimond, *Ce que les femmes reclament* (Paris: Arthème Fayard Librairie, 1971).

4. Z. Staikov, "Modelling and Programming of Time-Budgets," *Society and Leisure* 5, no. 1 (1973): 31–47.

5. A. Szalai et al., *The Use of Time: Daily Activities of Urban and Suburban Populations in Twelve Countries* (The Hague: Mouton, 1972).

6. E. O. Derow, "Married Women's Employment and Domestic Labour" (Ph.D. thesis, University of Toronto, 1977).

7. Derow; W. Michelson, *Environmental Choice, Human Behavior, and Residential Satisfaction* (New York: Oxford University Press, 1977).

8. Michelson, chap. 6.

But even when we comprehend the dynamics of time and its general relation to space, we all too rarely assess the facilitating and constraining properties of our urban communities. What temporal and spatial *opportunities* make a day fluid or frantic? What we can do on a given day, for example, is predicated on the linkage of opening and closing hours of desired or needed services. It is also related to how close and clustered these places are. Mårtensson, for example, demonstrates absolute differences between residents of two regions in Sweden in their physical opportunity to participate in community activities in the evening, given the time and space parameters of those areas.[9] She similarly shows how much time is needed to get medical treatment, depending also on where one lives.[10] Both differences are major. Indeed, I do not believe it is coincidental that the levels of routine pediatric checkups and immunization have recently dropped in North America, while evening use of hospital emergency facilities for acute illnesses has increased. The public has more fixed obligations during regular working hours, while primary-care physicians have not adapted by making their services available when their patients are.

We doubtless adapt to the given system in which we live, weaving our desires and the available opportunities into habits.[11] Yet, these habits are not purely personal constructs, as they reflect the fixed hours of, for example, food stores, day-care centers, banks, pools, doctors, employers, restaurants, bars, television programs, public transportation—external community factors.[12] Manz assessed empirically the effects of selectively planned services for employed mothers in the German Democratic Republic; these women were shown to gain an extra half hour's sleep per night after implementation of these supports.[13] People's habits reflect as well the ease or difficulty in reaching these places. Simonsen, for example, showed the differential use of city facilities in Denmark which accompanied differential proximity to them.[14]

Melbin astutely indicated the revolutionary impact of making more activities and services available at night.[15] If viewed in our perspective,

9. S. Mårtensson, "Time Allocation and Daily Living Conditions: Comparing Regions," in *Human Activity and Time Geography,* ed. T. Carlstein, Don Parkes, and Nigel Thrift (London: Edward Arnold, Ltd., 1978).

10. Ibid., pp. 189–90.

11. I. Cullen and E. Phelps, "Patterns of Behavior and Responses to the Urban Environment," in *Public Policy in Temporal Perspective,* ed. W. Michelson (The Hague: Mouton, 1978).

12. M. Shapcott and P. Steadman, "Rhythms of Urban Activity," in Carlstein et al.

13. G. Manz, "The Time-Budget in National Economic Planning," in Michelson, *Public Policy in Temporal Perspective.* Increased participation in adult education had been hypothesized; see G. Manz, "Way of Life and Leisure Time Use," *Society and Leisure* 6, no. 2 (1974): 75–86.

14. K. Simonsen, "Household Activities and Environmental Constraints" (paper presented to the Ninth World Congress of Sociology, Uppsala, August 1978).

15. M. Melbin, "The Colonization of Time," in Carlstein et al.

what he called "the colonization of time" makes possible increments in individual flexibility and, hence, in the ability to fulfill daily needs; these increments, in effect, increase personal freedom. More can be accomplished with less time pressure if someone working from nine to five is not forced to shop, mail, consult, pick up, repair, or bank in almost exactly those same hours. The private sector has responded more sensitively in this regard than the public sector, but coordinated response by any sector is still lacking. Such distribution of activities throughout available time is paralleled by the need for a similarly sensitive distribution in space.[16] Decentralization, wherever possible, gives greater access and, hence, more flexible use.

There is evidence that unresolved time pressures can be detrimental, despite people's adaptive capacities. Researchers dealing with such pressures in the lives of working mothers, for example, have noted consequences like dissatisfaction,[17] stress,[18] and intrafamilial conflict[19] among women, and nervousness[20] and hostility[21] among their children. All the purported effects of time pressures cannot be ascribed to contextual time and space parameters, nor do all who fight the clock suffer from it. Nonetheless, how we arrange and timetable our communities has definite implications for the lives we can lead within them.[22] Some segments of the population, undertaking multiple roles, are more subject to constraining effects from rigid or irrational timetabling and land-use patterns. Some members of families are more affected than others, without compensating intrafamilial adjustment.

A continuing interest in urban time-space dimensions, and association with a research program tracing the implications for children of recent social and physical trends in urban areas,[23] has led me to study

16. See, e.g., K. Hapgood and J. Getzels, eds., *Planning, Women and Change* (Chicago: American Society of Planning Officials, 1974); and R. Peterson, G. R. Wekerle, and D. Morley, "Women and Environments," *Environment and Behavior* 10, no. 4 (1978): 511–34.

17. D. T. Hall, "Pressures from Work, Self, and Home in the Life Stages of Married Women," *Journal of Vocational Behavior* 6, no. 1 (1975): 121–32.

18. A. D. Ross, "Some Comments on the Home Roles of Businesswomen in India, Australia, and Canada," *Journal of Comparative Family Studies* 8, no. 3 (1977): 327–40.

19. B. L. Lobodzinska, "Married Women's Gainful Employment and Housework in Contemporary Poland," *Journal of Marriage and the Family* 39, no. 2 (1977): 405–15; M. Young and P. Willmott, *The Symmetrical Family* (London: Routledge & Kegan Paul, 1973).

20. P. H. Chombart de Lauwe, *Famille et habitation* (Paris: Centre National de la Recherche Scientifique, 1960), vol. 2.

21. F. E. Nye and L. W. Hoffman, *The Employed Mother in America* (Chicago: Rand McNally & Co., 1963).

22. The pioneer theoretical work on this topic is by T. Hägerstrand and associates. The most lucid explanation of this work in English may be T. Carlstein, "A Time-Geographic Approach to Time Allocation and Socio-Ecological Systems," in Michelson, *Public Policy in Temporal Perspective*.

23. The Child in the City Programme, University of Toronto, under a supporting grant from the Hospital for Sick Children Foundation, Toronto.

the characteristic daily time demands on parents; the challenges and roadblocks to getting what is felt to be necessary and desirable; types of adaptation; the consequences of unresolved pressures; and, in particular, the implications for children of the time and space dynamics of the other members of what must be regarded as a family *system*. We are comparing the daily conditions among traditional, two-career, and single-parent families. The place of various child-care services in the daily routine is examined in talking with families using different forms (centers, family day care, siblings, mother at home, etc.). As in previous studies dealing with temporal and spatial factors in everyday life, a major methodological feature of this study is the time budget.[24] This technique can be used to gather data on the content of selected periods of time (usually one or more days): activity, duration of activity, location, persons with the respondent, secondary simultaneous activity, and subjective responses to or evaluations of one or another aspect of the activity.

Our current study may be distinguished from others on its component parts by its integrated focus on (1) all members of the family; (2) activities that may not take place; (3) the daily life conditions of children assessed directly (though in the family context); (4) the basis for ease or difficulty in carrying out the daily round in view of community time-space parameters; and (5) the place of child-care services in a wider context than availability or program content. Because many outcome measures like adaptation or stress are also likely to reflect other causes, such as socioeconomic status or coping style, singly or in combination, a variety of other data are being gathered as well. These cover sources of time demands, aspects of employment and family economics, parenting arrangements, social network and support considerations, and measures of and explanations for the hypothesized dependent behaviors, attitudes, and health conditions of family members.

There are three phases in this study. The first, on a heterogeneous but nonrandom or representative sample of forty families, combines observation and both structured and unstructured interviewing. The second phase is one of systematic data gathering among a representative sample of families in Metropolitan Toronto, during winter and early spring, using standardized interviewing and some systematic observation. A stratified, random sample of 800 families deals with the need for sufficiently large, though independent, categories regarding the main independent and mediating variables. A subsample of seventy-five families is to be reinterviewed during the summer to assess seasonal differences. The third phase will occur after the results of the first two have been tentatively determined. Discussion sessions with previous respon-

---

24. W. Michelson and P. B. Reed, "The Time Budget," in *Behavioral Research Methods in Environmental Design*, ed. W. Michelson (Stroudsburg, Pa.: Dowden, Hutchinson, & Ross, 1975).

dents will be organized to assess the accuracy and subjective meanings of the conclusions drawn.

We expect that this study, if successful, will lead to recommendations concerning hours for employment and other enterprises and services, strategic and needed parental supports (particularly, but not exclusively, for single parents), and the articulation of child care into a wider set of community considerations.

Department of Sociology and
The Child in the City Programme
University of Toronto

A Women's Self-Help Network as a Response to Service Needs in the Suburbs

Rosalie G. Genovese

The failure of urban researchers to make women's daily lives a topic for serious investigation hampers efforts to plan communities responsive to women's changing life-styles. There is a crucial lack of studies exploring women's diverse concerns and ways of dealing with unmet needs for services. What explanations are offered for the lack of research on urban and suburban women? As Lofland so perceptively argued, women are just "there" in urban studies—in the background like furniture or the unobtrusive butler in an English murder mystery.[1] This "thereness" is attributable to three factors. First, the "community" emphasis of urban studies leads researchers to study ethnic or working-class communities in which the woman's role is home-centered, segregated, and circumscribed. Since her overt participation in the community's public life is usually limited, her life is not readily visible, especially to the male researcher. His limited opportunity to observe and study women's lives and activities, then, is a second explanation for the lack of studies. A third reason for the paucity of studies on women in cities and suburbs is that government and foundation funding is largely allocated to the study of "problems," particularly those associated with social disorganization and crime.[2] In these studies, the focus tends to be on men, although

---

1. Lyn H. Lofland, "The 'Thereness' of Women: A Selective Review of Urban Sociology," in *Another Voice: Feminist Perspectives on Social Life and Social Science,* ed. Marcia Millman and Rosabeth Moss Kanter (New York: Anchor Books, 1975), p. 145.
2. Ibid., pp. 146–62.

there is now a burgeoning literature on crime committed by women. Daniels advances still another explanation for the dearth of work on women's lives—that women's worlds are "invisible" because traditional social scientists consider them unimportant.[3]

The gaps in the literature include a lack of research on well-to-do urban and suburban women whose life-styles contrast sharply with the neighborhood-based world of ethnic or working-class women portrayed in such classics as *Street Corner Society* or *The Urban Villagers*.[4] For example, suburban women may travel long distances to take advantage of diverse facilities and resources located both in the city and in the suburbs. Since their activities take them away from their immediate residential community, these aspects of women's lives fall outside the parameters of neighborhood or community studies.[5] This need to travel, whether for greater intellectual stimulation or higher-quality services, gives women in most income groups and life-cycle stages the common task of working from within their environments to fulfill their needs. As Boulding has noted, unless they can do this, they face a kind of death.[6]

How do women cope with these limitations in their environment? Women in upper-income categories can most easily remedy deficiencies, since they can afford to pay for services or facilities and can select from a variety of alternatives. They can choose the most advantageous location in the city and, if they live in the suburbs, they can take advantage of both the city and the suburb, although they may have to travel considerable distances for jobs, cultural activities, and so on.[7] At the other extreme, low-income women are least able to satisfy their need for services. Women who head families are especially hard-pressed and, with high divorce rates, increasing numbers of previously middle- or upper-

3. Arlene Kaplan Daniels, "Women's Worlds," *Society* (September/October 1978), pp. 44–46, see p. 44.

4. William F. Whyte, *Street Corner Society* (Chicago: University of Chicago Press, 1943); Herbert J. Gans, *The Urban Villagers* (New York: Free Press, 1962).

5. Lofland, pp. 154–55, suggests that a translocal approach would avoid the limits imposed by a community model and would provide an in-depth picture of the complex lives, diverse activities, and social relationships of women which go far beyond local community boundaries. Barry Wellman and Barry Leighton discuss the network approach as an alternative to a neighborhood or community focus in "Networks, Neighborhoods and Communities," *Urban Affairs Quarterly* 14, no. 3 (March 1959): 363–90.

6. Elise Boulding made these remarks in her comments on the papers presented at a community section session, "Spatial Inequalities in American Urban Life: Consequences for Women," at the annual meetings of the American Sociological Association, San Francisco, September 1978.

7. See the discussion of the impact that distance has on women in Sylvia Fleis Fava, "Woman's Place in the New Suburbia" (paper presented at the annual meetings of the American Sociological Association, San Francisco, September 1978). For a general analysis of how suburban planning affects women, see Marilyn M. Pray, "Planning and Women in the Suburban Setting," in *Planning, Women, and Change,* ed. Karen Hapgood and Judith Getzels (Chicago: American Society of Planning Officials, 1974), pp. 51–56.

income women face adjusting to drastically reduced incomes, limiting their ability to afford services. Brown's study of divorced women in the Greater Boston area revealed that they spent a considerable portion of their time just meeting basic service needs.[8] Their primary problems were in the areas of transportation, child care, home maintenance and repair, and low-cost, easily accessible education. One way of coping is through collective services: "Collective services are needed by people who cannot provide services themselves or hire a private individual to do it for them. Collective services are useful for everyone, but for a single parent they become crucial since there is no longer the labor or material resource within the family."[9] Several women in the study, for example, started day-care centers.

Suburban living, despite its often stereotyped carefree image, may also leave the woman with unmet service and resource needs. According to Popenoe, women in the suburbs often suffer from "deprivation of access," a condition they share with the elderly and teenagers.[10] Without a car, individuals of all ages have lesser mobility and fewer options than their neighbors. In rare instances when the woman's needs *have* been taken into account, such as new town planning, these needs have been narrowly defined in terms of the wife-and-mother role.[11] Such an approach does not realize the interests and needs of married women who work; the single, widowed, or divorced; and the elderly. Moreover, some married women with children find themselves forced to obtain essential resources and services within a limited family budget.

My study of how one group of women met their needs was conducted between September 1975 and August 1976 in the townhouse complex where I lived. As a peripheral participant in the network, I had the opportunity to observe the women's activities and relationships, both in informal interaction and at more formal, planned events. My location in the complex was strategic—behind the playground and two doors

8. Carol A. Brown, "Spatial Inequities and Divorced Mothers" (paper presented at the annual meetings of the American Sociological Association, San Francisco, September 1978). For data on the economic status and other characteristics of households headed by women, see Heather Ross and Isabel V. Sawhill, *Time of Transition: The Growth of Families Headed by Women* (Washington, D.C.: Urban Institute, 1975).

9. Brown, p. 10.

10. David Popenoe's comments were made at the annual meetings of the Eastern Sociological Society, New York City, March 1977. For a detailed comparison of life in the Swedish suburb of Vallingby and Levittown in the United States, see Popenoe's *The Suburban Environment* (Chicago: University of Chicago Press, 1977). For a critical view of more recent Swedish suburbs, especially their impact on people, see Rosalie G. Genovese, "Social Factors in Planning New Suburbs: The Swedish Experience," *Sociological Symposium* (Spring 1975), pp. 53–61.

11. See, for example, Charlotte Temple, "Planning and the Married Woman with Children—a New Town Perspective," in Hapgood and Getzels, eds., pp. 43–50. Also see Sylvia Fleis Fava, "Beyond Suburbia," *Annals of the American Academy of Political and Social Science* (November 1975), pp. 21–23.

away from the woman who was a central figure in the network. During that year, the network was beginning to dissolve. One original network family moved away early in the year. Two other families moved out at the end of the observation period, as did I.

The townhouse condominium complex was located in a small town about twelve miles outside a large western New York city. The moderately priced houses attracted two major resident groups—young married couples buying their first home and individuals or couples in their middle years or nearing retirement. A townhouse gave young couples their first experience with home ownership, and many were already planning their next move to a single-family house. Older couples had often sold homes to buy the townhouses, which eliminated much individual responsibility for maintenance. All owners paid a fee to the homeowners' association for such services as landscape maintenance, snow plowing, and garbage removal.

The townhouses' location was extremely convenient to one of the area's largest employers and a short drive from a city with major corporations. However, mobility within the surrounding parts of the county was almost entirely dependent on use of a car. There was no local bus service. Although a supermarket was within walking distance, a half-mile stretch along a road without sidewalks presented an impractical way to do major shopping. Buses to and from the city stopped near the supermarket seven or eight times a day. Since mobility without a car was difficult, facilities close to home were important. A proposed clubhouse with year-round swimming pool and sauna had been an important selling point to buyers, but the financial difficulties of a series of builders kept it from becoming a reality. Families were expected to use their own resources for day care and baby-sitting. No laundry facilities were provided. While there were occasional functions for all residents, like an annual picnic, for the most part residents had to meet their own needs.

Common interests of residents, newness of the area, and proximity were all favorable conditions to the formation of the self-help network. The women were at the same life-cycle stage, with similar life-styles and incomes. Moreover, since they lived practically next door to each other, communication was not only easy, but almost unavoidable. The network's nucleus consisted of five women, with a secondary larger group of six to ten who participated in some activities. Obviously, women who worked outside the home could not be included in the informal daytime gatherings and outings. Participants ranged in age from their late twenties to early thirties, and their children from infants to those in the early school years. At the time of the study, three women were pregnant with their second or third child.

The families that moved in when the development was first occupied had the greatest chance of becoming friends. Research indicates that neighboring tends to be at its peak in the early stages of a new community when the neighborhood represents the most available source of friends.[12] Among the first residents of the complex were three women in the nucleus; two of the couples had known each other before moving in. Two families in the nucleus belonged to the same church, giving them additional mutual interests.

The backgrounds of the women were quite varied. Some had college educations; others did not. Their work experience also differed. Only one of the women in the nucleus worked outside the home during the study. She had returned to her job as a computer analyst for several months after a maternity leave, but decided that she preferred to be at home. Other nucleus members had experience in teaching, secretarial work, and hairdressing. Several women in the larger network had full- or part-time jobs close to home: in a bank, a publishing company, and a school. Only one woman had grown up in the same town as the townhouse tract. Her husband and one other couple had come from small towns in the surrounding region while others were from the Midwest, Virginia, and England.

There were fewer differences in the backgrounds of the spouses. Most had college degrees and worked in professional, technical, or managerial positions. One man worked in the post office. Four had moved their families to the area when they began to work for a large corporation. Perhaps this mobility helps explain differences in family attitudes toward their current residence. For some it was clearly temporary until they could afford to buy a one-family house. For others the townhouses seemed a more permanent arrangement.

The network seemed unusual in its ability to include women with these differing backgrounds without making noticeable status distinctions. Moreover, several women who moved into the units vacated by nucleus members became part of the network, despite differences in their marital status and cultural background. Considering these rather sharp differences in the women's employment, residential history, and aspirations, the network's success appeared to be based primarily on residents' current sharing of both time of life and life-style. For example, older women in the immediate vicinity were not part of the network, although it is not clear whether by choice or lack of invitation. Localism, often described as characteristic of suburban dwellers, was also a prevalent orientation of the network.[13] Moreover, the close relationships with neighbors probably took the place of distant families for some women.

The physical layout of the tract definitely contributed to the evolution of the network. The playground was a common meeting place for mothers with small children. Since the woman whose home was the unofficial headquarters for the network lived next to it, mothers could

12. Suzanne Keller, *The Urban Neighborhood* (New York: Random House, 1968).
13. See Fava, "Women's Place in the New Suburbia," p. 7.

easily keep an eye on their children from her house. It was not unusual to find several women sitting around the table in the dining area of her home, with numerous children playing downstairs or on the patio. The arrival of several more women usually started an impromptu coffee klatch. As children wandered in and out looking for their mothers, the overall impression was one of noise, bustle, and sometimes confusion, but most importantly one of informal support and mutual enjoyment.

To a large extent, the persistence of this loosely organized network seems attributable to the efforts of the woman whose home became its meeting place. She was the one person to whom everyone seemed to come. She gave the impression of competence and could be counted on to plan and follow through on activities. In addition to her previous experience as an elementary schoolteacher, she was active in church activities with her husband. More recently, she was named a deacon, an unusual honor for a person of her age. Apart from her position as the informal center, there were no formally designated statuses or roles in the network. However, when it came to a planned event, everyone made an agreed-upon contribution. The resulting spontaneous character of many activities made the group quite open to newcomers, an important characteristic in light of the frequent turnover in residents.

The network provided numerous needed services to all members. Without the network, child care could have been a serious problem. Working women relied on network participants to supervise their children after school. While older children only needed someone nearby to answer questions or provide assistance, younger children needed more attention. Women also took turns baby-sitting for each other. Since there was no public transportation, access to a car was crucial and the network played an important role here as well. A woman with a car would drive another woman without one to the doctor or dentist. Women also shopped for each other.

This quasi-communal character carried over to other interactions. Participants frequently shared household equipment, and sometimes they bought food or gardening products in bulk and divided them. One participant even gave her maternity clothes to two pregnant women in the network. Several women developed cottage industries. The most successful was a hairdresser who worked out of her home, an arrangement that suited everyone, as her customers found her haircuts convenient and less expensive than a trip to a commercial establishment. Another woman ran a successful business altering clothes for other families, in addition to holding a full-time job. (Her children were looked after by other participants while she was at work.) A third woman, a newcomer, sold cosmetics. Her neighbors represented a captive market for her products and referred her to friends outside the complex.

In addition to services and the pooling of resources, the network afforded its residents many of the same social activities associated with small-town and suburban living. There was constant visiting back and forth and during the summer frequent get-togethers took place at the playground or on someone's patio. These informal social gatherings provided a welcome break from the daily domestic routines, giving the women a chance to discuss their lives and concerns. Product parties—devoted to housewares, fabrics, plants, and cosmetics—were also frequent. Sometimes the get-togethers were instrumental as well as social, as when the women formed a group to learn macramé.

More formal events were planned at other meetings. These special events included an annual Christmas luncheon and a New Year's Eve party. For the former everyone contributed a dish, and for the latter there was a progressive dinner party for about twelve couples, followed by a larger party with friends and acquaintances. At some social functions, the easy interaction so characteristic of the daily meetings among the women seemed to break down. Women might congregate in one part of the room and men in another. This sex segregation seemed more typical of behavior found in working-class communities than of middle-income suburban neighborhoods.[14] Men had an embryonic network of their own. Husbands often shared tools or rented equipment together, two of the men drove to work together, and there were regular card games. When several families moved away from the complex, they rented a truck and helped each other to move, aided by some other network spouses. Nevertheless, the network was clearly woman-centered and performed a major function in providing women with social and psychological support. Its importance in this area stands out to me even more sharply in retrospect.

I do not want to imply that there were no undercurrents of annoyance or factions among participants. On occasion, a participant would express resentment toward another who did not do her share. Criticism was also passed in remarks about other women's sloppy housekeeping or questionable child-rearing practices. While some women would clearly have been friends regardless of whether they lived next door, proximity was the basis for interaction among other women. Proof, however, of the network's strength was visible in its survival in modified form even after three women in the nucleus moved out to houses in the vicinity.

The case study I have presented had significance for the women themselves and implications for planners and policymakers. Not only did it satisfy the women's need for services with little money changing hands, but it also met their expressive needs through friendships and social support. It was able to include women who worked outside the home and those who did not. And, because it absorbed new residents,

14. See, for example, Gans, *The Urban Villagers,* pp. 38–39.

the network did not dissolve completely when members moved away. In contrast to current research, which indicates that many suburban women suffer from isolation and boredom, network activities kept these women too busy to experience prolonged feelings of isolation or depression. Since those who stayed home apparently chose to do so, little frustration about achieving career fulfillment was evident. Overall, the women's attitudes seemed to be that the townhouse tract was a good place to live during that stage of their lives.

Therefore, although such a network is a partial rather than a complete substitute for extensive formal services, it is an important way for women to gain mastery over environments which otherwise narrow their options. This control and its accompanying sense of accomplishment could be vital to women in other socioeconomic circumstances and life-cycle stages—for example, the elderly, those with low incomes, and single parents. Networks formed by women with differing needs and interests confirm this. Hochschild's study of elderly apartment residents, most of whom were women, illustrates how they developed "sibling bonds" as they participated in collective activities and helped less able neighbors perform their daily chores.[15] Networks of neighbors may also be an important resource for blue-collar women, as Warren's study shows.[16] Similarly, women who have relocated can derive support and an essential community orientation from a network, facilitating their adjustment to the new location.

A question for the future is whether networks will widen their sphere of interest from the small area in which they are embedded to collective action efforts at the local, state, or national levels. In her study, Brown found that a "good" neighborhood for divorced mothers was one with a concentration of others in the same situation. Then, they were not labeled "different" or "deviant" by neighbors and, equally important, they were strong enough as a group to lobby for the services and facilities they lacked.[17] Some networks might well move in this direction. However, the localism of networks like the one studied might work against the likelihood that participants would place their immediate concerns within a broader national framework. Such a network might also be so successful in meeting participants' more pressing needs that they would not see the continued lack of services as part of a larger problem. These self-help efforts, then, could actually work to "cool out" women who might otherwise become activists for policy changes to benefit all women.

15. Arlie Russell Hochschild, "Communal Life-Styles for the Old," *Transaction/Society* (July–August 1973), pp. 50–57.

16. Rachelle Warren, "The Work Role and Problem Coping: Sex Differentials in the Use of Helping Systems in Urban Communities" (paper presented at the annual meetings of the American Sociological Association, San Francisco, August 1975).

17. Brown, p. 12.

This study of a women's network also demonstrates the importance of considering women as being more than just "there," or all having the same needs. The interests and needs of career-oriented women in a suburban complex are different from those of the women studied, apart from universal needs like transportation. Inner-city women's most urgent concerns are also somewhat divergent. Therefore, planners need to provide a range of services to meet these diverse requirements. Participation by residents in planning is an important way to ensure that a neighborhood's needs are effectively met. Carin Boalt, a Swedish sociologist with many years of experience in urban planning and architecture, thinks that participation would help eliminate the problems of "suburban areas with their concrete sameness which have taken over significant parts of the industrialized world."[18]

Given their flexibility and self-help aspects, networks provide a feasible way to keep service costs down. By building on existing networks, government agencies could eliminate additional bureaucratic structures and the personnel to administer large programs. Expensive construction could also be avoided, with funding confined primarily to renting space and supplying equipment. Moreover, the small area locus of such programs would eliminate travel for participants and save energy. Programs could be arranged so that they relied on a combination of volunteer and paid staff. Women could either volunteer their time and skills in return for services, in a "sweat equity" arrangement, or pay for the services if they preferred. If additional staff were needed, neighborhood women who sought jobs with flexible hours close to home might be hired.

In light of current concerns about government spending and the energy crisis, along with "big government" complaints, networks deserve serious consideration as a mechanism for providing alternative services.

Empire State College of the State University of New York (Rochester)

18. Carin Boalt, "Flexible Living," *Sweden Now* 2 (1977): 39–40, see p. 40.

The Role of Women's Social Networks in the Adoption of Innovations at the Grass-Roots Level

Lois Saxelby Steinberg

Social science theory and research have not kept pace with recent changes that are redefining the role of parents in the educational decision-making process. These changes have special significance for women, since responsibility for the child's educational achievement in this society has been traditionally assigned to mothers who, for the most part, have been socialized to passive, supportive behaviors in their relationships with educators.

Most of the literature on educational decision making provides little information on the participation of women. Findings based on data collected before the mid-1960s document the effects of the school-board reform movement and the growth of professionalism. By that time most school districts had instituted procedures originally intended to eliminate patronage and insulate educators from the particularistic demands of parents as well as community subgroups. One consequence of these changes is revealed in numerous studies reporting low levels of parent involvement, interest, and knowledge of school affairs.[1]

To a large extent, professional control of educational decisions was due to the type of citizens selected as school-board members, the increasing complexity of the educational enterprise, and the development of

This study is sponsored by the National Institute of Education, Contract no. 400-79-0005.

1. Roscoe C. Martin, *Government and the Suburban Schools* (Syracuse, N.Y.: Syracuse University Press, 1962); Marilyn Gittell, *Participants and Participation* (New York: Center for Urban Education, 1966).

educational technology. Professional domination was justified by the belief that educational practices were based on scientific expertise and the "cult of efficiency."[2] Most parent organizations, such as the PTA, adopted policies which prohibited parents from challenging administrative decisions.

Since the mid-1960s, following the resistance of many local school districts to a new series of reforms designed to promote equal opportunity for minority students, a number of events have led to a dismantling of these beliefs and a search for new strategies to make educators accountable for the services delivered to their clients—particularly those from poor and minority homes in inner-city districts. A series of innovations promoted at the national level have created the basis for parents to mobilize around special issues at the local school level. These innovations include mandated parent advisory committees in federally funded compensatory programs, laws and court decisions that require local districts to provide a variety of programs for children with specific needs, as well as movements that have endorsed or encouraged the active participation of parents such as decentralization, feminism, and alternative schools.

This paper describes an exploratory study which is examining the impact of these innovations on grass-roots participation. The study focus is on groups organized by women around issues that have been previously rejected or ignored by local school authorities and whose activation is supported, directly or indirectly, by the above innovations. Although the study concentrates on educational issues, a major objective is to identify the factors that promote effective citizen participation in an era when decisions affecting many public service delivery systems are being made increasingly at the state and federal level and where program implementation is dominated by professional educators.

The study is based on a theoretical perspective derived from three sources: (1) a review of an extensive body of theory and research on citizen participation, community power, and social networks;[3] (2) a seven-year participant-observer study of changes in participation in a northeast suburban school district which documented the experience of mothers whose children's educational needs are not represented by local school authorities;[4] and (3) a four-year study of the politics of implementing bilingual programs in the New York City school system.[5]

2. Raymond E. Callahan, "The American Board of Education 1789–1960," in *Understanding School Boards*, ed. Peter J. Cistone (Lexington, Mass.: D.C. Heath & Co., 1975).

3. Lois S. Steinberg, *Social Science Theory and Research on Participation and Voluntary Associations: A Bibliographic Essay* (Boston: Institute for Responsive Education, 1977).

4. Lois S. Steinberg, "Some Structural Determinants of Citizen Participation in Educational Policy-Making in Suburbia" (paper presented at the American Educational Research Association annual meeting, New York, New York, 1971, ERIC Document 046 841).

5. Lois S. Steinberg, "The Bilingual Education Act and Puerto Rican Community: The Role of a Network in the Implementation of Federal Legislation at the Local Level" (Ph.D. diss., Fordham University, 1978).

The literature review suggested that many analysts have recognized the significance of informal social networks in connection with individual decisions—such as the adoption of innovation and voting in national elections. On the other hand, the research on collective decisions (influenced primarily by the assumptions of "pluralism") has concentrated on formal relationships between elected or appointed officials. When constituents have been included they are typically leaders or elites representing established formal organizations (e.g., voluntary associations). As a result, our knowledge about the role of informal social processes, the participation of nonelites, and the methods by which excluded groups organize and develop influence is extremely limited. Besides their neglect of informal social processes, the community-power studies do not consider the impact of increased federal initiatives. Nor do they deal with the participation of women.

Findings from the suburban and urban studies suggested that informal social processes are an important aspect in the development of influence. The suburban study also suggested that the external innovations, particularly school decentralization and feminism, have had a profound effect on the participation of women around educational issues. Starting in the early 1970s, several parent groups emerged to promote reforms which had previously been rejected by local school authorities. These groups were all initiated by mothers, and, although some groups included fathers, most of the activists were mothers. So far, the data reinforce the view that this is another area where women are assuming more responsibility with little or no change in the father's role—when he is present. Many of these women are working at part- or full-time jobs or preparing to return to work when their children are older. The major change in the fathers seems to be that some are more willing to baby-sit and "permit" their wives to go to evening meetings.

The ability to mobilize support appeared to be largely dependent on the mother's social network—specifically her preexisting social ties and access to opportunities to interact with other mothers at the community level. A majority of these ties appear to have been formed through school activities, community organizations, the neighborhood, and a variety of recreational facilities shared by the children.

To explore the impact of external reforms on grass-roots participation of women, we have selected six groups from the suburban district for an in-depth analysis. They reflect differences in social class, ethnicity, and religion. The focus is on community and school-related factors that provide opportunities for mothers to utilize the resources created by the external events and differential access to these resources.

In addition to investigating the sociological characteristics of the personal networks of those recruited to the groups, the basis of the preexisting relationships, and the resources brought to the group by each recruit, we will consider the following questions: How did the women hear about the external innovations? What school- and community-related factors influence the structure of these actions groups? What types of resources are provided by external agents? In what ways do the women become linked to external agents? To what extent does employment outside the community affect the women's opportunities to develop informal local networks?

An inventory of school and community contexts that enable the suburban women to create policy-relevant social ties will be derived from the findings. In the Midwest city we will select five neighborhoods (differing in terms of social class and ethnicity) to compare variations in school and community contexts that provide opportunities for women to develop similar social networks and to explore the feasibility of replicating the suburban study in urban settings.

A longitudinal, comparative design based on a network approach will be employed to reconstruct the history of the six groups in terms of issue development, group formation, division of labor, strategy, conflict, and goal attainment. Data-collection methods include open-ended interviews with parent activists and school representatives, sociometric questionnaires, observation of meetings, and content analysis of school records.

Results will be used to develop hypotheses that can be tested in future research on change-oriented social networks. Findings will be applied to a discussion of the types of resources that foster informal social networks at the grass-roots level. This discussion will be geared to policymakers concerned with women's influence in general and minority women in particular. The author is interested in hearing from other researchers working in this area.

National Opinion Research Center

Some Trends in the Community Participation of Women in Their Neighborhoods

Sandra Perlman Schoenberg

The research that my colleagues and I have done in a core city over the past five years supports the conviction that the urban neighborhood has altered significantly and necessarily for women because of changes in the nature of city life and in the roles women play. Among those historical developments are changes in work patterns, family structure, and life expectancy; patterns of metropolitanization and dispersion of population; and new technologies. Questions still remain about the effects of these occurrences on American social life. For example, who will maintain the voluntary associations that have continued to play an important role in urban social life? Who will develop and maintain the social networks of kinship and friendship that women have nurtured traditionally?

Four studies that my colleagues and I have completed provide some data which address such questions. In this paper I will report some of the findings of these studies and suggest areas for further research. In the first study of ethnicity and race in urban neighborhoods, the role of older women is examined. From two studies of community involvement in two working-class neighborhoods, we offer some suggestions on the relations of paid work to volunteer work among working-class women. Finally, from a set of interviews of twenty middle-class married women with school-aged children who live in a suburban enclave near a large city, we offer some additional information that points to changes in social roles.

Older Women and City Neighborhoods

Although the literature on aging is rich with programs to integrate the older adult into neighborhood activities,[1] there is little attention to the role older adults play in the city neighborhoods in which they remain long after more affluent and younger family members have moved to new housing in the suburbs. The data we report were gathered as part of an Ethnic Heritage Studies program[2] which included the collection of taped oral histories from older residents; the collection and analysis of letters, newspapers, and census data; and participant observation in four urban neighborhoods that were the centers of primary settlements for Italians, Eastern Europeans, and black residents between 1880 and 1920. Although the neighborhoods are very different today in terms of their social structure and level of affluence, the role of older women in two of them is strikingly similar.

In each of these communities, there is dependence on older women to maintain the social networks that sustain community action. Intensive study of the Italian neighborhood indicates that a concentration of people over sixty who speak Italian has been important to the local storekeepers and to the small flow of immigrants who continue to come to this city and to settle in this neighborhood.[3] The older women have been mobilized by the associate pastor of the major church to fight the encroachment on the neighborhood character. Pictures of women in black shawls picketing a pool hall and speaking on television against a drive-in movie were effective deterrents in the local area to changes to which the church objects.[4]

Natural barriers and political acumen have acted together to protect this neighborhood from the type of physical decay that has occurred in the other neighborhoods we studied. Political affiliations have guaranteed better city service provisions than others receive; but these services are supported by diligent homeowners, many of whom are over sixty years old. Italianism is symbolically embodied in the generation of women who gather for the Italian language service at the church and who walk to the market daily to shop and to speak Italian.

1. G. F. Streib and R. B. Streib, "Communes and the Aging: Utopian Dream and Gerontological Reality," *American Behavior Scientist* 19 (1975): 176–89; I. Welfeld and R. Struyk, *Options to Serve the Elderly Better,* Occasional Papers in Housing and Community Affairs, vol. 3, Office of Policy Development and Research, U.S. Department of HUD (Washington, D.C.: Government Printing Office, 1978), pp. 63–86.

2. Ethnic Heritage Studies Program, 1974–75, Washington University, St. Louis. This study was supported by a grant from the Ethnic Heritage Studies section of the Division of International Education, U.S. Office of Education.

3. Neal Barkan, "Structural Determinants: Their Effects on the Crystallization of an Ethnic Identification in an Urban Neighborhood" (senior honors thesis, Urban Studies Department, Washington University, 1975).

4. Timothy O'Leary, "Ethnicity in Defense of Class" (Ph.D. diss., Washington University, 1977).

The older women play a similar function in the black neighborhood we studied. The Ville, an elite black community formed around 1900, became the center for black educational institutions from kindergarten through law school by the 1930s. As a resident of the Ville stated in an oral history session, "You knew you were somebody if you lived in the Ville."[5] In this midwestern city, black women were admitted before men to teacher training, so there were many women in professional roles who chose to live near schools in the neighborhood through the years of segregated education.[6] In this neighborhood, the loss of elite symbolic meaning paralleled the end of segregated housing, schools, and hospitals. The institutions that had served a captive population were diluted by the reassignment of black teachers to other schools and by the opportunity for students to move to suburban communities.

Older residents were entrapped by their homeownership and their inability to sell their property in a deflated market following the Second World War.[7] For two decades, the community deteriorated and home ownership and property maintenance dropped. In the last five years there has been a renewed interest in the neighborhood, spearheaded by women who remember the community when it was the center of cultural life. They have participated in the creation of several organizations whose task it is to reconstruct the neighborhood. The historic meaning of this older enclave may be a reasonable beginning in the work for local rebirth.

In these two communities older women are the collective memory of a more cohesive period in neighborhood history. Their political and social mobilization for service to the community is a rarely observed phenomenon. Comparative studies that document its presence in older cities across the country would be of interest to social scientists. The symbolic importance of multigeneration communities has been discussed in many studies on community revitalization,[8] but the public policies that actively solicit the participation of older men and women in community life have been slow to form.

Working-Class Women and Community Involvement

The second and third studies I report concern working-class women. They have maintained a tradition of participation in church and

5. Ethnic Heritage Data Bank, Tape no. 5, Ville Collection, Washington University.

6. Board of Directors of the St. Louis Public Schools, *The Printed Record, Annual Reports 1906–1912* (St. Louis: n.p., 1975); and *The History of Charles Sumner High School* (St. Louis: n.p., 1975).

7. Charles Bailey, "The Symbolic Meaning of an Urban Neighborhood: The Ville in St. Louis" (Ph.D. diss., Washington University, 1978).

8. Jane Jacobs, *The Death and Life of Great American Cities* (New York: Random House, 1961).

school organizations that complemented their roles as wives and mothers. Unlike their middle-class counterparts, working-class and low-income women have not been a force in voluntary associations with community or city-wide agendas. Until recently, research has supported the position that working-class women prefer to stay at home.[9] Recent studies that probe the relationship of levels of satisfaction afforded working-class women by both housework and paid work indicate that there is reason to question this generalization.[10] Part-time paid work is the favored alternative to both full-time housekeeping and full-time paid work. The social isolation of the home and the social role conflict of full-time paid work and housework have high costs, which have led researchers to miss the subtlety of the relationship between these roles. Our findings suggest that working-class women may prefer other forms of social participation when these options are open to them.

Our completed studies address the question of what individual characteristics of women appear to facilitate or inhibit community involvement in voluntary associations and neighborhood affairs. In a survey of a random sample of seventy-six women in a working-class and low-income neighborhood, we examined the relationship of income, education, homeownership, age, presence of children, paid work, and marital status to neighboring, community involvement, and organizational participation.[11] The most striking relationship we have noted is the importance of paid work to the social involvement of women. Unlike other studies that have examined the social life space of women, the educational experience of these women has less salience than the work experience.

Twenty-two women in the sample do paid work. Forty-eight women are not in the labor force. The data are missing for six women. Four indicators of community involvement were designed to provide information on the informal participation of women in neighborhood activities. Of the four, more women had contacted a city official than any other type of community involvement.[12] Women who do paid work were significantly more likely to attend a neighborhood meeting and to have made an effort for a neighborhood organization in the previous six

9. Carol Slater, "Class Differences in the Definition of Role and Membership in Voluntary Associations among Urban Unmarried Women," *American Sociological Review* 65, no. 6 (1960): 616–19; Patricia Cayo Sexton, "Speaking for the Working-Class Wife," *Harpers* (October 1962), pp. 130–34; Nancy Seifer, *Absent from the Majority* (New York: National Project on Ethnicity of the American Jewish Committee, 1973).

10. Myra Marx Ferree, "Working-Class Jobs: Housework and Paid Work as Sources of Satisfaction," *Social Problems* 23 (April 1976): 431–41.

11. The other indicators of community involvement are: (1) attendance at a neighborhood meeting in the last six months; (2) effort for a community organization in the past six months; and (3) initiation of an activity in the neighborhood.

12. Sandra Schoenberg and Patricia Rosenbaum, "Prerequisites to Participation by the Poor in an Urban Neighborhood" (paper presented at the annual meeting of the American Sociological Society, Chicago, September 6, 1977).

months. Initiation of an activity in the neighborhood was low for the total sample.

The low level of participation in actual organizations in the neighborhood by all members of the sample was in striking contrast to the levels of neighboring and informal community involvement. This finding is particularly interesting when we note that 75 percent of the women interviewed think that there are enough people who are active in the neighborhood to effect change. Our data suggest that residents of the neighborhood are aware of the moderately high level of informal activity going on in their area.

Events in the neighborhood support this perception. Through the efforts of the neighborhood organizations, the area has been designated as a historic district; a meals-on-wheels program has been inaugurated; Title VIII housing for the elderly is being constructed; and annual neighborhood celebrations have been conducted. What we might have recorded as low participation by women in this neighborhood is more correctly recorded as low institutional participation.

The lack of relationship between neighboring and community involvement and length of residence, homeownership, education, marital status, and presence of children in the household is worthy of further study. The relationship between paid work and some level of social involvement suggests that, contrary to prediction, for working-class women and women with low incomes, paid work may provide an enlargement of their social participation.

Further evidence for this conclusion is provided by Irene Dabrowski's study of forty working-class women in an adjacent neighborhood.[13] Here a large number of commonweal and service organizations exist. Groups that address such general community concerns as the historical society, the general neighborhood federation, the political party, and the businessmen's association, are designated as commonweal. By service organizations Dabrowski meant the Family Health Service, the PTA, and La Leche—a mother's organization.

Four groups of women were selected for study: ten who work and volunteer; ten who do paid but not volunteer work; ten who do only volunteer work; and ten who neither work nor volunteer. A content analysis of forty two-hour interviews with the respondents reveals that part-time paid work and part-time volunteer work provide a rich social world for these working wives and mothers. Dabrowski fully describes the expansion of the social world that paid work provides both in terms of self-assurance and the skills necessary for voluntary group participation. As working-class women continue to enter the work force at increasing numbers, we can examine this suggestion that voluntary group participation will grow when appropriate outlets are available in the

13. Irene Dabrowski, "Working-Class Women, Paid Work, and Volunteer Work" (Ph.D. diss., Department of Sociology, Washington University, 1979).

neighborhood. This research suggests that for working-class women paid work precedes voluntary group participation. Paid part-time work may serve the function of social role expansion for working-class women that we associate with education for middle-class women.

Middle-Class Women, Paid Work, and Volunteer Work

The fourth study I report, just completed by Sandra Holmes, replicates Dabrowski's study with middle-class women. Holmes[14] interviewed the universe of presently married women with elementary age schoolchildren who live in one school district in a suburban enclave near a midwestern city. She hypothesized that middle-class women with young children participate in volunteer work before they do paid work. For them, education provides the skills for volunteer work and for paid work. In essence, she suggests that middle-class women reverse the pattern we observed for working-class women.

Through a set of twenty two-hour interviews, Holmes found that the majority of women do volunteer work and paid work (eleven out of twenty). This segment of the group is from a higher socioeconomic position as measured by education and by the socioeconomic index[15] for mothers and fathers. Both paid work and volunteer work occur simultaneously in this group. Of the three women who do only paid work, all volunteered at an earlier period. Of the three women who only volunteer at present, all did paid work at an earlier time. Like the working-class women in Dabrowski's study, the three women who neither work nor volunteer at the present time saw paid work at earlier time periods as temporary. Unlike Dabrowski's sample, the women in this group who work and volunteer have a career commitment to their work that has increased since the birth of their first child.

The picture of volunteer work for this group indicates a high involvement in service- and family-oriented organizations, which women have joined from personal interest and because of the opportunities they afford for socializing. A third reason that explained involvement in community and professional organizations was commitment to a cause. The lowest participation is reported between marriage and the birth of the first child. The highest period of involvement reported was between the birth of the first child and the present.

Women who do both paid and volunteer work report more hours spent at volunteer work than those who only volunteer. Neither school nor paid work is seen as a source of skills used in volunteer work. Par-

14. Sandra Holmes, "Middle-Class Women, Paid Work, and Volunteer Work" (fieldwork project, Department of Sociology, Washington University, 1979).
15. Otis Dudley Duncan, "A Socioeconomic Index for All Occupations," in *Occupations and Social Status*, ed. A. J. Reiss, Jr. (New York: Free Press, 1961), pp. 109–38.

ticipation in volunteer work appears to be related to the mother's work history: the mothers of women who volunteer were themselves volunteers (twelve out of fourteen); the women who work and volunteer have mothers who worked.

Skills learned in school were most frequently related to paid employment. Holmes's findings do not support the hypothesis that volunteer work is a prerequisite to paid work for middle-class women. For these middle-class women, education is the source of skills for paid work. Personal qualities learned at home were used in their volunteer experiences. These interviews do not support the hypothesis that women stop doing volunteer work when they do paid work; however, the type of volunteer work they do may be changing. When women do paid work in an area of personal interest they may not look for voluntary experience to fill this personal need. Instead they appear to be participating in family related activities that support their wife and mother roles.

Like the working-class women, the women in this group who relate to their neighbors the most and who consider themselves best informed are the ones who do paid and volunteer work. Unlike the working-class women, these women do not see paid work as a source of skills that enhance their ability to do volunteer work. They see education as the major resource that affects their paid-work opportunities. Again unlike the working-class women, these middle-class respondents agree that it is possible to be a good wife and mother and, at the same time, to pursue a career. They also agree that husbands of women who work should share homemaking and child-rearing activities.

These findings suggest that decreasing membership by younger women in such traditionally middle-class pursuits as the League of Women Voters and the Junior League may represent a change in priorities. Paid work may absorb the time spent on community activities that fulfilled personal interest. When the middle-class woman who does paid work looks for volunteer work, she may choose activities that support her familial roles. If this small study represents a trend, we suggest that paid work will not reduce voluntary group participation by women who do paid work, but it may change the nature of the organizational ties. Further study of middle-class women at different points in the life cycle, in central cities, and in other suburban communities would precede such generalization.

The availability of organizations with open membership to which women can belong may bear an important relationship to the likelihood that working-class women will participate in voluntary organizations. In the neighborhood in which the first survey was conducted, there were few service organizations, although a commonweal organization had existed for some time. A new organization, which is service oriented, has mobilized many residents in the two years following the survey. In the working-class neighborhood in which Dabrowski's study was conducted, a rich array of commonweal and service organizations welcome participants of either sex. In the middle-class community of Holmes's study, commonweal and service organizations are readily available. These data suggest that the structure of organizations may facilitate participation, at least in working-class communities. In middle-class communities, commonweal organizations may lose ground to those groups which support familial roles.

Policy Implications of These Suggestions

Our finding about older women in ethnic and racial enclaves may be an isolated instance of participation by an unusual group of people caught by structural changes. Studies of older neighborhoods in other cities to examine the role of the older adult as a community participant are worthy of consideration at a time when organizations seek a stable population of participants. However, our findings about work and community activity may not be so isolated. At a time when full-time paid work is becoming the norm in American society, we are caught in a dilemma. Many women voice a preference for part-time work. The structure of many jobs does not allow for two workers to accept/share one job. Work that is close to the place of residence and part-time opportunities may have positive benefits for community organizations who reap the voluntary labor of the part-time paid worker. In an effort to enhance opportunities for women to do whatever paid work they choose, we may err on the side of forcing women into full-time paid work with but one alternative: to stay at home. The social expansion for working-class women from community participation that Dabrowski documents suggests that we need a careful examination of the opportunity structure for paid work with attention to an increase in the options for part-time work and volunteer work opportunities for working-class women.

Finally, community-oriented organizations and special interest groups may find that paid staff will have to replace the volunteer labor on which they depended during the years when middle-class women with young children did not do paid work. Rather than allowing important community functions to die, we may find that it is necessary to pay for services offered, previously, through volunteer networks. Parent-teacher organizations, church groups, and family-oriented groups may find that they still have volunteers among women who do paid work and who wish to spend their leisure time on activities that complement their familial roles.

Department of Sociology
Washington University

Reviews of Current Literature

The American Woman in Transition: The Urban Influence, 1870–1920. By Margaret Gibbons Wilson. Westport, Conn.: Greenwood Press, 1979. Pp. 252. $19.95.

Clyde Griffen, Vassar College

Professor Wilson's interest is the enlargement in the sphere of activity for women between, roughly, 1870 and 1920. As her subtitle suggests, she finds the explanation in "the phenomenal upsurge in urbanization and industrialization" (p. 3); she regards her own book as an attempt to remedy the lack of "systematic study of the ways urban living affected women's lives" (p. 4). She limits her investigation primarily to middle-class white women, however, on the presumption that they set the pattern for others.

Within the limits of her focus, Wilson performs a useful service. A large part of her brief, clearly written book draws together the literature on trends affecting middle-class women during her period. Separate chapters discuss changes in the character of urban life and the urban home, marriage and fertility patterns, and organizations and employment for women.

Wilson's original contribution is her attempt to test some hypotheses about the influence of urban living and of urbanization on women's lives by quantitative analysis of selected traits through the censuses of 1890–1920. She includes an interesting appendix in which she analyzes variables such as child/woman ratio and proportion of women employed to show (1) regional differences, (2) temporal convergence or divergence between 1890 and 1920, and (3) the relation of these temporal trends to urbanization.

Two limitations in Wilson's working definition of urban and rural areas raise doubts about the significance of some of her quantitative results. First, her decision to treat only places of 25,000 or more inhabitants as urban classifies many small cities and large towns as rural. That classification may, for example, be the explanation of her finding of a consistently lower urban/rural difference in employment of women in her North Atlantic region since that region had a disproportionate share of small urban settlements.

Second, the use of any definition by size alone skirts the larger question of whether many apparently rural localities are primarily urban in orientation. In their collaborative study of Essex County, Massachusetts, in 1880, Tamara Hareven and Maris Vinovskis found that two rural villages had different patterns of fertility which seemed to depend upon whether they were related primarily to agriculture or to manufacturing in an adjacent industrial city like Lynn.[1] The likelihood of such an urban orientation in rural villages increased during the period Wilson covers. As late as 1910 only 40 percent of the people of the United States lived in towns with 2,500 or more inhabitants, but a large majority already were urban *if* we include localities with less than 2,500 which adjoined cities of 50,000 or more.

Wilson's most promising innovation is her attempt to distinguish among urban environments by social and economic characteristics rather than simply by size. Her results show distinctive patterns in women's employment and fertility between cities, with a concentration in manufacturing and mechanical industries and in cities more involved with trade and transportation. I wish that Wilson had extended and refined this analysis since it seems much more fruitful than her emphasis upon urban and rural differences. For example, since we know that manufacturing industries varied greatly in the frequency with which they employed women, it would have been revealing to divide manufacturing cities by industrial mix to see the range in variation in such traits as sex ratio, conjugal condition, and child/woman ratio.

Wilson's focus upon native white middle-class women is understandable, given the earlier emphasis upon them in women's history. But in 1979 her rationale seems complacent and unhistorical: "a study of middle-class behavior patterns and values . . . presumably reflects the dominant mores of the nation" (p. 11). The title of her book, *The American Woman in Transition,* expresses her apparent conviction that the enlargement of the women's sphere was a middle-class achievement. The "True Woman" became the "New Woman." Wilson seems to presume what has not been shown, that overwhelmingly it was the daughters of the middle class rather than of the working class who filled the new white-collar jobs which increased so dramatically during the period she studies. Wilson's failure to grapple seriously with the problem of whether there were significant class differences in behavior among native white women is suggested by her use of the category "Native White of Native Parentage" as a rough indicator of the middle class.

Wilson shows no curiosity about precisely how and when women of other ethnic groups enlarged their sphere of activity, so the reader is left

1. Tamara Hareven and Maris Vinovskis, "Patterns of Childbearing in Late Nineteenth-Century America: The Determinants of Marital Fertility in Five Massachusetts Towns in 1880," in *Family and Population in Nineteenth-Century America,* ed. Tamara Hareven and Maris Vinovskis (Princeton, N.J.: Princeton University Press, 1978), pp. 85–125.

to assume some simple process of emulation, however delayed. Yet her own data on the frequency of employment among women of other groups invite more consideration of the meaning of group differences in behavior and a more complex interpretation of convergence in behavior over time. Readers will wish that Wilson had had the benefit of such recent studies as Miriam Cohen's "Italian Women in New York City, 1900–1950: Work and School" or—for an explicit comparison of ethnic differences in adaptation—John Modell's "Patterns of Consumption, Acculturation, and Family Income Strategies in Late Nineteenth-Century America."[2]

In general, readers acquainted with the research in women's history and related fields published during the past five years will be disappointed by this book's lack of acquaintance with important new directions, evident in the text as well as in the bibliography. Although this lack must be blamed in large part upon a rapidly changing field, it will limit the usefulness of Wilson's book. Perhaps the most striking absence are results from recent research on the life course for women, and especially on changes from 1870 to 1920 in the timing of such transitions as entry into work, leaving the family of origin, marriage, and the formation of new households.

Women and the City. Special issue of *International Journal of Urban and Regional Research.* Vol. 2, no. 3 (1978).

Mary Lindenstein Walshok, University of California, San Diego

This special issue of the British *International Journal of Urban and Regional Research* is the result of a collective editorial process reflective of a commitment to integrate feminist practices with academic work. The issue emphasizes feminist urban research and, in particular, work identified with the Women's Caucus of the British Sociological Association. As such, as Eva Gamarnikow's introduction points out, it does not include the contributions of scholars from a variety of other fields concerned with studies of the city, such as political scientists, planners, architects, geographers, and economists. Although the introduction asserts no theoretical or political consensus among the contributors, from the point of view of an American sociologist, steeped in our varied traditions of empirical research, the issue does reflect a single style of analysis and

2. Miriam Cohen, "Italian Women in New York City, 1900–1950: Work and School," in *Class, Sex, and the Woman Worker,* ed. Milton Cantor and Bruce Laurie (Westport, Conn.: Greenwood Press, 1977); John Modell, "Patterns of Consumption, Acculturation, and Family Income Strategies in Late Nineteenth-Century America," in Hareven and Vinovskis, pp. 206–40.

discourse. In addition, it is frequently polemical in its various discussions of the ways in which patriarchy and capitalism contribute to sexist generalizations about the character of the city. Such polemics would be less of a problem if the issue had lived up to its promise to shed light on a range of issues pertinent to research on cities from which women have been excluded. The introduction states compellingly that "urban studies must confront the theoretical issues arising out of the space occupied by patriarchy in the urban environment. Research projects must include, as a central figure of any analysis, the position of women and the role played by marriage, the family, the sexual division of labor and patriarchal social relations in the urban system. Within existing theories, however, women constitute an absence, and this very fact results, politically, in perpetuating patriarchy, and theoretically, in producing only a partial understanding of the structure of the urban system." I had expected this issue to contribute more broadly to my understanding of this problem. Because the articles tended to focus on issues such as cooperative experiments in the city, aspects of the women's movement, and services for women, it did not provide the breadth of feminist perspective for which I hoped.

The issue consists of three articles written in French, six in English, and the introduction, which is in English. It also includes a short review essay in English by Madge Dresser of the essay by Davidoff, L'Esperance, and Newby on the idealized images of home and community in English society, "Landscape with Figures: Home and Community in English Society" (reprinted in Juliet Mitchell and Ann Oakley, *The Rights and Wrongs of Women*). The first article, by Dolores Hayden, describes the life and work of Melusina Fay Peirce. In the 1860s Peirce suggested that unpaid and unspecialized domestic work was at the root of women's economic and intellectual oppression. Hayden's discussion of Peirce's ideas is interesting and gives her a proper place next to more well-known advocates of collective housekeeping such as Gilman.

Hayden's piece is followed by two articles on aspects of French life in urban settings. The first, by Danielle Chabaud and Dominique Fougeyrollas, is entitled "Travail domestique et espace-temps des femmes" and deals with the relationship between women's reproductive roles in the family, their productive roles in the paid labor force, and the spatial and temporal proximity of medical and educational services, for example, to the domestic role. They also point out how the design of housing and urban structure reflects a dominant perception of the female role as domestic. They urge a reformulation of space and time dimensions in urban settings which recognizes the duality of women's roles rather than the current definition of women in primarily wife-mother roles. J. Coutras and J. Fagnani are the authors of the piece "Femmes et transports en milieu urbain," which, like the preceding article, treats the general problems of the ideological norms of a patriarchal society which bind women to paid employment in ways which are difficult to combine with domestic roles. Their piece describes, in particular, the problems with transportation faced by women in France and their somewhat unequal access, for example, to the automobile. The situation differs from the United States, but the problems associated with adequate forms of public transportation are similar.

The fourth article, by Miriam David, reviews policies and practices affecting women caring for preschool children in the United States. However, the purpose of her piece is not merely descriptive, and she presents her overview in terms of the role of the state and its policies—taxation, social security, income maintenance—in reproducing one aspect of the capitalist system, the traditional family. Her article is an excellent review of the development of social policy vis-à-vis child care, but her implicit suggestion that the state self-consciously perpetuates dual jobs for women and a sexual division of labor is developed less convincingly. Examples of social policies which might overcome such distinctions would be useful. David's piece is followed by Regina Fodor's discussion of "Day Care Policy in France and Its Consequences for Women." Fodor points out that despite a century of day-care centers and state support, family ideology and the importance of the mother-child relationship has never been seriously questioned in France. The Fodor piece shares some interesting data (although it is in places dated) and some provocative ideas. However, it deals simultaneously with so many issues and levels of analysis that it is ultimately unsatisfying.

The remaining four articles in the collection each deal in one way or another with collectivist-cooperative movements and issues pertinent to the women's movement as a social movement. They include an essay, in French, by Michele Morville-Descolonges, "A propos de la socialisation du travail domestique," focusing on collective experiments with domestic work; an analysis by E. M. Ettorre of the women's liberation movement, and, in particular, a case study of a lesbian ghetto as an example of women's emergent political power in urban environments; an account by Hilary Rose of the problems encountered by Women's Aid in Great Britain in trying to deal with family violence; and an analysis by Anna Whyatt of the underlying reasons for the problems and generally poor success among both working-class and feminist groups in experiments with cooperative living and governance. Each of these pieces is interesting in itself, but its role in the collection and thus its far-reaching implications for urban studies is less clear. The Whyatt article is more useful because of its thoughtful observation that cooperative movements depend for their success on a certain level of skills—communication, governance, business. These skills are not typical to female socialization; so the unsuccessful cooperative ventures should not be surprising. The potential validity of the cooperative concept as a force in urban society remains to be tested.

In some ways the title of this special issue is a misnomer, for it suggests more than it delivers. It provides the reader with a number of interesting articles on the consequences of patriarchy and capitalism for the general status of women in urban society and offers some perspectives on cooperative movements, past and present. It is, however, at such a level of generality that the reader does not come away with a better understanding of the everyday problems of living, working, caring, and effecting change as a woman and for women in the urban environment. Many issues need to be discussed with reference to urban planning: the design of housing and work environments; the provision of child care; domestic support services; the character of employment opportunities for women; the organization of life at work; the hours, benefits, and pacing of paid employment; the political process in urban environments; and the obstacles and avenues for change facing women. If one is concerned with these questions, this collection will do little to help. If one is interested in a theoretical critique and an analysis of alternative structures to patriarchy and capitalism, this collection is both provocative and useful.

Index

Abrams, C., 91
Activism, 208–9
Addams, Jane, 67, 68
Adolescents, in immigrant families, 47
A Fool There Was (movie), 56
American Institute of Planners, 223
The American Woman in Transition: The Urban Influence, 266–68

Baldwin Hills project, 183
Bara, Theda, 56
Barton, S., 208
Battered wives, 172
Berkeley, E. P., 191
Bernard, J., 96
Birch, E. L., 208
Birkby, N. P., 188–89
Blenkner, M., 137
Boalt, C., 253
Boulding, E., 187, 192, 193
Brown, C., 106, 197

Capitalism, and household production, 27–28
CASSR, 235–38
Central Park, New York, 78
CETA, 11
Chapin, R., 45
Charity Organization Society, 65
Chicago: fear of crime in, 145–46; mobility of women in, 158–66; urban parks in, 78
Childbirth, for poor women, 120–21
Child care, 14–15, 40, 173; and time and space, 237–44. *See also* Day care
Children, and choice of home location, 100, 101, 102
Cities, identified as masculine, 93
City structure, and working women, 217–22. *See also* Urban life, Urban planning
Civil rights movement, and political involvement of women, 70–71
Collective services, 247
Community activism, 208–9

Community involvement, and working-class women, 260–63
Community organizations, 71–73
Commuting costs, 218. *See also* Public transportation, Transportation,
Congress of Neighborhood Women, 73
Consumption, and suburban life, 169—70
Cools, A., 207
Crime: fear of, 141–57; measures of fear of, 143; and older women, 129–32; and self protective behavior, 144, 148–49, 154; and urban life, 141–57. *See also* Fear of crime, Rape
Cuban Family Code of 1974, 173

Dabrowski, I., 262
David, A., 67
Davidoff, P., 94
Day care, and parks, 88, 92
Delinquency, and parks, 83
DeMille, Cecil B., 58
Demography: changes in, 31–33, 104–6; and fear of crime, 145–46; statistics on, 2–5; statistics on and older women, 124–25
Depression (Economic), 13
Dewson, M., 69
DiLeonardo, M., 28
Discrimination, in housing, 204–7
Divorce, 12. *See also* Single parents
"The domestic mystique," 170
Dreis, R., 203

Economic analysis, of housework, 23
Education, and parental involvement, 254–57
Elderly. *See* Older women
Eleventh Hour (movie), 50
Employed women, statistics on, 171, 172. *See also* Working women
Employment: need for, 13–14; suburban *v.* urban, 105–6; suburban-